CALI GIRL,
How Did I Make It in the Treacherous Streets of Detroit?

TIANNA JONES

Copyright © 2017 Tianna Jones
All rights reserved
First Edition

PAGE PUBLISHING, INC.
New York, NY

First originally published by Page Publishing, Inc. 2017

ISBN 978-1-64082-474-4 (Paperback)
ISBN 978-1-64082-475-1 (Digital)

Printed in the United States of America

I dedicate this book to all the people in our world who need to be heard. Rest in peace to all my friends who didn't get a chance to be heard. Everyone has a story of their own, as life is a cause and effect. A higher power over myself blessed me with the faith to keep believing. I will never doubt the power of love. I strongly bless you all with it. Just keep believing.

When I was younger, I didn't know what it was like to be loved. I was lost for the understanding of love. Searching for love at a young age, first I looked for it from my parents who were absent. Later on in life, I had discovered love while I was searching all along through God.

God was reaching out to me, trying to tell me to stop searching.

The first person who scarred my heart was my mother. Her self-centered actions caused us to part when I was only two. After my father was imprisoned, my mother decided to choose a different path, so she left me and him. My father was imprisoned for a crime he committed for his family. He later on in life taught me how valuable family was and wasn't at the same time. As a child, my heart was empty from two missing parents.

The truth of love lies deeper than this story can be explained, as the realest experiences I had ever felt. I've prayed to God to help my life be great. Everything I am about to tell you is the truth about my life. As you read this story, understand that I do not care what anyone thinks about me but the Almighty God above who has been watching over my shoulder, whispering his words of surrender and mercy.

My story is unlike your's. My story is unlike anyone's I had ever known, but I hope that you readers will be able to relate to the love that is running through my veins. I realize that everyone has a dream that they do not follow. I am living proof that if your heart is in your dreams, it all will follow through.

Chapter 1

It was a matter of time before I realized that I actually had a father. One of my earliest memories was when I was a little over two years old going to visit my father. At the time, he was incarcerated.

As my grandfather and I crossed a bridge to get to the prison, all I could see around me were mountains. When we got there, my father was a tall, brown-skinned man with broad shoulders and long hair that was slicked back into a ponytail. He held me tight with care, which reassured me that he was my father.

During this visit, he bought me a vanilla ice cream cone. As I was eating it, my father also licked the ice cream cone, causing some of the ice cream to fall on the ground. I immediately started crying, and he bought me another ice cream. This visit was the first memory I had of my father.

We all lived in the Bay Area up until my grandfather up and moved us to Kingsville, Texas. Trying to provide for his family, my grandfather slowly became absent and was never home, which caused him to leave me with his girlfriend during the days.

From what I could remember, at a small age, was the way my grandmother would light up a room with her smile and appearance. My face would brighten up right along with hers whenever she was near. My grandmother was an adventurous woman who liked to express herself. My grandmother would always spoil my cousin and me, saying that we were her favorite grandchildren.

My cousin Junior was brave and adventurous like Grandma. People who didn't know us swore up and down that we were brother and sister. Junior would always stand by my side, protecting me. We got throughout our childhood together. I never met anyone in my life who was like my cousin. He wasn't afraid of anything at all and was ready for any danger that came his way. When my father went to prison, I went to stay with his younger brother, and his girlfriend, and my uncles son. My cousin was just like his father who was adventurous and brave. Junior resembled his father in so many ways.

My uncle was a big kid that never wanted to grow up. There had been an incident where the music at my uncle's friends apartment ways to loud. They must have gotten a few complaints prior because CPS came, and took me to foster care.

My father was in prison and my mother was absent. My grandmother wasn't notified. Who was notified was my father's father. My grandfather came and got me, taking me in his home to raise me from that time on. My grandmother was upset because, by the time she found out, it was too late. My grandfather had custody of me.

My grandfather started dating an ex-junky. He was trying to save them by taking her and her son in trying to make a better life for them. He met them while he was driving the transit bus for a living in the Bay Area.

She became pregnant, claiming she didn't know she was, up until the point of having my grandfather's child. My uncle was two years younger than me.

As a child, living with my grandfather was very confusing. I was a child with missing emotions. The missed emotions were from lack of love needed from my parents who were absent.

Most of my childhood with my grandfather I have mentally blocked out, trying not to remember what I went through. I know he tried his very best to provide a good life for me, but I felt he had the wrong woman as a life partner. I didn't understand my grandfather's situation until later on in life when I got older and was around other family who could explain it to me.

Even though my parents were absent, I always thought about them. They were constantly on my mind, every second of every day. I was not allowed to know anything about my missing mother. Any time I brought her up, I was immediately shut down by my grandfather's girlfriend, Deb. She was a step-grandmother to me, but they were not married.

I was upset with my mother because my father had a reason why we were not together, but she had no reason why she was missing from my childhood. Not knowing where she was or who she was, it wasn't until almost a decade later when my father was released, all my questions that I craved were answered.

My grandfather loved me very much. He never had a daughter. He mainly left it up to Deb to take care of me. I remember a time in my life, at around four or five years old, when my grandparents had a hook nail lock on the outside of my bedroom door, that was my great grandfathers old room. The hook lock was used to lock me in at night. I never understood why the lock was on there or whose idea it was to put it there. I think it was because I would sneak out of my room, around bedtime, going in the kitchen, taking our food. I remember banging on the wall, screaming and crying, "I need to use the bathroom! Let me out!"

They wouldn't let me out of my bedroom. I remember pooping and peeing on myself because no one would get up in the middle of the night to open the door to let me use the bathroom.

I remember my grandfather being aware of the lock on the door because he came in my room in the middle of the night and cleaned me up. One occasion that I can remember. I assumed they had the lock on there because of my nightmares that caused me to unintentionally scream and try to escape out of the room. Eventually my grandfather had the lock taken off. I figured he was tired of having to clean up most of my messes. A lot of these memories I have mentally blocked out, but I could remember for a fact the abuse I went through.

I was either four or five years old when I remember Deb's son Brandon's friend coming down to visit him from California. He came in my bedroom asking me where Brandon was. He stuck his finger inside me. I felt the most forced discomfort. I wasn't able to be accountable for my actions as a five-year-old by allowing him to do that to me.

I'm disgusted by the thought of remembering Brandon, telling me that he had candy on his penis so that I would suck his penis. I did more than once. Things started escalating to more situations. I remember him fingering me many different times when my grandfather wasn't home. When I didn't want to be subjected to the molestation, he would hit me while abusing me, slapping me around.

I told Brandon what his friend had done to me when no one was around. He caught an attitude and walked away. I was so confused to what was right and what was wrong. Writing this is very hard for me. It makes me sick to my stomach.

Looking back at my childhood makes me disappointed that I was disgustingly abused and oblivious to the wrongness of the abuse, blaming myself for it.

A memory that I could actually remember, that my mind lets me not block out, was when my great-grandfather was being personally cared for and treated in our home by Deb before I took over his room that had a hook lock on the outside of the door.. Great-grandpa and I talked often. We both felt like prisoners dealing with the same crazy woman. I would sneak to his room and hide under his bed from her. She was very mean too me as a child and resented me for having to raise me while my grandfather worked. My great-grandfather told me with great care that he remembered meeting my mother, she was a beautiful nice woman. I loved my great-grandfather for indulging those kind words that set me at peace, because I knew she was out there somewhere waiting for me.

I watched my great-grandfather constantly being mistreated by Deb. When she would change his diaper, she was very rough and would talk all kinds of crap to him as he moaned and groaned for help. Those were the moments I knew that she was an evil woman who hated herself, which is why she hated us so. She never showed me any compassion or love the whole time I was there. If she did, it was just her putting on a front for my grandfather.

She became the least of my worries as I stayed there with them. Most of my mind has blocked out the times I was molested by her son Brandon, who was nine years older than I was. Here we were, in another state, with no family near to come visit and check on me. I felt alone as a child and never told a soul what was going on while I was in their home.

At one point in time, I thought that it was my fault and normal for me to be sexually active with this step-uncle. I was only between the ages of four and seven when I was aware of this all happening to me.

I would have nightmares and wake up screaming trying to rush out of my bedroom. I was never aware of what I was doing until I was scolded by Deb the next day.

I remember around the time I was six or seven, I would still be hungry and thirsty so I would sneak out of my room and steal pieces of white bread and drink from the faucet in the bathroom. Barely being able to reach the faucet, I quenched my thirsty mouth. She wouldn't give me anything more than the dinner she would make.

I would write my father tons and tons of letters, telling him I wanted to leave my grandfather's house.

I would give them to Deb, and eventually, the older I got, I caught on that most of my letters would never reach my father since I never got any answers back from him.

Feeling neglected, I turned to God and the stars for hope. Wishing on a star through my bedroom window sill. It was my only way to release my emotions that I had left, saying, "Star light, star bright, first star I see tonight. I wish I may, I wish I might, have this star I wish tonight. I wish that my dad or grandmother would come take me away from there." I would pray and pray every night.

Finally, the God from above did me a favor when I heard the knock on the front door. Running through the hallway to see who was at the front door, I watched Deb open the door. There, standing beautifully, I knew the familiar face. It was my father's mother. The grandmother I had been wishing for night after night on the brightest star was standing on my front porch.

However, Deb shut the door on my grandmother's face and yelled at me to go to my room. I ran back to my room straight to my window sill, staring hard at the brightest star. Thanking the God above and the star for making my wish come true, I smiled because my wish came true.

Since my grandmother flew all the way from California to spend time with me, my grandfather allowed her to take me out for the time that she was there. Happy to see my grandmother, I also resented her for taking so long to come and visit me. I enjoyed the time we spent together, but I knew I was going to have to say goodbye to her eventually. She spoiled me the whole time she was in town. My grandmother bought me a horse collection, clothes, shoes, and much more.

She also took me to my very first dentist appointment where I had to get a filling. It was the last day she had me and I didn't want to go back to my grandfather's house. I couldn't tell my grandmother what had been going on, because I was very confused about everything that was happening to me. I ran from my grandmother outside the hotel and hid behind a wall. I didn't want to go back to that God-awful place. All I could hear was my grandmother saying my name with frantic worry in her voice, "Tianna, Tianna, Tianna." I didn't want to worry her any longer so I came out from behind the wall saying, "Grandma, here I am."

She was so upset with me because she loved me so much and she didn't know what had happened to me. She had no idea that inside I was hurting because she was leaving me there returning to California.

We eventually had an understanding that she loved me, and when my father would be released, I would be coming home to California where my grandmother would be.

I knew there was nothing that I could do except be patient and wait for my time to be away from abuse.

Chapter Two

My grandfather would go away on trips for little league football where he was one of the main people who coached and took care of the treasury. In his absence, it started feeling like he didn't even live there at all.

My grandfather, after some years, had put me in Pop Warner cheerleading for the Bronco little league team. My grandfather was really dedicated to throwing his fundraisers for the football teams. I remember there was an occasion around the time when my grandfather's family and I went to a trip where the little league and cheerleading competitions were being held. My grandfather was out with my step-grandmother. I remember clear what I had been used to knowing. I started running to my predator for love.

I snuck into the hotel room where my predator was staying. Brandon was my grandfather's child's mother's son she had before they met. There I was, seven years old running down the hall of the cemented hotel. I snagged my toe on the upper level outside of the hotel halls, causing my toe to bleed. The pain from the cut was excruciating. I knew that I was subjecting myself to being molested. I was a child still feeding into the abuse because that's all I had ever known.

The reason I realized that I had subjected myself to the sexual abuse was because I was trying to feel a void of love I wasn't getting from my parents. Confused of the feeling of loneliness, I replaced my feelings by feeding my predator sexually.

A happy memory of my grandfather, that I could never forget, was when I had to go on a field trip to the country fair. He surprised me and ended up being my bus driver. He got off the bus and went with us to see all the animals. I hugged my grandfather, happy to finally spend some time with him away from home. It was one of the best gifts he had ever given me.

I loved my grandfather dearly, and he was the first person to show me love that I never had from my dad. I never blamed my grandfather for what had happened to me. I knew it wasn't his fault because he had to make money and out working to feed us. I was ashamed as a young child and never said anything to him, because I felt degrading, running to my predator after so many years of this going on. I started thinking this was normal, and really, it was sick. There I was, a young child who blamed myself for my sexual abuse.

After a while, Brandon laid off me because his mom walked in on seeing me on top of him in the bed. She told him that he better stop or she would tell my grandfather. She closed the door without removing me. Later on I started to come to her, telling her that my vagina was sore and hurting. She would put Vaseline on it, never asking why. It started becoming a routine, coming to her for help. I knew it was caused from humping on Brandon or vice versa or him sticking his penis inside my child private parts.

I blocked so many memories out of my mind and heart as a child. It seemed the younger I was, the harder it was to remember these foul accounts.

After a while, I knew Deb was aware of what was going on and was trying to protect her oldest son. She was aware of the situation and withheld the truth from my grandfather, with malicious intent.

One night, I snuck out of my bedroom into the living room where he had been laying on a pull-out spring mattress. We heard my grandfather coming out of his bedroom so I hid underneath his bed. When my grandfather went back to his room, I climbed back on top of the bed. Felt that this was expected from me, I came onto Brandon. The response from him was completely different, not wanting to rub his penis on me anymore. He told me that we couldn't do that act anymore.

Now that I am older, I am able to heal and reflect. The experience has helped me understand to have acceptance and forgiveness as to what has happened to me as child. Although this experience had been extremely painful in my life, I will not allow it to damage me permanently. This experience has helped me be able to understand that victims are not accountable for being abused. From then on in my life, time was passing by so fast.

Growing up I was a tomboy who spent my days hanging with boys and climbing trees. My uncle who was two years younger than me always hung out with me after school, riding our bikes or wrestling with boys. A lot of the older boys my age would try and pick on my little uncle. He would always come and get me when they were messing with him. I would fight three of them off at a time.

I loved my uncle very much because he looked up to me and was all I really had to play with when I was growing up. That all ended when my father was released from prison when I was eight years old turning nine.

In 1999, my father was released. He was in California, home only for two weeks when he decided to send my great uncle to pick me up and fly back with me to California. I was happy to be leaving but knew I was going to miss my little uncle who always needed me to protect him.

Even though I would beat him up and break his glasses when he got on my nerves, I knew that he was just like a brother to me for so many years. He was always known to me as a miracle baby since we were little because he had a lot of medical issues. Being separated from him was one of the hardest things I could have done as a child. He was all I ever knew besides the family that never came to visit me.

My father's younger brother was waiting there at the airport for me with my dad. I felt like I didn't have any clue who my father was but knew that this was one of the most important days of my life. My heart was still feeling emotionless. I had anger built up inside of me for the years I spent in Texas away from family with pretty much no friends.

This anger built up in me was from my parents being absent, and my mother not wanting to be with me. I didn't know what was going to happen next, but I knew it couldn't have been anymore worse than what I had already been through.

All I could do was cry as my father told me that he would always be there for me. That day I knew that my father meant his words and I hugged him and went to bed. After that time on, I knew that my father loved me and I wanted to be there with him and my family. I knew that his words of "this too shall pass" had meaning to it, and one day, all of what I was going through would pass.

Most of my stepmother's troubles were based on her drug issues and her accusing my father of cheating on her. I had a very dysfunctional relationship with my stepmother at any early age. I experienced, as a child, my stepmother having known to turn to about her issues with my father. At a young age, my stepmother started involving me by confiding in a child about her mind-theories about my father and would always try catching my father doing something wrong. I didn't know what to do as a child but to try to be there for my stepmother and my father. I was very confused who to believe and whose side to take. My stepmother was the only real mother I had ever known. Although my stepmother treated me as if I wasn't her child at times, it seemed clear why. My stepmother resented my father's love that he expressed still for my mother. I was my mother's child at the end of the day. Since my stepmother didn't give birth to me, we would always carry that non-connected relationship.

As a child, I ached for love from a mother so I tried to adjust to having a stepmother and what dysfunctional relationship came with it. Life was changing fast before my eyes, when I felt hurt from waiting for a calm time of peace I would start to pray. The day we moved out of our four-bedroom house, I was sad, but ready to see what God had in store for my family's future.

Chapter Three

Ever since I was nine years old, my grandmother had me around her best friend, who I called Aunt K.

Aunt K was married and stayed in a nice hilltop area in a three-story, four-bedroom house with a garden wrapped around the entire house. The house was beautiful and we would come over quite often for lunches, dinners, and just to visit. In order to get to my grandmother's best friend's front door, people would have to climb up almost 50 steps up the hill. Across from her front door, she had a tree that had an old tree house connected to it with a rope that had a seat at the end of it.

My cousin Junior and I would swing sitting on the seat overviewing the hilltop.

My favorite thing as a child to do was spend time with my grandmother, her best friend, or my grandmother's sister who introduced me to going to church.

The older I got, I realized I had many talents. My grandmother and her best friend saw the most potential in my talents. I was enrolled in ice skating, modeling, acting, math, and taekwondo classes at the age of eleven. My acting and modeling classes were held at John Robert Powers in a mall close to my grandmother's house.

I went to New York to do some competitions through an organization called IMTA. There, I ended up winning two trophies and one ribbon.

One of my trophies that I won was for little miss actress of the year. I was so impressed to be so young and so good at acting. There were literally thousands of people enrolled for the competitions and I was the one who actually won.

I knew I was blessed when I had just missed being in 9/11 a month before the terrorists' planes crashed into the Twin Towers.

That was very significant to me as I got older because I always felt it was a miracle that I was alive and didn't die in that tragedy. The same year, my grandmother took me to LA for a photoshoot and some more competitions.

My grandmother's best friend loved seeing me in extra activities. The faith I saw running through their eyes made me have the confidence that I was going to be a star one day. They boosted my self-confidence sky high as each day went by, telling me great things about myself. Growing up in Texas, I had never heard that before from any woman in my life. It was from that moment on I knew I wanted to be a star.

I set in my mind that nothing was going to stand in the way of me being able to make my family proud of me. All the extra classes and skills I had picked up helped me set dreams for myself.

Looking back, I know that it was my grandmother's and her best friend's dream to see my dreams come true. The skills helped me later on in life. I knew in my heart that my grandmother knew I was always going to be someone great one day! The next adventure my grandmother and I went on was later on down the road when I was thirteen years old.

My grandmother was close to her retirement from the light rail services in the Bay Area in California. That year, my grandma took a job in San Juan, Puerto Rico, as a dispatch supervisor for their transit system. She stayed out in Puerto Rico and worked for a couple months for the light rail train system.

When my grandma came home to California to close a deal she had with one of her homes that was being sold, she had every intent of going back to Puerto Rico for work. After selling one of her homes, my grandma ended up with a hundred thousand-dollar profit.

Around that time, my grandma convinced my cousin's father and my father to let my cousin and I go on a vacation for only a couple weeks. There was my ultimate getaway it seemed from all my problems.

In Puerto Rico, my grandma had her own apartment with beautiful trees all around. At night it would rain very hard. As it rained warm drops on my face, I knew I found the peace I had wanted. Visiting the beaches was really nice! I could never forget the beach's color and how it was really blue, warm, and clear. The atmosphere was an adventure we had never experienced before. I never wanted to go back home to my dull life.

While my cousin and I adventured in the jungle trees around the apartment, we became friends with the neighbors. Eventually a month went by when my grandmother was getting phone calls that my cousin's mother was going to call the police on her if he was not returned home immediately.

My grandmother spoiled us when we were there, with no choice but to send my cousin back home. When he left, my grandmother showed me more of an adventure.

Even though she had an apartment we were living in, we went to stay at the El Conquistador resort, which was $200 a night.

My family and I stayed at the resort for three days. In the resort my grandmother spent twenty thousand dollars in jewelry for me and her.

Out of the resort she spent more money on three motorcycles. Out of the three bikes, one was mine that I would ride around town on. I had never experienced anything more amazing than the time we spent there. I felt as if I was on the best get away ever, and at that point I never wanted to go home.

    My grandmother had befriended a dark man from the Dominican Republic named Roberto. He was very kind to my grandmother and me, always making us laugh. He looked after me while my grandmother rested, showing me around the towns. She even went to try to enroll me in school but failed because it was already the middle of a semester. All the schools were private, and very hard to get accepted into in this beautiful place called "Puerto Rico." Originally, I was only supposed to go for Spring break, but then I turned out living in Puerto Rico for two and a half months.

Eventually, my father was threatening to call the police also on my grandmother so she decided it was time for us to return. It was a lifetime event that I would never forget. My grandmother didn't like anyone telling her how to live her life, especially her sons. She decided that it was her money, and she spent it the way she wanted!

Chapter Four

By the time we returned home, she had spent a little more than half of her money from her house she sold. It caused my dear grandmother to fall into a deep depression that lasted for about three years.

When my grandmother changed, we all changed with her. My family who was so used to my grandmother picking up the pieces of their financial issues, were all in an uproar, ready to blame me for part of the reason my grandmother had spent so much money. I stood by her side as I never heard the end of my father and uncle's views on my grandmother's actions.

My father was angry with me because I really didn't want to come home and went with my grandmother. I was my grandmother's favorite granddaughter. I was treated like I washer real daughter. Even though my baby brother was born with a different mother, I loved him from the bottom of my heart from the moment he was born. It wasn't until I was in high school, already on our fourth home since being with my father in California, that I found out my stepmother was a drug addict, just like my real mother.

    At a young age, I would watch my baby brother and my stepsisters. It felt as if I was a mother at a young age nurturing my sibling's and watching them grow while their mom was working. We then moved thirty minutes away from my grandmother to stay in a ghetto apartment complex that she had owned and wanted my father to manage for her.

My father always told me that the most important thing for me to do was to be successful in school so I wouldn't have to struggle or want for things later on in life. I always strived in high school to get good grades, which became my escape.

Still upset with how my life had been going, I didn't really understand at the time that my father was doing the best he could for me and my siblings all on his own. I kept myself busy so I wouldn't have to come home after school to deal with my stepmother. I involved myself in track, cross country, and basketball. Living thirty minutes away from my grandmother, I hardly was able to see her because she never wanted to come out of her bedroom.

Every time I would go see my grandmother, it hurt me that she wasn't her lively self, who wanted to go out and do things.

Throughout the school year, I noticed a girl that was in my gym class that was known around school to be bisexual. I started conversation with her off and on but found myself staying my distance from her because I was judging her for being bisexual. I knew it wasn't right to judge her, but I knew that there must have been a reason I was feeling that way. I started catching myself staring at her in the gym's locker room. I was so inexperienced to the understanding of my sexuality.

Throughout the whole year, I saw myself caught in a stare with this bisexual girl.

I knew at that moment I was bisexual. I didn't know who to turn to. None of my friends were bisexual or gay. It was the last day of school so I finally went up to the girl. I smiled at her as I started writing in her yearbook.

I wrote my phone number, telling her to call me. I was in a rush so I left. That summer we became close. I admitted to her that I like girls.

I didn't know what it was like to be involved with one but knew the girl I admitted my sexuality to was also the girl I had my eye on the whole entire school year. We dated each other over the summer mainly through the phone. I spent my summer meeting my mother and her family for the first time out of state.

My father was sick of my mother's same old stories. He felt that it was time to see who she was and what she had become for myself. My father paid for a round-trip plane ticket for me to go see my mother. I was nervous to meet my mother because I knew what I had been through in the past was nothing but disappointment with her. My mother was a drug addict for so many years, which caused her facial skin to be very wrinkled.

The first two weeks I couldn't even look my mother in her face. I didn't know her and part of me resented her for the hurt that she caused me while I had been growing up for her absence. She was still not off of drugs, but I didn't know what signs to look for at the time. My mother had introduced me to her husband. He was very nice and funny. They were both recovering from drugs.

I started hinting to my mother that I was bisexual not knowing how she was going to take the news. I had heard from my family back in California that my mother was bisexual as well.

I spent a lot of my time trying to study my mother's movements in order to see if we were similar in ways. My mother introduced me to my little brother and sister who had heard so much about me from our mother.

My brother and I bonded by playing basketball together. That experience helped me get a lot of closure to who my mother was and what other life she had. Even though, in the beginning, I wasn't too fond of seeing the mother who let me down so much, I was glad I did go visit so I could know about the other part of me. I returned home with so much to talk about. Right before the summer ended, my grandfather, Deb, and my little uncle came to visit us.

My family wanted me to finally tell my grandfather what his stepson had done to me through my childhood. Somehow the adults already were discussing it. I heard Deb say that I was lying about the situation.

My grandfather and I had been going to walk the track at my old high school when my grandfather and I went off by ourselves, so I could talk to him. I was an emotional wreck, not knowing how to explain the truth to him. I was ashamed for so long and really didn't want to discuss it. Finally, I burst into tears, and my grandfather kept asking me what was wrong with me. I told him I didn't want him to be mad at me. He asked me if Brandon had messed with me. With tears all over my face and my mouth flooded with spit, I didn't hold it in any longer. I told him he had raped and molested me. I blocked out the difference between the two words as a young kid. I vaguely told him the details, not knowing how my grandfather would act.

I told my grandfather that I was not lying. I told him about how he pretended there was candy on his penis, but I used the word *thing*, telling him he said that so that I would suck on it.

I also told my grandfather that when Brandon's friend from California came to visit us in Texas, he had stuck his finger inside of me when he was there in our home. The nasty boy snuck into my room abusing me. Somehow, no one was paying any attention to me.

Thinking it was okay, I went along with the abuse. I told my grandfather that I told Brandon what his friend did to me.

I was crying really hard at that moment. I told my grandfather I was sorry for not telling him what was going on.

I was scared my grandfather didn't believe me. I had really cared about his opinion over me. I always wanted to make him proud. I felt sick for going along with it and never telling my grandfather when it was happening.

I told my grandfather that Deb had walked in on an incident between me and her son Brandon. Deb's exact words to her son was that he better stop or she would tell my grandfather. I loved my grandfather so much because, for so long, he was the only one I felt that loved me when I was little. I knew it wasn't his fault because he was unaware. My grandfather hugged me and told me he was sorry for what had happened to me. He told me he loved me.

The moment he said it, I cried harder in his arms than when I told him. I knew that when he came originally to come visit that I would have to admit the truth to him but didn't know how with Deb around all the time. My family told me later on that Deb convinced him that I was lying and he did not believe me.

Their trip didn't last long after that. They returned home, and after I heard my grandfather didn't believe me, I resented him, not wanting him in my world ever again.

I was hurt that one of my favorite people let an evil woman ruin his relationship with his family by denying the one person who loved him with the upmost respect. We didn't speak again for years after that until later on I was long gone as a young adult. Hurt again by family, I chose to stay far away from them.

Soon my love affair with the bisexual girl came to a halt. I knew the school year was coming up again. I didn't want anyone to judge me once we returned back to school, so I put an end to it. The girl and I continued to be friends but usually, my family didn't stay in one place long so I knew sooner or later we would have to move.

It was my sophomore year when my father was having many partial problems with my stepmother. My stepmother was leaving notes on my pillow before I would get home from school saying things like I wish you weren't here.

My stepmother was acting petty, feeding me less portions than everyone else, trying to turn my sisters against me, throwing bleach all over my jeans and clothes, and expecting me to go to high school wearing them. I understood why my father stayed out working in his shop fixing cars to make a living for us, as well as, trying to escape her mouth. I was trying to escape my home life it seemed. I continued do cross country as a sport I really enjoyed. I found myself my sophomore year finding an interest in a huge linebacker named Stephen. It would rain a lot where we lived. Stephen would walk me from class to class holding an umbrella over my head. He was tall and muscular with a big heart for me. I was still a virgin and was scared to have sex because I didn't want to be a young teen with a baby.

My father and I always had talks of my future and what would happen if I made poor choices. My father never allowed me to date. It was one of his biggest rules.

When I started admitting to him that I liked girls, he thought I was just saying it to get attention. I was still not able to really do much outside of our home. I was required by my father to go to school and get home after school. He occasionally would let me go to football games and basketball games through my high school.

Everything at home was affecting me. My feelings inside were starting to feel very angry toward my stepmother. I wanted my father to leave her but didn't understand the results that were going to happen because of it. I started seeing changes in my stepmother's face a lot. She had her skin on her face always picked to where you could see her flesh mainly next to her mouth. I didn't know what it meant but caught her smoking herb a few times. My father and stepmother had enough of each other. I constantly told my father how she was taunting and harassing me. My father beat his parole. After nine years of being on parole, my father never violated not once. We moved out of the three-bedroom house we had been staying in.

My step mother got a one-bedroom apartment that my father and I would visit, while they were trying to work out their marriage. The apartment was near my high school and my sister's school. Finally, my sisters and I would watch my stepmother locking herself in her room as we smelt drugs seeping through the door. My father was never home when this was going on.

All I could remember is my sisters banging on her door to let them in. My younger sister would throw a tantrum, yelling at her mother calling her disgusting, saying after with tears flowing down her face that she would never be like her! My youngest sister was my stepmother's favorite and was always spoiled and praised more than my other sister.

At that point I knew she was a drug addict and had a problem that only she could cure herself. My father finally had enough of her and didn't want to put himself in a situation to cause him to go back to prison. Around this time, my stepmother started seeing some dude who was supplying her drugs whenever we were at school and my father was working.

Enough was enough when my father had an altercation with the dude and decided it was time to move. My father drove me up to the school, telling me that we were going to move in with my grandmother. I was upset because I didn't want to leave my high school. I had actually been going to school with some of those people since the end of middle school.

My father would tell me that I wouldn't know any of these people when I got older. It was Valentine's Day. I had Valentine's cards that I wanted to give out that day but ended up throwing them in the garbage as I walked through the school grounds. I was being rushed by my father to get my transcripts and come straight back to the car.

With great disappointment that another move was about to be made, I only said goodbye to who I could at the time. I was able to give my information to only a couple people to reach me online before I left. I started to see a change in my father's attitude toward me.

Chapter Five

The things that would come out of his mouth basically explained that he was blaming me for ruining his marriage, because his wife started to hate me while the more drugged out she got. I didn't know what to do to make things better. I was sixteen years old, trying to belong somewhere but didn't know where I belonged because we would move every couple years. To help me get my emotions out, I would spend my time rapping, writing poetry, and singing. I knew I had great talent but had so many talents that it was hard for me to put my focus in just one spot.

My first inspiration when it came to rapping was my father, and uncle's friend Todd. Todd taught me a very important thing when it came to rapping, which was not to care about what other people had to say. When I was in sixth grade, I had my first rap battle after school by the bike racks with all my friends around me, spitting off the top of my head against a boy named Bryan.

My sisters were then sent back to Nevada and I never saw them again. I continued my junior year down the street from my grandmother's house where she hardly came out of her bedroom. I was so selfish at the time and didn't want to be around my sisters caused from resent I had for their mother based on how she treated me. The moment they were gone, I missed them like crazy. As the months went by, I started seeing a change in my brother. I started missing what I had lost. I knew no family was perfect but missed the family I had been around for so long.

All I could remember is my stepmother's words, telling us kids that the portrait of us was going to be the last one we ever took together as a family because our family was soon going to be over with. My father only wanted me to be successful by staying in school. He really didn't see my talents except when it came to academics.

I knew it wasn't easy for my father to raise four kids. I started being in my rebellious stage. The last time I saw Stephen, he met me on the corner of my court hugging me, kissing me, and watching the stars with me. I knew if my father would have pulled up he would have killed me. Stephen was almost three years older than me and fully developed like a grown man. I told Stephen that I couldn't see him anymore because it would be too risky, plus he lived thirty minutes away. We talked about our future of him playing college ball. He was going to college that following year. I figured he would forget all about me. Even after time had passed I never forgot about the only real boyfriend I had ever known.

I still didn't understand fully that God had loved me all along. I didn't need anyone else but Him to guide me to the heavens above after getting through all the obstacles the world had to offer me.

That summer was the last summer I had seen my mom and her family once again. She was staying in a big house that my grandfather, her father had owned. The house was really old but was in great shape. There was a pond connected to the property. My little brother and sister would play with me as we would use a little raft to go out on the pond. My brother and I became very close that summer. I was the big sister that he had always wanted. He looked up to me and saw me as an amazing person.

I still didn't know who I was or who I was going to become. I just knew that I didn't want to let my siblings down. I was the eldest child on both sides of my family. It was hard being me at times. I had to grow up at a young age. By seventeen years old, after school, I found myself coming home to get online on a site that would let you talk to people all over the world. The site helped me meet new people and keep contact of old people that I had known through my childhood.

Still sheltered from the world, my father had me on a strict scheduled to come straight home from school. I found myself looking for someone to share my thoughts with. I had started talking to this girl from Michigan. The girl had claimed she was nineteen and went to Michigan State University. I was still new to being in any relationships, especially any gay relationships. I found interest in talking with the blonde hair beauty. One thing escalated to another. I found myself coming home every day to either get on the internet, house phone, or my cell phone to talk to Megs, this girl no one knew from Michigan. I loved talking to her about anything and everything. She became close to me. She and I spent every second of everyday on the phone in between my breaks from school.

It was the first time I had ever felt in love with someone who I had never met before online. Still young and growing, I didn't know what love was. It became an interest to me as well as it became an interest to her to have contact every day with each other. Now that I think about it, we were each other's security from the world we had in front of us. Things started getting really serious as time started passing us by.

Chapter Six

It was April 24, 2007, the day we officially called ourselves a couple. At one point of time, whenever I got disciplined, my father chose to take my privileges away.

When my dad started taking my cell phone away, I would sneak from the house phone when everyone was asleep. Megs and I would end up falling asleep together on the phone. Sometimes my father would pick up the other phone line and notice we were on the phone and yell at me the next day. Our phone conversations took up most of my time throughout my day. I didn't mind sharing my heart with someone else.

It seemed like whenever Megs felt that my interest wasn't her, we would always end up fighting. A lot of games were played between us, on and off. At one point of time, she called my house phone and told my father to have me stop calling her. No matter what, she always ended up telling me that she loved me and fixed whatever argument we were in. She told me that she was bipolar. I really didn't know what that meant but knew that she had many mood swings. She would go from angry to mad very quickly especially if she saw I was talking to other females online.

I was young and I would usually feed into playing games with her for attention. One thing she did a lot was give me attention that I felt like I was lacking.

Everything seemed to be going pretty smooth. My little brother was finally playing with the kids who lived across the street. He spent his time riding his scooter around the court. I spent a lot of my time with him trying to keep an eye on him. He started spending more time with my grandma the more we lived there.

Instead of him falling asleep with me being my baby, my brother started falling asleep with my grandma being her baby. I didn't mind it because I enjoyed being able to worry about my own life by having friends.

Having friends started being my main priority besides the online relationship I was having. My grades were being maintained but they were slipping. My priority had been changing. I was still searching for who I was and where I belonged. I didn't know what was going to happen next.

The crowd that I started hanging around was different than the crowd I was hanging around my sophomore and junior year at a different high school. I found myself riding around with friends drinking gallons of liquor on the weekends, and whenever I could get out. I started going to a lot of death metal shows in downtown San Jose, California.

Around that time, they called the crowd I hung with scene kids. I never really experienced much because I was always in the house.

My cousin Junior came to live with us for a short while. He didn't know anyone in the area, so after I had been around for a while, I had introduced him to some people. Junior and I hung out with the same crowd.

He started dating a girl who was older than me and went to my high school. She hung with the same crowd that we had been hanging out with. My cousin had been very talented in skate boarding. It was one of the biggest dreams to become pro, ever since we were small kids. He practiced almost every day.

I started getting into skate boarding too. I was not by far as good as my cousin, but I was able to keep up when he and the neighborhood boys would skate far distances.

Junior and I started partying hard. We were in our experimental stages where we were trying mushrooms, ex, weed and coke.

I finally got away for the summer going to visit my father's cousin who I barely knew in Clovis, California. There, I had went to summer school and worked a full-time job opening up the kiosk and closing it for a company that sold sunglasses. Early in the morning starting at 5:00 A.M till the store closed in the evening was when I had to work. The heat was 116-degree weather. I was still dating Megs online off and on as I was experiencing a falling out with my dad's cousin.

One of my cousin's ex-boyfriends ended up feeling sorry for me, so he helped me. My cousin had been trying to put me out of her house knowing I was far from home. He decided to take me home to his mother to help me. Still so young, I was very inexperienced in many degrees. I ended up falling for the trap and sleeping with him.

He then introduced me to one of his friends who was a truck driver who let me stay at his house. He was never home and was always on the road. He wanted someone to watch over his apartment so that no one would break in. The community mainly consisted of Hispanics.

I only knew a little Spanish and tried to stay away from all trouble. I remodeled the truck driver's apartment for him by making it more comfortable and clean. He put me on the lease. He treated me like I was one of his daughters. I later on met a beautiful Hispanic girl who was older than me with no kids. She was a beautiful young woman who lived in a really ghetto area around Fresno, California. I had never been exposed to much back in the Bay Area and wanted to escape.

I ended up staying out there all summer but felt that someone was watching me at the apartment because I was all alone.

I decided to return home instead of running away from my problems, trying to find who I was. The beautiful girl and I parted but always kept contact online. That was the first time in my life I felt some type of independence.

It was the first time in my life I felt free to make decisions on my own even if they weren't the best. I wanted to grow and felt that at home I couldn't grow because I was being controlled by my father.

That summer I had learned how to survive in another area other than home. Blessed by God that my friend's mother was making sure I was okay throughout my journey. I knew from that instant that I was blessed by the Lord above who guided me out of that situation. It taught me how to approach new situations with a little more knowledge and care.

When I returned back to the Bay Area, I felt a bit more experienced in life. Not being able to comprehend that I had much more to learn from life, I still assumed I knew it all. My family was upset with me for not coming home right away.

We were trying to work out our dysfunction but didn't have the right way to do so. Immediately I turned to drugs and alcohol to try, and overlook my reality of my past abuse.

My cousin Junior was doing the same thing it seemed. I knew one day I would be at peace with my past.

Hoping for the same peace for my cousin it seemed it was easier for me to forgive than my cousin Junior. We started growing apart as our friends and hobbies started to change. I wasn't getting along with my father because of some of the poor choices I had made. I was going to be eighteen in two months.

I knew that my family was angry with me because I had failed in school to be successful. The more me and my father fought, the more I resented him.

I then decided to move in with a guy friend of mine who was very loyal to me named Vince. Vince was a hippie at heart who was raised by his mother.

He was a sweetheart that wanted to save me out of my home life. He ended up taking me back and forth to school. I hung out with him and his best friend Jackson.

I spent my weekends with them, spending nights with them on a private beach called Davenport Beach that not many people knew about. The beach was off the coast and very well hidden. We had to climb down the rocky mountain to get to it. Once we got to it though, it was one of the most beautiful sites with a cliff in the water that people would jump off of. Sometimes my cousin would meet us there because we had the same acquaintances.

One person who had my back besides Vince was my cousin's friend Corey. Corey would drive me around and let me stay at his house when I needed a place to crash. He was about six or seven years older than me. No matter what, he looked out for me though. I finally felt like I was wanted around someone in what felt like a tough time in my life.

There were many other friends that I had that were real friends, but they all had different views on life. Around those times I wasn't the best person to be around. My state of mind was weak and selfish. Megs and I continued to talk over the phone.

We went back and forth wanting to be in a relationship with each other but didn't know how.

When I moved out of Vince's house, I ended up moving on the block with a boy who was interested in me named Jim. Jim was a sweet guy who lived with his parents who were fairly older, around my grandparents' age. He was about six years older than I was. Somehow I convinced him to book me a plane ticket to Michigan so I could see this girl who had a part of me that I couldn't let go. He was interested in me and respected me.

My cousin hung out on that same block with all the same people I had been hanging out with. He really wanted me to move back home, but I was being so rebellious at the time. I didn't want to go back. The plane ticket was booked for a week. I left all my belongings at his house.

I had every intention to go visit the girl I had been talking to for so long and then to come right back. Around this time in my life I was very confused. I was lost, wanting to know who I was and where I truly belonged. I didn't know what I was going to do when I came back to California because, it seemed like I had pretty much no options.

I burnt a lot of bridges for being selfish and making poor choices. Many people I was friends with stayed with their parents. People I knew couldn't pick up the slack of having another mouth to feed. I knew, from that moment on, that I had to do something positive or my life was going to be going down a bad road.

Chapter Seven

October 16, 2008, was when my plane arrived in Michigan. I had a round trip plane ticket that had a set date and time for when I was supposed to return in California. I only had ten dollars in my pocket when I arrived in Michigan. I was very excited to see Megs. We always had talked about being engaged and our future together. I believed every word she had told me about her life. I believed that she was really nineteen and went to Michigan State University.

I was polite to her mother when she pulled up to pick me up from the airport outside. She helped me put my bags in the trunk. On the drive to their home, I asked her mother if it was true that she was her adopted mother. Her mother laughed a little and then told me no, and that she was her real birth mother. That was the first lie that I discovered wasn't the truth. The airport was a forty-five-minute drive from their home. By the time we got to their home, I was exhausted from the eight hours of traveling. There she was laying in her living room floor with her comforter. She looked exactly like she did online, beautiful with platinum blonde hair and baby blue eyes. Even though she was laying down, she had her make up done. We both smiled at each other because we had joy in our hearts knowing we had waited so long to finally be next to each other. I ran up to her, tackling her, giving her a huge hug immediately. I thought it was so cute the way she giggled when I did so.

Everything had seemed so perfect at that very moment. I reached in my bag for what I had brought her. I gave her a ring that I had, hoping that we would be able to establish some type of engagement. She then gave me a ring that she had as well.

I found out from her mother that she was fifteen turning sixteen in two months. That wasn't the only thing she had lied to me about now. She also didn't attend Michigan State University. I didn't know how to act toward her. Here I was eight states away from home, visiting a girl that I had believed was someone she wasn't. What could I expect? I was talking to practically a complete stranger.

    I should have noticed some signs when we had our own problems in the past through long distance. In a sense, you could say I was holding on to someone who I really never knew anything about. I was eighteen years old at that time, able to make grown-up decisions but didn't know where to start. I had a gut nervous feeling about the rest of my trip there.

After confronting Megs about who she really was made my stomach drop while questioning her. My instinct knew things weren't what I had been told for the past couple years. Megs's mom was in the medical field. They had an upscale apartment right by the water in the city of Harrison Township. Harrison Township was outside of Detroit in the suburb area. I talked to my friends in California daily because my cell phone had worked there.

    My father had no idea I had planned to come to Michigan. Even though I didn't live with him anymore, he would have never allowed me to travel across country for some chick I met online. As the days grew staying at Megs house, things were getting a bit confusing. We were from two different worlds with a relationship that was formed based on lies. We didn't really know each other as much as we thought we did. All we knew was that we thought we were in love with each other.

    I had been talking to her for so long. Even though she lied about who she was, the feelings that we had grew from each other weren't going away. What Megs and I shared was different from any love that I had experienced in my future. Later on in life I realized what we shared was lust, and infatuation for the thought of us being in love.

This feeling seemed to shine so bright like a light that wouldn't be able to go out. The more we started to argue about the pettiest things such as my relationships with other people I knew that I had to shut her out of my heart. As much as I tried to shut her out, somehow the feelings I had for her would always find their way back into my heart. The few days we spent together were very unstable. We found ourselves fighting off and on one minute and then loving on each other the next.

At one point of time, she showed me how bipolar she really was. She had been working on her homework and got mad at me about something. She started stabbing her homework screaming angrily. Another day she had locked me on her balcony and asked me how was the weather. Thank God the snow hadn't come yet. She thought it was funny but, I really didn't especially after she left me out there for fifteen minutes.

My plane was leaving that following Wednesday. Even after all the drama we had experienced, we both really didn't want me to leave to return to California. We hugged each other tight, crying with pain of the thought of losing what we had held together for so long. We stood holding each other tight telling each other we didn't want to leave each other. Somehow I knew that I had to leave and had ever intention in returning but something held me back. I missed my plane going back home. Thinking that I would be able to rebook it for another time, I called the travel agent. The airline had my ticket as nonrefundable ticket.

Even though I didn't want to leave her, a sense of panic came over my body. I called my father telling him the truth that I was in Michigan. He was angry when I told him. He wanted to pay for me to come home instantly. I told him that I would get back to him on that. I continued to live my fairy tale for the moment. We were living in a fairytale that we didn't want to break.

We were two totally different people who experienced a lot as children that we really didn't have any control of. She had a twin sister who had been around for part of the time I was in there home. They were two opposites of each other. Her sister had understanding of mercy from her experiences with the Lord. Megs really didn't have the same dreams her sister did. Her sister's dreams were to go out of the country to help people change for the better through teaching them Christianity.

Meg's sister seemed more, humble than she was. I started to think of how much better things would have been if I met her online instead of the twin who had so much pain in her heart. I knew I wasn't anyone to judge her for her mental issues, but I knew that I loved her. Soon I was to learn that she was never going to change unless she wanted to change. It was also hard for her to change her train of thought when she was naturally mentally sick, taking medicine that she was required to take from the doctor.

A week had finally passed in Michigan! Toward the end of the week things got worse. We had experienced drama that was unnecessary. By me missing my plane, I had no choice. I was stuck with this Barbie looking girl for a few days until my dad's cousin Frances who was like an aunt to me, could figure out how to get a ticket home for me. Megs had homecoming in a week or so for her high school. She had a boy named Lex who she had befriended at school who asked her to go with him to homecoming.

When he came over to fix her computer one day, I was extremely jealous of the fact he was taking the girl I loved to the dance. She decided that we were going to go to the mall with Lex and her twin so she could shop for her dress. When he picked us up, I was mad beyond belief. Here I was in another state visiting a girl that I fell in love with and she was here purposely trying to make me jealous with this short, stocky boy who drove an '07 white Charger that was juiced up with tinted windows, rims, and a loud banging system. I was still in shock as we arrived at the mall.

The boy was very polite to me. The whole time we were at the mall, I had felt very uncomfortable based on the fact that we were arguing and not getting along at her house. I knew the real reason that we were going through the trouble we were. She didn't want me to go home and I made it clear to her that I wanted to go especially after she started treating me bad. I was sad along with her but knew my home was in California.

The mall was very small. I had never seen a mall as small as that. Coming from California, there was many malls near where I had lived that were a big size with many stores to offer. The first place we went was a place called Coney Island, a diner that seemed extremely busy. The fighting back and forth took my appetite away. She ordered a desert. I couldn't remember what her sister had ordered.

The boy Lex ordered a meal. When we got up to pay at the front register, I asked the girl who ran us up if they were hiring. She replied no and said the chef, but that I was pretty. I looked at him and said thank you. That compliment made my night a bit better until Megs got angry, grabbing my hand, yelling while she was pulling me out of the restaurant. I was extremely embarrassed.

I started holding my tears back, rushing the boy Lex to let me get my purse out of the trunk of his car so I could have a cigarette. While I was having my cigarette, it started to sprinkle a little. He told me that I was too pretty to be upset, as he could tell I was struggling with my emotions. The minute he begged me not to cry, my eyes started pouring. It hit me that I was stuck in Michigan being mistreated. I felt stupid for leaving my friends and family to come to another state to be only put down and hurt.

Lex told me that if I wanted, I could come and stay at his house knowing I was all alone with not many options on my hands. I wanted to get away from here. My heart felt so broken because this wasn't the first time she had been acting the way she was with me. Not thinking everything through, when we got to her house, I packed up most of my belongings. I wrote her the fastest letter I had ever written, letting her know that she had hurt me and I couldn't take it any longer. Attached with the letter I enclosed the ring, giving it back to her to let her know I was serious. The ring resembled our plans of marriage in our future. I knew if I couldn't deal with being treated that way for a week, I wouldn't be able to marry her. Tears flowed down my face dripping all over the letter. Meg's mother was sleeping because she had to be at work the next day. Her sister was very cooperative with my decision. Feeling bad for me, she took the letter to give to her sister. I grabbed my suitcase, rushing down the three flight of stairs fast with tears flowing down my face. What was bothering me the most was that she seemed like she didn't care while she slammed her front door. As I left, it felt like she never loved me at all because she let me leave so easily. We drove away fast blaring Gucci Mane. I had no idea where I was.

Chapter Eight

Lex took me to his house. Before we went inside, I had my last cigarette for the night. His mother was asleep and didn't know that I was there. He snuck me in his basement quietly, giving me a blanket to sleep with. His basement seemed a bit cold. My eyes were very sore from crying and my heart was weak. Megs kept calling with ridiculous amounts of phone calls. I chose to ignore her. Lex started receiving texts from her telling him that his mother and her mother were going to exchange words if I wasn't returned to her at once. I ended up texting her back a few times telling her to leave me alone. Neither of us paid any mind to her.

I finally was able to fall asleep on his mini couch. The next morning Lex had me go upstairs and speak to his mother. At first his mother was a bit rude to me, but once I explained my situation to her, she said that I could live with them as long as I went to school. I knew I had the potential to be great in school. I felt that there was my chance to actually graduate high school even though I was starting late in the school year. I listened to his mother, respecting her rules and wishes. I signed up for school at an adult education learning center. His mother laid down the law as if I was her own birth daughter. Even though I was so used to doing what I wanted to do, it felt good to actually have a woman role model who cared about my future. I never experienced a mother's view like this woman had viewed things. She was upset with my family back in California.

Mainly the woman after talking to my father over the phone didn't understand my father for not wanting to support me based on the fact that I was eighteen years old, with a past full of mistakes.

I resembled my mom in many ways but never wanted to admit it. In my past, some of my family would tell me that I looked like my mother. As a child I despised her for her absence, not wanting any part of her genes. The main reason that I had never wanted to be a drug addict was from feeling so alone from knowing my mother chose drugs over me. She really had done nothing for me my whole life. I didn't know how to accept her in my life as my birth mother because she had never been a real mother to me. I was scared of turning into my worst nightmare like my mother had done to herself. She struggled with her drug addiction back and forth, trying to keep herself clean. I heard stories about my mother not understanding who she really was. The stories I heard I had tried to ignore because they were all negative. Self-consciously, I knew after meeting her some of the stories had to be true. I felt that she never loved me.

There I was mentally still a child, sitting waiting for someone at that moment to lead me in the right direction, a mother figure like Lex's mother. My mother was a completely different character than her. My mother abandoned me and never looked back, building her own family forgetting that she had me. My father was bitter toward my mother for abandoning us and destroyed everything that they had built together. My experiences with my mother scarred me to never want a motherly bond with any other woman. That all changed when Lex's mom started accepting me as her own. Stepmother as my second mother, and then I experienced Lex's mother as a third mother was all very overwhelming.

Lex's mother helped me and supported me better than any of my other mothers. Besides my stepmother helping my father raise me, She showed an interest in me and my future. She mother clothed, fed, and spoiled me. Showing me a mother-daughter relationship based on time and money. Everything that my third mother did for me, she did out of the kindness of her heart to see me succeed. After a few months of living there, it felt very natural to call her mom.

As time progressed and I went to school, I spent most of my time with her. She gave me advice to let Megs go because it was nothing but constant drama with the girl. I really didn't know what type of medical and mental issues his mother had. I soon was to realize that most of her mental issues were caused from being abused and mistreated by people. The more she opened up to me, she told me stories of when men mistreating her. I started getting friends at my adult education school that I was attending. I soon started seeing a change in his mother of jealousy because she was so used to us spending time together. I started to feel weird about her train of thought. She seemed not to care that I was living there.

Lex started to like me a bit more than a friend. Once I established a mother-daughter relationship with his mother, I felt it odd to be anything more than a sister to him. He started resenting me for the way I thought of him. I started to realize that when he decided to help me, it was because he liked me and saw potential in a relationship with me. In school, I did very well because the education level was way lower than the level in California. I also believed it was because I was focused in my work. California education had more expectations from its students. Lex was two years younger than I was. The feeling for Megs still was there inside of me.

Most of my days consisted of spending time at home on the computer. I was doing it again. I was going back to the same patterns of getting online to seek love from Megs. We never hung out though because she was bitter toward me for moving in with Lex. Going our separate ways was extremely hard to do. She was all I ever knew for so long. The dream of our love was all I ever knew for so long. Lex's mother turned the basement into his room and his old room into my room. She bought us both brand-new queen-sized mattresses. Some friends I had who were in the automotive class helped me fix up a '97 Camaro that Lex's mother bought me from a kid at my school for two hundred dollars.

The boy I befriended worked very hard to help me. I didn't know him well but he lived down the street from me. My car ended up getting fixed by him and another boy in his garage. I thought I knew about cars but really didn't know much. They were able to get my car running with the help of my new mother.

His mom provided the finances for my vehicle. She made sure she took me shopping for clothes right before Christmas because I needed winter clothes. She made me feel really great about myself by helping me. I started changing in so many ways. I was so use to being sheltered growing up. Then something amazing changed for me. I guess you could call it life. I decided to start doing my make-up, wearing the brand MAC, which was an expensive brand of make-up. I also finally was done having the same hairdo.

I dyed my hair blonde with pink in it. Eventually I had someone who took classes cut all my hair off, giving me a cute Mohawk look with platinum blonde hair with hot pink at the top. I liked my new look and felt that I could actually be my own person without my father's opinion. My style was completely different from others at school. People knew I was from California, especially with the way I presented myself.

Once everything seemed to be going smooth with school and at home, I started searching again for some compassion. Somehow I ended up talking to another girl online. She lived about four hours away from my current address. I still didn't know my way around that much, but I had learned the basic routes that I needed to know.

Megs ended up throwing soda on my car, leaving behind her glove after hanging with some people late at night. She continued to make little minor threats, and my mom said that she wanted to report her to the police station. The police said that the only thing I could do was get a restraining order on her. I really didn't want to go through with it because I still loved her. We ended up going back and forth, arguing and not getting anywhere until one day I went skiing a couple hours north with a guy friend I had met. My new mom supported all the things I wanted to do. I told her that Megs and I were going to try and work things out. She had love for me so she said it was okay for the ex-girlfriend to come spend the night. She really didn't care for her at all though and preferred me to let that part of my life go.

On the way home from skiing, we picked up Megs at Pontiac from her grandmother's house. I wanted to fix things with her. I had hope that we could fix what we had. She told me that she was going through a situation with her mom's ex-boyfriend and the courts.

I was not told many details, but after we had talked, we chose not to have any sexual relationship from that time on. My mom didn't want her there any longer, so I told her that she had to leave. My mom and I dropped her off at her mom's house the next day. I was told she wasn't allowed to come over any longer.

I could tell that the girl I loved was jealous of the fact that someone was helping me trying to see me succeed. My bedroom was nice. I had nice sheets, blankets, pillows, and a computer in my bedroom. It was the first time in years that I felt peace. At my grandmother's house in California, I had a twin mattress. I finally experienced the true meaning of comfort at Lex's home.

Still trying to be a part of my ex-girlfriend's life, I ended up befriending people who ended up knowing her. We would hang out with the same people but never around the same time.

My new mom thought it would be a great idea to take me and her niece to the Li'l Wayne and Keisha Cole concert. It was a really good concert that was held at the Joe Arena concert hall located in downtown Detroit. That was one of the first times I had been to Detroit. It was my first concert that I had ever been to. I was so excited and felt such love for this woman who wanted to show me that she could provide a better life than my own family in California. We ended up taking the boy that fixed my car who went to school with me. He and I were close but never messed around.

Eventually he started dating his ex-girlfriend again and we ended up growing apart. I was still talking to the girl who called herself Jersey. I should have learned my lesson about meeting people online because of the situation I had just been in with my ex-girlfriend.

Chapter Nine

I finally went up to visit Jersey, assuming that she was going to be a different situation than the last. I took a boy with me to protect me I was becoming really close with named Reg who went to school with me. Reg was one of my first black friends. Reg actually was the first person who called me Cali. Later on, I started just calling myself "Cali Girl" when I hung out with the black community.

We had known that things were divided by race still in Michigan. We both knew that black people mainly lived in Detroit or out where we lived. People up north were mainly white and retired with families. There was a lot of racism in Michigan that I hardly knew anything about. White people and black people were still struggling with racism, hating on each other, finding no understanding that it was the millennium.

Later on as time progressed, and I met so many people, I then realized that black and whites weren't the only races hating on each other. Many races were so separated into their own cities and areas. People I talked to would say California was ten years ahead of Michigan in many ways.

I honestly believed that based on what I ended up seeing. On the way there, about twenty miles before we got to her town, my car broke down. I ended up running out of gas. It was night time and raining off and on. Reg was a little nervous because, he was a tall young dark skinned man in a random town where he knew black people were not liked. We ended up being able to have someone stop to take us to a gas station to get gas, for my car.

CALI GIRL, HOW DID I MAKE IT IN THE TREACHEROUS STREETS OF DETROIT?

My car still needed a lot of work and I should have never chosen to drive it that far. Once we were able to get the car running we drove it straight to her house. Jersey's home was small. Her mother's home was over a hundred years old and was falling down. The inside of it was really creepy because it was a home that needed so much work done to it. The staircase was collapsing and so was the balcony. Her background was she was from Michigan but moved to Arizona for some guy then ended up moving back. I really didn't know her but wanted a new girlfriend who could keep me busy. It was very beautiful up north. I loved the scenery.

We spent the night at her house. In the morning we got up and got her things. I drove my car a couple miles from her house, heading to one of her friends' houses where I was able to have my car checked out. I really had no idea what sort of girl she was until that trip. It ended up being a nightmare. I gave the girl too much credit assuming that she wasn't nasty.

Along the way, I met this amazing guy that she had told me after the fact that she was involved with. My car was being looked at across the street. I needed some work done before we were to return back home. I went independently across the street, leaving Reg and the girl Jersey to handle my business. My new mom paid $150 for my fuel pump to be fixed. When I was gone, the boy Zeek, Reg and the girl Jersey ended up sexually messing around. By the time I went back to knock on the apartment door, none of them would answer the door. I was really mad because I felt like I got played once again. I was told by Reg and Zeek later on that the girl was nasty and ended up giving Reg head right along with Zeek having sex with her. They called her a bustos. That was my first time understanding what that word meant.

The word was another term for a slut. Part of me wanted to leave Reg there for betraying me. Here he was getting close to me as a friend, and then disregarding my feelings for the girl and still messed around with her. At first I was mad at him, but we ended up having an understanding that the girl was worthless. The girl started fighting with Zeek. He was in a messed up situation like I was in with my family back in California. He didn't have anywhere to go. I found an interest in him. He and I talked about different things that we could relate to mainly being hurt by our exes. I felt bad but wanted to know him more.

I decided to take him to his grandma's house to get his things so he could return with me. Irritated with Reg for what went down, he sat in the back seat while me and Zeek got to know each other.

When we got back home, I dropped Reg off and told him I'd see him around school. In the back of my mind, I was hurt that he did something like that to me but knew what I had been taught about most men being deceiving.

Zeek was handsome and had a tattoo on the right side of his neck, saying his real name in Spanish. He was half black and half Mexican. I was scared to get close to him but was tired of dealing with girls. I never had a real boyfriend but my high school sweetheart.

We soon connected really fast and close.

At school I had really only hung with two African American girls. One was named Nini and the other was Kimmy. We also hung with a boy we would smoke herb with named Nae. When I returned introducing them to the boy I had brought back with me, they really weren't all too fond of the idea of me dating this boy.

Zeek and I found ourselves inseparable. My high school prom was coming up and mom wanted it to be an amazing experience for me. She bought Zeek and me our attire and paid for our tickets.

It wasn't a nice experience the first time I let a girl put a sew in in my hair. I didn't know how it was supposed to look, but people told me later on that it terrible really hated the idea of a boy living with us. Zeek had a similar story like mine, but it was very different. We both lacked the support from our families.

Lex's mother was what he needed as for what I needed. Around that time, Lex's mother spoke to my father in California, telling him that he basically owed her child support for supporting me for the past time. He laughed at her, thinking she was crazy. I just understood in a sense where she was coming from.

The woman had helped me so much and wanted a kickback in return for the help. He felt that I was eighteen and wanted to leave so it wasn't his responsibility. His bond with me grew the more time we spent together. A boy struggling to become a man changed my interest in caring for another person. My heart was confused. I was getting scared the more I started to love Zeek. I knew I just wasn't in love with him. The old love I already had for a girl was stopping me from moving on with him. We became a couple, Zeek and I.

I decided to stay with him even though part of my heart belonged to someone else. I stayed in a relationship with him until things started to get tough at home with my new mom.

My relationships were crashing and now I understand I was being extremely selfish letting friends become an importance. On the freeway one day, when school went back into session from the holiday break, I was coming up the ramp on Metro parkway and ended up getting into a car accident with my car losing control spinning all the way around facing traffic.

I had Zeek with me because, while I was at school, he would sometimes wait for me until in my car or he would go put in applications. I immediately saw my life flash before my eyes and jumped into the passenger seat with my boyfriend. I ended up getting whiplash when the car spun around.

I was so grateful that the semi-truck coming our way did not hit us. The police came and dropped us off at school. I called my mom immediately, telling her that my tired were bald and I had just been in a terrible accident. The tow yard came and got my car. My mom didn't want to get it out because she had felt that she was already spending too much money as it was on me. We decided to let it go rather than get it out to repair it.

My new mom didn't want to drop me off at school any longer so she looked online and found a car for me that was a '97 Saturn for 2,500. She told me that it was a steal and she encouraged me to go with her to look at it. I really didn't want her to buy me anything else, but I knew I needed another form of transportation instead of relying on her to always drive me around.

I was really excited to get a nicer car that was more efficient. She went to the ATM and then we headed out to Pontiac. There a man showed me the car. It was very clean with a little system in the trunk and a nice set of rims. I loved the car and watched her purchase it in cash.

Two or three months went by when my new mom was getting depressed all the time because she was single. She wanted to share her life with someone. The more she saw me happy, it seemed the more she was unhappy. Seeing this change in her attitude I started to not want to be around.

I ended up getting into an argument with her and decided to move out with no plan. I went from a stage of being fed to going hungry. I needed to stay focus, and at that point, school was not in season so I lost all focus by hanging out with the wrong people. I had Zeek carry my things to my car. My new mom offered him to stay at the house. I didn't want to leave him because I had brought him all the way there but knew it was best for him to stay with her so she could take care of him.

My car and insurance was in my name. I didn't know where I was going to go but made a couple friends along the way. I knew I had to think fast because my actions were going to reflect my future. I felt really bad one day when I didn't want to be around Zeek from having a bad day dealing with stress not being at home staying at friends' houses. I yelled at him and told him to go home. I told him that I wanted to break up with him that it wasn't working out. I couldn't take care of him because I could barely take care of myself now that I was on my own and that's how I explained it to him.

When he called me later that day, I told him that I was going to stay in Detroit with my friend Nini from my school's sister. He told me immediately he wanted to come with me. My friend told me that he could not come with me, and I told him that. I cared about him and told him that it was better for him to stay with my new mom because he wouldn't have to struggle with me. I told him that I could not go back and live with her.

Chapter Ten

I was scared and had no idea what I was getting myself into. The next time I called my new mom, I asked her to check up on Zeek. I heard that he had returned on a bus back up north because he had a court date coming up.

From that moment on, we lost contact and I never heard from him again. He had no cell phone. I felt bad for not letting him love me. It was one of the biggest mistakes I had ever made. I knew that he was going to find a nice girl somewhere that he could spend his life with. He claimed that he and his ex were talking back and forth, so I didn't know what he wanted to actually do with himself. I always cared for him and sometimes wondered how different things would have been for me if I didn't run away from him and my new mom didn't change the course of my future.

Nini was younger than me but was a black girl who cared for me as if I was one of her best friends. Her older sister lived on Six Mile Road and Goulburn, which was one of the worst areas on the east side of Detroit. I knew Detroit was bad but had no idea where I was about to be staying. I was still really fresh to being in Michigan. Here I was a pretty young light-skinned mixed girl who had dyed bleach blonde hair. I stood out in an area that mainly were all blacks unless they were crack addicts. People would call this area the hood. My friendship with Nini grew. We became inseparable. It was known that everywhere I went, she went. I still didn't know her very much but relied on her for food and shelter.

Meeting my friend's sister was a different experience. Her plans for me were not logical in my mind. Every day for a week and a half, I drove me and Nini to school to Riverside Academy. My high school's policies were extremely strict. If you attended there and missed five days without making time up, you were dropped. If you missed seven days, you were still dropped. Nini was dropped before I was. It was hard for me to attend school with no money for gas because school was twenty minutes away from her sister's house.

Finally, after the long struggle of trying to stay in school, I dropped. I was so close to graduation with only one credit to achieve, but I had to wait to reenroll when a new term began.

An incident happened one morning when Nini's sister's ex-convict boyfriend stole my cell phone when I was taking a shower. I wasn't sure who to trust. My mind was weary of Nini and her family. In the hood they looked at white people as suckers. I wasn't all black. I actually could pass for a white girl faster than a black girl. In the hood people thought that they could manipulate white people to do what they wanted because they felt that white people were stupid. From my experience, Detroit is a very racist place.

Never expecting to be treated the way I had gotten treated in Detroit, I had to remind myself that it was all over the news that Detroit was one of the most dangerous areas in the country. If I would have known that I was going to be living in a place that was known as the murder capital of the world, I would have never come. Detroit was difference from what I had ever experienced.

People there were street hustlers, with street smarts that they had been born with from being in a dangerous city. Everywhere you went in the city, people had alternative motives up their sleeves.

After I left Nini's sister's house, I went to live with her mother and other sister in the suburbs of Fifteen Mile Road. I was only there a few weeks until a bunch of drama occurred. Nini and my relationship was more based on her wanting her way. Most of the time I gave her that to avoid conflicts. I was what people would tell me was too nice.

Staying with her mother was different. Her mother seemed to be a sweet, gentle woman who looked at life in a religious aspect. Nini had three sisters. The sister above her was a lesbian who perceived herself as a man by dressing like one with a buzzed cut hairdo.

CALI GIRL, HOW DID I MAKE IT IN THE TREACHEROUS STREETS OF DETROIT?

The type of lesbian she was labeled as in the community was called a stud.

Even though I like females I was never attracted to that type of girl. I was never interested in a woman who wanted or felt like she was a man. I enjoyed women who knew they were women, who were proud to express themselves by looking and acting like one. Even though it wasn't something that interested me. I never judged her sister for her interests.

At first it seemed as if the family I had been living with was nice. It wasn't until the first time I branched off from her to hang with a girl me and Nini's sister had met in Detroit at a gas station was when I got to see things on my own.

The next day her sister and I planned to hang out with the girl because her sister wanted to protect me from getting myself in any bad predicaments. Her sister took a liking to me wanting to see me hurt. We had met her on Connor and Jefferson in one of the deadliest areas at around ten o'clock at night. It was pitch-black and the cold pressed up against my face. I called the girl Ciara and she came to meet us outside. We walked to the back of the house where we were greeted by a staircase entrance to the back door. Inside when we finally got there she introduced us to twelve young African Americans.

The moment I counted all those guys, my heart creeped up on me with a thump. I was worried until I saw Ciara's face smiling right at me. While she was staring at me with her smile, she said, "You straight." I noticed there was wooden big logs put up against the front and back door locking it from anyone trying to kick the door in. I figured it might have just been because, the area we were in was bad. We hung out there with them for about an hour until my nerves started getting bad noticing some of the guys waving guns in the air. I started questioning in my mind what were we doing there? My friend Nini's sister started, panicking me, telling me she wanted to go.

Watching her manly sister who always acted so tough made me laugh inside a little but then again was not laughing at all. At that moment I knew I was in a trap house. Next we heard bump, bump, and then a thump at the front door, watching the guys rushing to the door. We heard it again.

At that time my friend's sister and I got up running to the back door where we came in at, moving the log from the door as quickly as possible. We then were approached by all the guys that they wanted us to stay. The people at the front door were people that they already knew but, we felt it was time for us to go. Ciara told me everything was all right. I told her I wasn't comfortable with staying any longer and asked her if she wanted me to drop her off at her boyfriend's where she was staying. She said yes. About five guys walked us outside to my car. I knew after talking to them that they were all right people. I just wasn't use to all of what was going on around me. It was pitch black outside as they made sure we got into our car safely I felt as if we had been escorted by some body guards. That night was the first night I learned to try and have faith that not everyone was bad and out to get me. Ciara sat in the back seat drunk.

Before we pulled off, she started throwing up outside my car. Still watching my surroundings, I helped her as much as I could, holding her hair back so she didn't throw up on it. She finally finished and we took off. When we got to her boyfriend's, she got out and went inside. On the way home I was confused at how to get home because I had never driven in that area before. All the way home I got scolded by my new friend Nini's sister. She yelled at me, saying I was naive for putting her in a situation with a bunch of niggas.'

I understand how she felt but was intrigued by how I never had been subjected to that. Ciara was brave and very experienced when it came to her city. One of the next places she had taken me to was an abandoned house on the east side of Detroit that she wanted to squat in to make her own. When we got to the abandoned house, it was really big. I was extremely scared as saw on the outside of the home yellow caution tape all throughout the front yard. I was really scared but thought the girl and I had a connection from jump street. We had also hung out a few times before we had gone there. I was scared and didn't want to go inside the house.

We walked around to the back door as I was grabbing on her arms terrified. The house had no electricity and it was already dark outside. I took a step foot in the back door taking a step out telling her I'm not going in there. She told me not to be scared so I trusted her holding on her tight. We held hands and went inside the house that which she had already been in. The house was actually really nice. I could tell a renter must have just moved out and remodeled it because it was freshly painted. I admired the carpet and bathroom too for being all remodeled. Ciara and I talked about my situation after being from California with no family. We talked about how things weren't working with the girl I was staying with and how I needed a new place to live. The grew and I had a lot in common but mostly the fact that we had to survive on our own. In the abandoned house, she and I had ended up getting really close to each other engaging in something I thought was never going to happen. I was attracted to her but knew she had just broke up with a boyfriend claiming she wasn't gay. The girl ended up coming onto me.

I was still scared thinking someone was going to bust right in since we were in an abandoned house. She told me she liked me and really didn't like girls. I was cold because there was no heat. She wanted me to try something new with her.

Chapter Eleven

Ciara was a beautiful brown-skinned girl that had a perfect fit body with her hair done up in some zillions always pinned up. She started touching all over me. I was still shy at really hooking up with anyone being so young and inexperienced in sex. I pulled my jeans down only a little, still watching the door, making sure no one bursts in. I let her lick me just a couple times, but got freaked out because of the atmosphere and told her to stop because I was leaving this creepy house.

I had never been in any abandoned house before. Driving I had passed by them but saw on the news how people were being murdered every day. Ciara and I started getting real cool. I started to feel like I had someone else that I could trust that may be able to help me get around in the city. I invited Ciara to Nin's mother's house for her older sister's baby shower. I didn't realize that Nini was getting jealous that whole time. It soon escalated to where Nini and Ciara had exchanged numbers.

When I had told Nini after the baby shower about the incident with Ciara, claiming she was straight, I guess it made Kimmy and Nini mad about my actions because they were the only girls I had hung out with. When I told them they seemed a little mad, but I really didn't see it at that Nini started trying to get close with Ciara. All the girls started hanging out as I started hanging out with Nini's sister a little bit more. Nini and I started having altercations to where she wanted to fight me. I didn't understand why except for the fact that she must have been hurt I wasn't spending much time with her anymore still staying at her house.

Not expecting what was going to happen next, I didn't want to put myself in a situation alone. I went over to Kimmy's house with a couple white girls that I had met through a friend that were not fighters.

Kimmy stayed on shady side, which was a hood area in Mount Clemens with nice houses that the black community worked hard to maintain. Many homeowners were established there for years. Kimmy was pregnant, about to have a baby in four months. When I pulled up, she waited on her porch. Who came out from behind the side of her house was Nini and Ciara running up with a baseball bat.

All the girls and I piled out of the car because I didn't want them to bash my window. The girls were scared and screaming. I was mad and couldn't do anything. I was outnumbered and they had a bat. Ciara kept saying, "So I ate you? I ate you?" She was acting like it never happened, trying to attack me verbally looking hurt. I was honest, saying yeah, not caring what anyone thought.

Nini snatched my keys and they both jumped in my car, taking off. By that time Kimmy went in her house acting as if she had no idea they were going to do that. Till this day, Kimmy says she had no idea they were going to take my car. I called the police; they showed up fast. I was not the type of chick to call the police but had no choice because I wanted my car back.

I told Kimmy to relay the message that the police were called. Nini later on called me, putting most the blame on Ciara. I understood why Ciara was scared about coming out about liking girls but I started questioning if the other two girls were curious about their sexuality.

Kimmy seemed like she was irritated with what I had done with Ciara, and so was Nini. I kept thinking over and over again why would any of these girls care what I did with this Ciara girl if they were straight? I told Nini's sister I was getting close with what had happened. She had taken the bus to meet me and return to her home.

I trusted her sister a little more than Nini because she was easy to talk to and had less drama. Everyone knew what happened. Ciara had contacted me on my cell phone. When we talked she told me she was upset for me telling the girls.

Ciara told me to meet her in Detroit on the east side and she would give me my car back. She didn't want me to bring the police or anyone with her because she felt I was going to set her up. At that time NiNi didn't want to take all the blame for that so if she went down she was taking Ciara down with her. Nini claimed Ciara dropped her off and she took the car hiding it on her own in the city.

When I got to Detroit, I hopped off the bus right after State Fair on Gratiot Avenue. Ciara had her green school uniform shirt on from just getting out of school. Her and I walked talking about everything that was happening. I told her it was stupid for her to feed into whatever the other girls were saying.

We walked for about six blocks one way and four blocks another. I really felt bad because I liked Ciara and didn't want to lose her as a friend. She told me she felt betrayed and didn't want to lose me as a friend either. She explained she wanted to help me survive out there in Detroit.

On the way to get my car, we had an older man named Luther and his nephew try and talk to us. I was still friendly from being from California. We ended up getting their number just so we could have more friends. By the time we got to the car, it was parked in the back yard of an abandoned house under a car port. I was so grateful everything wasn't tampered with except for my license plate. Ciara took me a couple houses down to where my license plate was given to me.

I screwed it back on my car, thanking her, apologizing for opening my mouth to the two girls I had trusted to be my only friends. Nini had convinced Ciara to give me my car back because, neither of them wanted any police contact. I knew I was alone again because Nini's sister I was growing to trust was looking at doing time in jail.

Once I moved out of Nini's mothers house she apologized to me for being shady towards me. I felt alone and missed having Nini as a best friend. She claimed she felt the same way so I forgave her. Nini had the same things on her mind that I had and that was money and love.

We started running the streets again staying where we could with each other. I couldn't stay at her mom's so we decided to stay back at her sister's house on Six Mile. Nini's sister ended up going back to jail for an old charge that I had not known too much about. Luthe had wanted me and Ciara to come over because a seventeen-year-old boy had found an interest in her. We ended up doing so, trying to still be friends. I kept it to myself about our friend though. Luthe was in his late thirty's finding himself infatuated with me.

Ciara started befriending Man-Man and his family just like I did. They knew my story and started becoming a stability I didn't anymore in Michigan.

At their home lived Man-Man's mother, Miss Robin, and a man we called named Uncle Ern who was his father. They were very polite to me, welcoming me in their home for meals. They lived in a black society many people considered the hood a couple blocks away from Seven Mile. Ciara had a problem. She had fallen for Man-Man and I had a problem too Luther had fallen for me. His heart that beat for me started making me dislike the thought of being around him, but needed someone to have my back in this cold city.

I became very close with him trying to think of ways we could make money. Being around that family started keeping me away from hanging with the wrong people as they would tell me "keep your ass out of the streets, Cali." The closer Ciara started getting to the boy Man-Man the more we started going our separate ways.

I started hanging out with Nini again back in forth from her sister's house. We continued to be in the hood with each other trying to grow into better friends because, it was hard for me to trust her but had no one. I hung out with Nini because she seemed street-smart to me and I wanted to survive.

One day Nini and I hung out with this guy named Kevin who threw dance parties and such other adult entertainment. They called the late-night affairs after hours. Since I was eighteen back at Lex's mother's house, she and I knew that I could dance at an upscale club making enough money to support myself. I knew at the time that I had no income and needed to support myself.

I planned to dance but didn't have any idea how to start. I asked Kevin to lend me the money for the dance outfits and he said yes.

In return I told him I would give him extra money after I worked my first night. He trusted me, and gave me ten dollars.

Nini and I went to the mall to find me something to wear. A hundred dollars was deep in my pocket. We found two outfits that were just my size. I told her I was ready to pay for them. She told me she wanted to steal them. Determined, she got caught ripping the tags off them. She then put the tags in her back pocket. Right before we walked out of the dressing room she put the tags in my purse swinging the purse over her shoulder. She walked around over by some clothes racks and I walked the opposite way not wanting to involved in her stealing.

In the end we both ended up right next to each other. A few steps into the next department, we were stopped by two women, saying, "Ladies, please come with us." They then told us, "We are in the top mall store security and we believe that you have been shoplifting. Not being too worried about it because I wasn't carrying the purse and had money on me I followed security to the basement. The feeling of mall security was making me feel as if I had already been sent to jail. The room was empty with cement seat toward the back of the room split up into cubicles. When the women security guards looked through my purse, they found two dance outfits and a couple tags. I wasn't realizing it—oh my they were charging me for shop-lifting. I immediately offered to pay for the two outfits.

The two women security guards told me no. The one security guard read me my rights and typed up their report for the both of us. Since she was only sixteen almost seventeen her mother was called to pick her up. She was sent a ticket to her home to notified her for court. Since I was nineteen years old the police were notified to come and pick me up to take me to jail.

I was scared. Here I was on my own in Michigan, with no one to get me out of jail. I didn't know how I was supposed to feel. I never thought I would get caught up so tough in some trouble like that. I was allowed us to make some phone calls.

Nini's mother answered the phone with disbelief. Thirty minutes later she was there to get her daughter. The look she gave me when she walked in the door was terrible. She looked at me disappointed from me hanging out with her daughter. She had told me before she didn't like how her daughters were treating me and wanted me for my best interest to move on with my life from hanging out with her children.

When the police officers came in, they cuffed me. As I sat in the back of the police car for the first time on my way to jail, all I could do was close my eyes because there was no turning back. We were on our way to the Harper Woods Police station.

The station was a small department with filthy cells. They had usually one cemented block with a dirty plastic thin blue matt on top of it. They brought me inside, booking my fingerprints, taking up to an hour. Then making me empty my pocket they also wanted me to take off my shoes and shoes laces out of my shoes.

The officers placed all my belongings in a Ziploc bag, labeled with my name. Not knowing anyone's number by heart, I asked the police officer if I could write down a few number from my cell phone. She allowed me to do so quickly.

Chapter Twelve

Once I was in the system, they showed me to where I was going to be staying. I was terrified about who was going to be locked up with me. The first hour I was placed in a cell with bars. It was so cold and disgusting. I remember freezing, not having any way to warm myself. The type of cold that creeped me out was running up my spine knowing I had no control. I knew I was in jail for real. At first I tried to stay very relaxed but, the colder it got the more I felt the panic.

It was all in my head, and I knew that if I stayed calm, I could make it through this situation. I picked up the phone in the cell I was in, trying to make a phone call. There was no dial tone. I started yelling for the guard. When I thought he heard me, I started yelling louder. Finally, the guard came and placed me in a warmer but still dirty, cold cell with an older woman.

The difference between that cell I was in and the cell I had just been in were the cell didn't have bars that had a thick cemented door that blocked you off from seeing anything. You could see a small window toward the top of the door with a sliding cover that only the guards could control if they wanted to look inside.

The holding cells had no way of escaping. The woman inside the cell started screaming that she wanted to speak to her lawyer. The woman would then would get louder demanding a phone call immediately.

The police seemed to be mocking her from what I could hear. The woman found a way by getting a different shift of guards as the night grew to allow her to make a phone call. There was no blanket in my cell so I layed down covering myself with toilet paper trying to keep warm. The poor lady that was in there didn't have her medication and started weeping for a while.

Automatically, my people skills shut right on, helping me calm her down. I was still scared she might attack me but just went with the flow of things. She told me about her life continuing to ramble on, laughing, yelling at the guards. My mind seemed to come to an ease because I amused myself by listening to the woman's stories.

The next day was a little worse for me when they took the lady out. It was the weekend and I wasn't able to see a judge until that coming up Monday. I really didn't know any of my rights. Day two became longer than I thought. My stomach started to growl and I knew I needed something to eat. Just because I was hungry didn't mean the police officers were going to feed me just like that. I happened to have to wait eight hours for a soggy cheese burger with nothing on it. It came with the smallest mini Sprite ever in a Styrofoam cup. Even though the meal was nasty I didn't care I was starving. I ate the meal in three seconds and drank the Sprite until it had no drops left in the cup. I fell asleep then finally and woke up the next day at five o'clock.

By that time, I had a blanket in my cell. I covered myself up, going back to sleep. I then woke up to the holding cell doors sliding open with the loudest noise that followed from them doing so. The guards then placed a girl inside the cell with me who was about eighteen years old. I didn't know what type of person this was, but hoped for the best.

The girl looked like she had been crying for days. She looked at me and I smiled while I asked her if she was all right. She told me she was airtight and wanted to go home.

The girl said she lived right down the street from the mall. She started to explain her crime to me as we sat in the germ hole cell. No offense to the girl but her story was dumb to me when she told me why she had gone to jail.

I was told by the girl that she had assaulted her mother after an argument they had. I didn't agree with her striking her mother. I was with no mother and she was trying to ruin things with hers. I found a way to keep things cool conversing with the girl exchanging stories. Come to find out she knew Nini, the girl I had been running around getting into trouble with. They were friend's prior at a high school a year before then together.

For the next two days, we spent talking about our families and lives, claiming we were sorry for the past screw-ups. At that point we both wanted to go home. I finally called my father in California telling him what had happened. He wasn't surprised I was in jail by the way my life had been going so far. My father had no way to help me because, they wouldn't take credit cards over the phone.

I was sentenced to see the judge after seventy-two hours. My father had nothing positive to say about me. He was disappointed in me for my actions in the past. A new friend in Mount Clemens a couple weeks earlier helped me taking me bail up to the station. I didn't have anyone else in my life at that time reliable and wanting to see me helped. It seemed like I was coming to a realization that everyone in my life at that time was not really my friend.

I wasn't able to be bailed out of jail because, I didn't have any identification so I had to wait for my prints to come back, identifying me from California.

The girl and I knew that we were going to see a judge soon but just didn't know when. The third day came and they took her to see the judge first. She was sentenced a move to the county jail in the city of Detroit where they would allow her to shower and have a bunk bed depending on her charge but couldn't hold her for more than a year.

A few hours passed and I was alone once again ready to be released. I was finally brought some food was told I would see the judge at nine in the morning. I was beyond ready to get out! I had no idea what was in store next for me but prayed to God that I could be able to leave.

I felt as if I had any goals they were being put on hold based off what decision the judge was going to make for me. People I considered my friends didn't answer any of my phone calls or even except them to come in.

Waking up the next morning with hardly no sleep from the night before, I was mentally making myself aware of anything that could have happened next. The guards came that morning taking me to court. I felt dirty from not being able to shower. The thought of doing more time made my stomach sick. As my eyes looked upon the court room, all I could see were the judge, a jury of seven, and a crowd of people in the audience who were scheduled to see the judge.

The judge was an older man with a grim on his face. When it was finally my turn to see the judge, I was very nervous. It caused me to forgot to say "yes, sir" and "no, sir" a few times. I explained my situation about being alone with no family from out of state. The judge got straight to the point and asked me, "Did you know the merchandise was in your purse?" Being truthful I said yes.

The judge then waited for my lawyer's verdict. I pleaded mute so the judge sent me to Wayne County Jail in Detroit until my next court date in five days. I looked the judge in the eyes and asked, "So what's supposed to happen to me?" He didn't answer and the guard took me away. I was locked back in the cell until the other Wayne County police came and got me. They cuffed me lightly.

I felt extremely dirty because I needed a shower. When I arrived in the city, I still had the hundred and ten dollars in my account. They had taken twelve dollars out to charge me for my wrist band. I was more worried about going to Detroit's county jail.

I knew there was a bunch of woman trying to fend for themselves in jail. I knew that the women would look at me for being a pushover because of what they were used to racism. I looked more white than black. It was a system that wouldn't seem to break in the streets. When I got to the jail, I had to go in one a holding cell to wait to be processed.

After I was processed, I had to wait in another cold cell with a bunch of girls to go upstairs. Some people were spilt up into different categories such as Quad A, Quad B, Quad C, Quad D. Mine was Quad A. When I got there, I was nervous but didn't cry because I didn't want to show weakness. I was polite to anyone who spoke to me but at first never spoke to anyone but the two girls.

One girl was next to the cell I was in to the right named Shonnie and another girl in my cell that I vaguely talked to. I ended up getting along with the girl next to my cell named Shonnie who told me she was from the west side of Detroit, had two kids, and was living in Taylor. She told me her kids were being watched by her brother and she had another thirty days to go. She was a pretty African American girl, fit, with blue contacts in her eyes. Her hair was extremely short like a guy's but it fit her face perfectly.

Part of me didn't mind being in jail feeling that it was better than being on the streets. It was true. I was homeless.

It gave me a time to reflect on my future and where I wanted to be. I knew I had to start using my brain about who I chose to bring in my life.

The next couple days went by fast. I spent most of my time talking with Shonnie or watching the news. We ate three times a day. We had to wake up early in the morning and stand up out of our beds by the time the guard came in to open the gates for us. I knew once the gates opened I wouldn't be able to sleep.

The next couple days, me and the girl Shonnie talked and were cool with each other. She told me right away when we first met to call her Shonnie. I respected her nickname and called her it even though I knew her real name from us being there in jail. The girl started treating me like I was her real friend. It was relaxing to have someone to talk to who had some sense of things even, about things I asked her about that didn't relate to jail. I knew I had to have some short of guidance in this new place I was in. One afternoon, this big burly dark-skinned African American woman with dirty hair, after being homeless from being homeless tried to take my food tray coming up to me asking me if I was done with my food.

Feeling very intimidated, I was uncomfortable so I gave her the tray. My new friend Shonnie came and sat next to me, asking me where was my food. I told her I gave it to the woman. She was irritated with me doing so and called the guard.

The guard was a beautiful white blonde. "Did you try to take that girl's food?" asked the guard. She noticed they were stealing trays and saw they had piles of trays in their cells. So she locked them in their cells.

My friend didn't care and was really loud making sure they knew she wasn't playing with the two women who were working together to steal trays.

These women treated the jail as if it was there home. They sat on the toilet bare not having a worry in the world. I never sat on the toilets in jail.

During the days when your cell doors were open and anyone could come in your room, it was quite awkward to even poop in there. I remember my celli next to me Shonnie, holding her blanket up for me blocking people from seeing me so I could use the bathroom. I never wanted to go to jail ever again. Shonnie never let anyone punk me and always had my back for the rest of my time in there. Jail had felt long, like I had been in there forever.

The last time me and Shonnie hung out was the day before I was sentenced up until they locked us in our cells that night. That day, she and I hung out and she told me some of her stories about her working the street corners to feed her children and she told me she was recovering from doing crack. She had been locked up for three months already basically detoxing the whole time. I was very proud of her for wanting to turn her life around by being able to reflect in jail.

I prayed to God at night that she would stay off drugs to improve to be a better mother for her kids. I really enjoyed her company so we exchanged contact information.

My new friend braided my hair that day into a Mohawk. My hair was growing out and the curls were finally showing. My hair was dirty blonde. To make rubber bands she took a new pair of plastic gloves, taking a pencil, stabbing, making her own rubber ties to finish my hair with. I was impressed what people did to survive. I couldn't sleep the night before I was transferred to Harper woods for court. I kept praying and thinking I didn't know where I belonged.

It was sad how easily I was adjusted to jail in nine days from being traumatized from the idea. I knew I never belonged in jail though. I thanked the girl one last time before actually falling asleep. I told her I promised I would come visit her in jail.

I always had intensions on doing so but too much happened to where it never happened. I never saw her again. After I was processed out, I was again not released yet I had to wait in a waiting cell with the same dirty clothes on that I came in.

Finally, when Harper Woods came, they cuffed me, putting me in the prisoner van, driving me over to the court house, which was connected to the police station. In the van there was a couple men who were looking so down and out. I remember riding with one of them men on the way up there. One guy on the way up there was trying to harass me, he told him to chill out. I guess the man was looking at a huge sentence because his face was terribly upset.

To cheer him up, I ended up sliding my hang cuffs off. I smiled at them t,easing them playing around for about five minutes. The men cheered up smiling and laughing. I was happy to be on my way out of jail because I knew I wasn't supposed to be caged up like an animal.

My heart was too kind to be in there. I had been a lot of things in my past but an animal wasn't one of them. I had to be processed in before seeing the judge. It took me an hour before I could see the judge. I could tell he was ready to see the change in me. When the judge asked me a few questions, I answered with yes sir, no sir every time.

I was polite and didn't have as much to say as last time I spoke to him. I owned up to my actions, making sure that I opened up my ears and listened to the old man. I went into that court room with faith. Shonnie had taught me how to have faith and rely on the one and only "God." The judge granted me permission to be released and told me to stay out of trouble. He wanted me to go back to California.

I knew that I didn't want to but told him I would. The guard walked me back to my cell. I couldn't help but to smile as tears flowing down my face. When I got in there, I had a cell mate actually two of them. They were polite to me. Both of them were exchanging their stories of both being in there for drunk driving.

CALI GIRL, HOW DID I MAKE IT IN THE TREACHEROUS STREETS OF DETROIT?

Both of them were exchanging their stories of both being in there for a DWI. The smaller girl in the cell with me had been drunk driving, stopping at Taco Bell to pee, and the cop followed her from there pulling her over in the drive through. She told me she was lit off Patron, which was a strong tequila and top-shelf liquor.

The other girl's story was simple why she was in jail, and it was because she cussed out a cop. She wasn't waiting long at all until her family came and bailed her out while I felt like this process for me needed to be over.

Finally, an hour later I was completely processed out and freed at last. The girl who got picked up from her mother gave me a lift to the Gratiot 560 bus so I could make my way back to Detroit. I had nowhere to go but, back to six-mile where Nini's sister had been letting me stay. I ended up first riding to downtown Detroit to pick up my check to the Wayne County police station for the money that was in my commissary that I took into jail with me. I signed for my check walked out with no idea of what to do next. I felt like the city of Detroit was staring at me. I had no idea what was out there nor where I belonged.

On my way to the bus station downtown, I stopped at the social security office to report a red flag on my social security card because, prior, someone stole my social security number. That's where I met officer Shank. The officer was tall with black hair and very handsome. He had a great smile that made me feel that everything was going to be alright. When I checked a person out I would always look at their teeth and his were white! He spoke softly and I could tell he had some interest in me. We sat around talking for forty minutest about my life. I felt good having someone to talk with who was concerned about my world.

The nice man tried making me a few phone calls to resource centers to try and help me figure out what I was going to do from there. He told me he had a girlfriend and two kids. He gave me his number and told me to call him if I ever needed help. He showed me the way to the bus station in order to get on the right bus. He told me how to get to Six Mile from there. I held my hand up high positive ready to make my way to a safe place. I knew believe it or not that Nini was the only one who could help me have a roof over my head.

I was mad I went to jail for so long. I knew I really couldn't be mad at her because, it was both of our faults. I knew I really didn't have anyone at all but her. I knew that I was the cause of our friendship in the ups and downs because, I had the tendency to want to do my own thing as I wandered off. I didn't think anything of it because, I thought I was protecting myself for meeting other people. I went while I was downtown to a pizza shop to get something to eat. It felt like I was starving from not eating properly in jail. I was able to build a conversation while my pizza was cooking with a guy that worked there. I was still shaken up from jail.

The men who worked at the pizzeria listened to my story, trying to cope with my situation. Damen, the Italian delivery boy, became friends with me that day. I still had no real place to go to be comfortable. After he got off work, he drove his BMW, taking me to Nini's sister's house. There was KK, Nini's cousin who I had met there once before.

She decided to come with us to hang out at another guy's apartment in downtown Detroit who worked at the pizzeria with dreads who was a black African American artist who had one of his nostrils pierced. He showed me pictures of him and Naima who was a young woman who won America's Next Top Model.

I was always a fan of her beauty. He had more pictures of her sister and her but the one picture he kept on his glass mirror warmed my heart. He never forgot about her. His art work was all over the apartment. He lived in an old apartment complex that use to be a hotel. It was over a hundred years old with great history of murder and chaotic moments. Its history of the mob being involved there intrigued me as I heard the stories.

There was security once you went inside the old-fashioned doors that spun you around till you reached inside. If you weren't expected, you wouldn't be getting into the elevator that led you to other people's rooms. You would have to get buzzed in by the front desk. KK and I became cool to where we didn't need Nini there when we hung out. We had hung out a few times without her from that day on. KK ended up knowing Ciara from school. It seemed like it was such a small world in Michigan.

I returned for a few days to reunite with Nini. We became close again, and it seemed like no matter what we went through, I always forgave her and we moved on. Since I had made some friends at the pizzeria place, she came downtown with me to check out who they were.

Chapter Thirteen

I started staying a couple days at a time with Damen as we got close and I wanted a safe, comfortable place to lay my head. He lived thirty minutes away on his family member's farm. I enjoyed his time and thought maybe we could grow even more found of each other. He was older than me and a young man. I wasn't used to that so I didn't let myself to get to close to him. Nini would take the bus as well as I would.

We met each other downtown by Capitol Park. It was directly across the street from the pizza joint. Nini made friends with a young kid that was a dope dealer selling crack posted up in capitol park. I didn't know the guy but really didn't want her going off with him. The park was no joke.

Dope was sold fast down there. We were smart enough not to ever do it! I, from my past experiences with my mother, never wanted to do it. I knew that it would become my fatal problem if I was to ever try it. One thing me and Nini had in common was that we had families who both taught us better than to be drug addicts.

I looked after her like she was my blood sister, not wanting anything to happen to her from watching her being naive by trusting people. She ended up leaving on the bus with this guy she met randomly from Capitol Park. He was around her age, but I still felt she should have left with me because she was my security at the time. I made sure when we were down there that most the time she didn't talk to people because, people were nuts.

As I was watching my friend leave on the bus with the boy from Capitol Park, it really broke my heart. I didn't know what to expect out of her next, if she would leave with a stranger that she didn't know.

I understood her because she liked boys with money but was scared not wanting anything to happen to her. I talked to her and told her she better be meeting me the next day. I waited for her downtown the next day to step foot of the bus. She knew she was wrong for leaving me. When she got off the bus, I yelled at her, telling her never to do that again. The boy was sixteen so he seemed safe to her, but she was still my best friend so I worried. We looked at things differently.

I wasn't going to let money or a guy change how close we were. She and I made a couple more friends while we were down there. We had met an Australian blue-eyed blonde-haired young man who was barely able to speak clear English. He ended up staying in the same apartment slash old hotel that the artistic man with dreads who worked at the pizzeria had stayed in.

I also met an African American girl named Tanisha down there who had been cut in her face by a girl with a blade some time in her lifetime. I met them one day when Nini was hanging with the boy she met down there, who sold dope. We both were jealous about the people around us but really didn't show it besides separating ourselves to find time to spend with other people. To me, it was really stupid but best for me because I needed more than one person to help me through being alone in a state with no family.

Nini and I stopped going downtown because she said she wanted to stop going down there. I let her call the shots because I wanted to continue our friendship.

Both the girl and I got attached to each other. We went back to downtown Detroit so I could visit Shonnie like I promised. I had no ID so I wasn't allowed to visit her.

I went across the street where I knew she could see me below from the window because I had once been up there with her. I waved my hands, trying to keep a promise I had made to the young woman. I think she knew in her heart that I would come there. She saw me waving my hands and waved back to me.

The police officers came across the street, asking me to stop. I couldn't help but keep waving. Shonnie was important to me and I we were friends. I looked at the situation like I wasn't fake. I just was lost in a city I knew nothing about with not much help.

Sadly, a few weeks later I lost her contact information. Nini and I only hung out a few times after that. That same day I went to see Shonnie when I was coming out of the county building I noticed a cute brown-skinned girl looking at me, smiling. She had a bright yellow pair of short shorts, a belly shirt on that showed her fit abs, and she had an orange sew in wrap in her hair. I thought she was cute. I could tell by how she was looking at me she was either bi-sexual or lesbian.

At first, because of the much attention she gave me. I had a cocky vibe, like, in a sense, I thought I was better than her. I snapped back into reality of me being extra nice, not judgmental, and I realized that I had never dated a black girl before.

The more she smiled at me, I approach her she told me her name was Marty. She made me laugh when we spoke, making me smile at her reaction of me. She told me she had just broken up with her girlfriend. We walked a couple blocks downtown and came right back to where Nini had been waiting.

My new acquaintance said that she was down there visiting her mom for trying to run someone over. She told me she was waiting for her sister because she forgot her ID.

Marty was not allowed in to see her mother without having identification like me. We talked for thirty minutes and exchanged each other contact information. I wanted to hang out feeling like talking to her some more. She seemed interesting so I thought why not? Nini wanted us to go back to her sisters on Six Mile.

I was still bitter she had left me a week ago to go with some guy so I figured what would it matter if I left with some girl. After meeting her sister, I decided to get on the bus with them to go back to their house with them. Nini was mad at me and got off at a different stop. I wasn't focused on her being mad because, she had been so shady towards me lately, I was still a bit hurt.

Marty had a big family of kids. They lived in the hoover hood off Grospect and Eight Mile. I still didn't know that area to well, but it wasn't too far from Nini's sister's house. She and her sister they called lady was responsible for the kids until her mother got released. Their house was small and I understood why she complained about how many people stayed with them based on that being a serious fact. She told me she was still talking to her ex-girlfriend, and it made me feel awkward for even coming over there. I still wanted to be her friend and started liking her more than as a friend.

The next day I met up with Nini at her sister's house. She was still mad at me. As we talked, she put her arm around my neck, hugging me, saying, "Come here. You're my bitch. Don't go off with any other bitches."

I laughed at her and knew she wasn't gay and like a sister to me but started wondering if we like each other a little. Throwing the idea out of my mind, we talked and made up giving each other a hug.

The more I started hanging over at Marty's house, Nini and I started doing our own thing. Nini told me the girl was a hood rat. A hood rat wasn't the best thing for her to be called. I didn't understand why she was looking at me like I was crazy.

A hood rat was a way of saying she was dirty looking or uneducated, ghetto, etc. I had never seen anything like the girl before who lived in the hood. Her personality was loud and out there. The girl intrigued me. After I chilled with her a little more, she started to change by disrespecting me, being on the phone while I was at her house with her ex-girlfriend. She started acting, which made me fed up with her very fast.

One day I had spent the night at her house. When I woke up, she was down the street at a friend's. I didn't know what to expect. I was irritated and pretty much had enough. I packed the things I had brought with me over there. I was irritated because, the night before, I tried to snuggle with her and she wigged out on me because she was still in love with her ex-girlfriend.

I sat on her porch and watched this brown-skinned girl with a nice booty in a white tight dress walk by with her aunt on their way to the corner grocery store a couple blocks down the way. I planned to leave anyways but since she was trying to talk to me I felt the need to meet someone new. I decided to walk to the store with her and the woman she called her aunt.

Marty saw the girl I exchange words with and yelled, "Where are you going?"

I told Marty I was going to the store. The girl who told me her name was Jaz tried to befriend her. She just looked at the girl like she was extremely mad. At that instant she told me not to come back to her house. She was mad at me for trying to talk to another girl. I was fed up with how the girl had been treating me.

On the way back to the store, I stopped at Marty's house and grabbed my stuff, which was a purse with some clothes in it and my phone charger. Jaz told me that she and her aunt were throwing a dance party. When I went to the aunt's house a couple blocks away, they had a bar downstairs and a stripper pole in the basement. Jaz told me she was going to dance so I decided to try it.

I really needed the money to feed myself so I agreed to do so. That day every man they saw they advertised the party for Father's Day. Jaz's aunt gave me a fish net body suit and some heels to wear. Right before we were supposed to dance, Jaz didn't want to and had a guy pick her up. I knew I had to stay and dance in order to earn some money.

By the time I was getting along with the aunt. I sat there and danced a little bit, and walked around looking as cute as possible. I made a phone call to Luthe to come and pick me up. I knew I didn't want to stick around there much longer. Luthe came with his cousin picking me up.

That night only through dancing, I made a hundred and fifty dollars. It wasn't enough for me, but it was enough for me to pay my cell phone bill and get something to eat. I made sure I paid the lady twenty-five dollars who through the party. Come to find out the woman actually wasn't her aunt.

I came back the next day and returned the body suit. I finally got a hold of Jaz and she later that day got dropped off at Luther's house by a woman and a man. She needed to get her clothes so we went to State Fair and Dresden for her things. Her mother was in jail and had no idea why. She had been moving around and when we got to her old house it was an abandoned house that was filthy inside.

The front door was half way off the hinges. She told me that crackheads were going in the home to smoke their dope. The crack heads had ruined her clothes and what was left of her furniture. I literally saw poop on her carpet. I had never experienced seeing anything like that before. It was unbelievable. We walked across the street to give what was left of her clothes to the neighbor to keep in his basement. She told him she would be back for it.

We then took the 560 Gratiot bus to Ten Mile to meet up with Nini. When I saw her, I told her the story of what had happened with Marty. She told me so acting as if she didn't care what I had went through. She made sure to remind me that she warned me, and it was my fault.

Nini had us meet her at Buba's house, a brother of one of her ex-boyfriends. She met Jaz and was somewhat polite to her. The young man's house was basically an apartment where people came and partied. There was a party almost every night there.

By this time of the summer, Nini and I came to a toll in our friendship. We were bitter toward each other for having others in our lives. I was mainly weary of her for the shady things she had done too me.

I remember there was a time when I was trying to make money at Buba's house by dancing. I gave someone a lap dance and only made about thirty dollars.

At that point I knew that if I wasn't dancing in a club, it wouldn't be worth dancing at all. There was a girl from Six Mile that Nini started to hang out with more and more.

The girl's name was Juicy, but believe me, she wasn't good looking at all. She always tried to punk on me because she thought I was a white girl.

Chapter Fourteen

I felt that she was jealous of me because I was pretty and she was a bigger chick who wasn't. A few times she approached me crazy and I had to put her in check. The more Nini hung out with her on Ten Mile, the more they tried to team up and give me problems. One day I had been at Bubba's hanging out when all of a sudden they came at me outside like they were going to jump me. I wigged out and had to stand up for myself. I grabbed the fire extinguisher, holding it up with two hands, telling them to back up. I said to them, "Oh, so you guys are going to try and jump me?"

I made it clear if they tried I was going to use that fire extinguisher to smack them across their heads. I could see it in their eyes that they knew I had had enough. They backed off, as neighbors were talking about calling the police. That night I knew that I couldn't keep bouncing around Bubba's family. Two sisters had told me to come with them to stay at their house. I decided to do so, not having much of an option. I was always so worried that someone was going to try and pimp me out so I told them I wasn't going to stay any longer but thanked them for their peaceful words of change. I was happy that someone was trying to encourage me to change my life, but was scared after what I had been through to trust them.

My days seemed to switch as each day sifted away so fast. Here I was having my clothes at one place, my car at another place, and myself always with Nini, where ever I could lay my head most of the time. After I slowly stopped hanging out with her, I heard she went back to live with her mother.

I continued search for something. I was searching for someone to accept and love me. Things started to change. I went to go meet NiNi once again, trying to stay in her life at her sister's house in the city. It was a hot summer day. I remember it like it just happened. I got off the 560 bus at Six Mile and Gratiot. I then walked to the gas station right off Six Mile. I knew I would have to walk about five blocks down to get to her sister's house.

At the gas station, I saw this beautiful dark-skinned girl with a bright colorful green, blue and yellow scarf around her head that wrapped her hair up. She was taller than me, about five ten, with a big booty and a size D breasts. I started to talk to a guy in the line named Philz. I could tell the young woman with the colorful scarf was checking me out. He told me, "Oh, she likes you." I looked into her eyes and then looked away. She was an angel standing in a war zone. Philz was her child's father's cousin.

I smiled being friendly with Philz, allowing him to walk with me on my way to Gould burn the street where Nini's sister had lived. We stopped to talk to the beautiful dark-skinned female who you could tell was strong and had been going through a lot in her lifetime. She was very nice and polite, showing some interest in me. We all talked for about an hour on her porch until of the four-family flat. The four-family flat was separated into four apartments.

Philz was a heavier-set guy who seemed nice with a smile on his face. I told him I was from California and that I was looking for my own place. He said he had a house near by that was vacant that he was fixing up on a street called Alcoy. The house was clean and fairly nice. It was big enough for me and a whole family. The house reminded me when I was a child of the San Leandro house that I had once lived in except this house was bigger. The house had a lot of potential to be extremely nice.

I still didn't know the neighbors or anything but knew that he had a house across the street that he had already fixed up. He showed me the house already fixed up. I was hoping to actually find out how I'd be able to rent it or fix it up because I currently had no place of my own so I felt like it was worth a try. It needed heat, water, and power. In the meantime, Nini was waiting for me at her sister's house.

I asked him if he knew any cute but gay girls he could introduce me to. He told me I had met one. The girl who I had met named Niki, which he called his cousin. I understood why he called her his cousin. It was because he was cousins with her two sons' father. He asked me if I saw the way she was looking at me? I told him yes. He then said, "She loves you!" He then chuckled with laughter after saying so. That made me smile because after talking with her, I grew a liking to her right away.

My clothes were janky from not having any of my own clothes. A lot of what I was bought from Lex's mom was stolen from me. I was living day to day. Philz offered to give me some old but clean clothes his girl gave him to sell. I then drove with him and his buddy to pick the clothes up.

After we left from there I told him I had to go to Nini's sisters house to meet up with her. I told him it was a couple blocks away from Six Mile and Alcoy. He drove me over to her sister's house. Nini jumped in the car with us coming to see what house I had told her I wanted to fix up to live in. She barely wanted to come in the car with us but wanted to see what had taken me so long.

When we got to Alcoy to see the house she asked me a couple questions, trying to understand where I met this guy I answered all her questions and we went inside the house looking at what needed to be done to make it livable.

I took the clothes he gave me and went in the house to go through them. She then told me she was going to stop hanging out in the hood. I got this feeling she didn't want me there either.

Nini said her mother had a discussion with her and wanted her to be there at home more. She told me then she was going to try to get a job. I was sad of the news because I was so used to her being there always by my side even after all we had gone through. This time I could tell she was ready to do her in a different way, which meant she wanted a positive change for herself. She didn't agree with me for wanting to stay in the hood. I just didn't have too many options as I thought at the time. We were still cool but just growing apart.

That day we went back to her mom's house. She loaned me an old pair of black and red forces. I ended up finding the girl I had befriended downtown named Tanisha's phone number. I told her to come meet me to look at the house with me. She agreed.

We then met up the next day and looked at the house. We decided that day that we were going to help each other. We both had no one who would help us and she was pregnant at the time. I was still a little upset from the day before from the news Nini gave me of planning to stay out of the hood to better her life. I wasn't mad she had a plan. I just was mad that we didn't have the same plan. I figured it wasn't anything new of us going our separate ways. I knew that one day we would be back hanging out with each other the way we had been before.

After we looked at the house, we went by Niki's so she could meet her. Philz wanted me to start getting at Niki because she received a check every month from social security for having seizures.

I sort of felt bad but knew that I was in survival mode. He basically said that if she liked me enough, she would cash me out, which meant she would give me money. I knew I didn't want any money from her once we started talking and I noticed I was falling for her. Every time she smiled at me, I smiled right back at her feeling very anxious.

When we went to her place, she had a neighborhood friend named day-day who was a heavyset stud with dark skin and a buzzed haircut over. We were all talking on the porch where there was a light blue paint bucket and one chair to sit on. My home girl sat down. I had nowhere to sit so I sat on her lap.

Niki started giving me a funny look. She really had no idea I liked girls after all. Her so-called cousins intentions were different from mine why I had actually wanted to know her. Don't take this the wrong way. I did consider the idea until I actually got to know her.

My focus was more a love affair with her. She seemed nice and was trying to get at my friend on the way to the bus stop. My friend asked me to switch shoes with her and I forgot they weren't mine so I switched with her earlier that day in the house I wanted. The bus that Tanisha got on Nini had got off and didn't notice the girl was wearing her shoes until after I brought it up. I told her I would get her shoes back.

Chapter Fifteen

The next day Nini was downtown and saw her there. She told her to put the shoes in the old house I wanted to fix up. My friend with no problem did so two days later. When I went back to Niki's house, I was drowsing off sitting on her porch still there to get to know her. She told me I could go lay down inside.

I told her no, I was okay even though I was extremely exhausted. I still wanted to figure her out but kept my heart guarded. We went over to Alcoy, the street where Philz and her kids' father were. She talked to him while I talked to Philz about what I had noticed that night when there was a big crowd of people drinking and partying. I thought that same night that I would never be able to have a permanent home there. When we got back to her house, her two boys were already asleep.

Niki got into the shower while I waited in her apartment that was on the lower flat. I hoped that she liked me but didn't know so I went into the bathroom with her while she was in the shower. I helped her scrub her body with a very big ego but didn't know what to expect. She allowed me to help her wash her up. I got into the shower with her and then she helped me wash myself up. I was so nervous because I had never done anything like that before. I was very spontaneous.

It was a different for me actually becoming woman. I wasn't too experienced with sex. I kissed her in the shower and she kissed me back. We got out of the shower going into the back bedroom where we were alone. The kids were sleeping safe and sound in the front room. I struck her body against mine.

CALI GIRL, HOW DID I MAKE IT IN THE TREACHEROUS STREETS OF DETROIT?

It was our first time making love with each other. I had this pretty chocolate woman right where I wanted her. My intentions weren't to get any money out of her. They were to show her the love I possessed. I didn't judge her because of where she was. I figured I could help her see a change by witnessing me, a girl from California. I had her squirming and breathing hard. At the end we kissed each other.

When we were finished, I put my clothes on and she put her night wear on. From that day on, I stayed with her in what they called the red zone of the east side of Detroit. She didn't have a boyfriend, but she had to deal with the abuse that her child's father had conflicted on her.

After I was there for the first month, what she called her baby daddy started showing up coming around all the time. He was a tall, bald black man that always had everything he wore matching. I remembered he wore solid colors a lot. The next few weeks, I barely went anywhere. I stayed inside watching the weather change, spending time with the two boys who became my kids as much as they were hers.

Their names were D and Dd. The boys were only four and five years old. They were very cute and polite. I finally felt like I belonged somewhere. I felt that God put me there with her and the boys for a reason. In my eyes they were just what I needed.

Stability was what I was looking for. The love that grew throughout my body for them wasn't going anywhere. The area were we had lived was known as the red zone or other words as a drug zone where police officers had patrolled. The community was full though of mainly African Americans.

Between the two streets, Pelkey and Greiner, is where I lay my head. You didn't hardly ever see any white people down in the hood unless they were doing drugs.

Crack and heroine were the major drugs down there being sold. I never tried hard drugs besides ecstasy, cocaine, and mushrooms but that was all in California.

Besides this one time that Niki ate half of a yellow pill and because I liked her, but knowing I didn't do drugs, I took it anyways by feeling some love for her. I knew after taking it I had made a terrible mistake.

Niki's child's father ended up coming over late in the morning, fighting and arguing with her. I ended up staying up all night in one of the other apartments that were vacant upstairs in the four-family flat. I felt like such a retard for doing this stupid drug.

I was raised better and knew better although, in California, when I was young and rebellious, I tried things and they weren't for me. Niki asking me to leave early in the morning was nothing new. Later in the day when I would return, I would witness her have bruises, cuts, and marks all over her body. As I was seeing the young woman I was falling in love with having all this going on hurt me but knew it became a routine that I didn't want any part of. She always protected me from being abused by her baby's daddy by getting me out of there before he could do anything foul to me. She told me stories of him.

As we got closer, she liked to pretend everything was fine, but I knew deep inside my heart they weren't. I knew she would have to leave that place in order to have a good life with my new sons. Thank God I had enough sense never to do any crack, heroin, cocaine, or any other drugs after that. Black people usually would call an herb smoker a puffer. I smoked marijuana for a couple years and didn't chase it.

I would smoke if people I was close with smoked with me. I knew that people could lace my weed and have me spun out so I made sure to keep my distance from people.

Naturally I was a nice, outgoing young girl trying to turn into a young woman with a bubbly personality that I couldn't help but have. Niki made it clear she wanted me to stay to myself, and for the most part, I tried to do that.

I didn't understand what a jungle it was out there and found myself once again meeting people along the way. That ended up being my biggest downfall, being naive to what was out there in the streets. I had no big understanding being a California girl that not everyone was friendly. People out there had motives for you.

My health was starting to become terrible the more weed I smoked. I went to the emergency room and found out I had bronchitis. So I started to lay off the cigarettes and weed. The doctor prescribed me medicine and treated it when I got back to Niki's house. I couldn't breathe really well, so I quit smoking cigarettes all together. The temperature was changing periodically, but that next week, I noticed it was getting warmer. My boys started playing outside with other boys from the neighborhood. The neighborhood seemed to be fond of me as the children were as well.

I started to realize by me being so friendly, it kept getting myself in more and more trouble. It wasn't like many other places I had ever been with people that I could understand. I wanted to change my life and people who heard how positive I would talk would hate on me for that.

People looked around and didn't understand what I had to smile about. They just didn't know it was a natural positive energy that ran inside my body. I wanted to see people do good, but most people in the hood wanted to drag you down right along with them. They had no faith or hope. I don't even think some of those people knew there was a God because they suffered most of their lives.

Where I was I felt good intentions to see people do great, but their intentions for me were different. Feeling as if the people around had intentions of soldiers trying to survive in a place of poverty, where people were starving, I knew what to expect out there after witnessing it. It started to seem to never amaze me what people would do for money. I had never been a prostitute before but knew that there was history in my family of people doing so.

I heard of people making these sacrifices to pay for college and provide better lives for their families. I never knocked those people for doing what they felt they had to do. I mean I had never done it before but knew people had to survive especially where I was at.

Most men in the city was hooked on becoming or being dope dealers. Most men with a lot of money called "baller" out there were some type of dealer. I learned early that the game was not told. It was to be sold. The saying was very truthful I heard it as a kid but never understood it until the days I met people living that lifestyle in the streets. I tried to keep myself pure by not having sex with men.

Men really weren't what I was after. I had been around those streets ever since Nini introduced them to me. For some reason, every step I took walking through that hood was another step toward a journey of making sure I made it to my destination alive. The streets were cold and the most hardship I had was keeping a roof over my head, making sure Niki and I were on the same page because by that time I loved her. I didn't just love her I loved the boys and wanted to show them a better life. She was a grown woman who I had fallen for whose personality was nothing like Megs the girl I came here for.

Niki was two years older than Megs, and in reality, her mentality was older, due to her hard life was a new love that lasted quite some time, Niki and I. I knew that she loved me and wanted to see me do something with myself. She really didn't want me in the hood with her. I never wanted to leave her though because I wanted to save her and the boys. Niki wanted a life for me that was stable and legit, which meant legal. She didn't want to see me suffer like people she had known her whole life. I started to venture off, visiting with people that I had once been aquatinted with. I crossed eight-mile on the 560 bus headed to sixteen mile and Gratiot. Once I made it there I walked from Sixteen Mile till I reached harper. My friends the twins had been holding my clothes for me. I decided to stay at their house for a couple days to get my mind off things back on Six Mile.

Nini and I met up out there once again to hang out. We seemed to be in two different worlds. She hung out with her stud sister and old friends that she seemed to have the same interests with. We all hung out for a day and then I decided to go back to Six Mile.

When I returned. Niki had started to be influenced by her neighbor and friend's perception of me. When I was gone, she started messing around with her baby daddy. The slang that people used was different from the slang I had ever been subjected to in California. People seemed to have different interests from me there in the city. It came to my attention that everyone was competing to be the best.

They had their own style. Another word for *style* was *swagger*. I also seen that there was a lot of rappers to. To me I perceived everything as people just trying to survive. I saw striving artists who had made their incomes but, hustling to support their dreams of becoming rich and famous in the music industry. Detroit was another life for a Cali girl. People were different from I had ever perceived from a distance for them to be. I would wake up taking a breath of the Detroit city's air starting my day. My days had no purpose.

The time started to pass and summer was almost over. The kids and Niki loved me as much as I loved them. I never thought I'd fall in love with a woman who was nothing like me. We came from two totally different worlds. Before I met them, I was searching for someone to love me. After meeting them and being around them so much I knew that what I thought was missing was full filled after being a part of their world.

I truly believe that the reason I never left Niki's house in that atmosphere was because I loved them. I felt that I finally found someone who would love me no matter what was going on around us. Amazing love I found, I put it in my head that I would never forget the way they captured my heart.

The day Niki told me she loved me first was clear view she was being honest. It was getting late and the sun was going down. Niki and I sat on the porch like we always did. I would stare into the sky trying to reflect on certain things when I would sit out on the porch. The boys were in the house. I started to do this eye staring thing I would do to her. I would stare in her eyes when she would talk to me to tell her without words that I loved her. I had to catch myself because I knew I was falling in love with her deeper than I had ever fallen for someone.

My eyes latching along with hers she started to say, "Cali, you silly." Then after that she told me that some things were wrong with me with a little laughter after that. I said after she told me that "I know!

She then told me, "That's why I love you." I then started to smile hard, blushing a little. I kept my eyes shut and then we kissed. Every moment we shared together changed my life in so many. I finally had my own little family that was worth sticking around to help and protect. From that moment on, I knew I would do whatever was needed to provide a good life for them and I if I was going to continue to be around. No matter how things got, I would always look back remembering the smile Niki and I would share that made everything around us disappear.

Looking back in time, I never regretted meeting or loving any of them. Our love was different from others around us. I knew from experience of her telling me that there would never be another Cali. She knew I felt that there would never be another Niki. Our area was not an area to raise a family.

For some reason though, after conversing with the different people around there, I was respected and looked out for. People knew who Cali girl was. Not everyone respected me. I had women judging me from jealousy and always basing how they felt about me because, of my skin color.

Everything happened so fast. For a while there it seemed like nothing was going right. My opinion was that every time I would cross eight-mile to the suburbs when I returned her baby daddy who would hurt her started to be excepted more in her life as someone she would chase in order to possibly keep her mind off me. I knew that wasn't completely true because, he had always been popping in and out of their lives.

The more I saw him, the more I decided to leave to stay out of drama. When I would come back, she could tell that I was irritated with the situation but kept my cool always. Niki started to tell me, "Cali, we are just friends." I hated that word "friend" she used so freely as if we had nothing there. Every time she said those words to me, it made me want to kiss her. I felt that it was my fault for her actions by leaving on the bus to continue having other people in my life.

I felt that maybe if I would have stayed my ground, I would have been able to change her mind about going that route feeding into her abuse. I hoped that since I was continued to live with her, she would see that I cared for her, giving me one more chance to be more than just friends. I figured if I gave her and the boys more attention, she would see I was right for them. We kept having a sexual relationship as if nothing were wrong. Knowing I had to keep my feelings controlled because of the situation.

Even though it felt as if I couldn't control it, I did my very best for my safety, not to get involved in Niki's relationship with her baby-daddy. Niki and I started to talk a lot of things out that we both kept inside.

My perception of our love seemed to be held together based on us both being hurt. She was hurt by him and I was hurt by my past. We clang on to each other because we truly only had the boys and us. She claimed after all the abuse she took that she had only love her child's father. She claimed that he was all she ever knew for so long. She had told me she had never experienced a love like our love.

I knew she was real about the way she had felt. I was told I was different than anyone she had ever met before. I felt what all she had told me was true and came from her heart.

I had a choice in life that was different from many others. Being from California, I knew there was another life somewhere that was better. I never had to stay down there in the pits of the city of Detroit. I kept witnessing people trying to treat other people around them like crap by putting them down always being negative.

In the city, people were always living day to day, treating life as if it was a party by indulging in alcohol and drugs. I loved to smoke weed because it kept me calm in the middle of most the drama around me. As the summer was coming to an end, I started seeing my situation there coming to an end as well. Niki and I were fighting, partying, and arguing. We never fist fought each other, but it seemed that when she would push me I would push her right on back feeding into the abuse that she had been use to with her baby daddy.

The more she drank the more our relationship started getting abusive. Her sisters were coming around. They didn't agree with me being around what so ever. It was the Fourth of July and the stud girl Day-day took me to her house to meet her sister a day prior. Her sister and I ended up walking for miles down Eight Mile to get to this strip club so we could dance and make some money.

The girl ended liking me allowing me to come with her to dance. The club was called All Stars. We were able to dance without proper license or ID. That day I was nervous to dance but danced in a sexy way. moving my upper body, watching myself in the mirror. I remember Day-day's sister was mad because she didn't make that much money.

All of a sudden I hid a hundred and fifty dollars in my locker. I didn't have a lock on the locker. I noticed she was in a rush to leave. I thought she may have stolen my money out of the locker. Even though I was irritated, I stayed and worked some more. The money ended up coming up missing night before she left.

I assumed later on that she stole the money. I was upset and knew I had to do something. I remember Niki let me go with the girl, but didn't want me to come home empty-handed. I had never turned a john before. While I was in there, I met a guy who wanted to pay me for a blow job. I was so irritated with the thought, but knew I needed to buy myself a new cell phone because my cell phone came up missing over at the four-family flat. I knew that the boys would need to eat just like I would need to eat. I decided to agree to give the man a blow job. He was good looking and very clean.

He put a condom on and I gave him the worst BJ ever because I didn't know what I was doing. I guess he didn't think it was so crappy because he came in less than two minutes. I was glad it was over with but proud of myself for making a sacrifice that didn't end up hurting me, physically. I had him drive me to KFC to get my boys and us some food. On the way home, I stopped to get some loose cigarettes for Niki, and I bought the boys some fireworks.

Chapter Sixteen

By the time I got to the four-family flat, I walked up the street with positive energy because I had enough money to get a new phone and I was able to show the boys how my family did fireworks in California. I noticed Niki's sister's car was there. Everything was pitch-black outside.

Right before I had gotten there, Niki had gotten jumped by two of her sisters all because they heard that Niki and I were messing around sexually. The thought of their sister being gay especially with a white girl made them mad.

Everything happened so fast. One sister grabbed everything out of my hand, throwing it on the ground. She then got into a car and ran over the fireworks and food I had for the kids.

I was so intimidated by the color black. I had never really been into a real fight before. I definitely hadn't fought a black girl before. Her other sister then tried to fight me, pushing me to the ground. I then balled up my body into a ball, trying to protect my face. Her one sister kicked me as I lay there. I was scared. I saw the girl say she had a gun in her trunk. I got up off the ground. She was drunk popping her trunk. I then heard Niki say, "Run, Cali, run!" I ran fast for my life through the four-family flat. There I hid in the basement waiting for the girls to leave.

Eventually they left and Niki told me what happened. She told me they jumped her before I got there. She was upset because she loved me so much and didn't want me to be in that environment. I was scared, but I wanted to stay with her no matter what. I really didn't know what to expect next.

I didn't know who to trust after a while of being in that jungle. All I wanted to do was love her, and all she kept doing was listening to other people. My friend started pushing me away. I think she figured one day I would leave her. I had an option of going home to California and she knew that. Niki hated thinking I would go back across Eight Mile.

I started going back across Eight Mile after that, a lot more trying to avoid the crew of sisters that were a problem for not just me but also Niki. I knew she loved me but really didn't know how to love me. Niki's intentions for me seemed good, but her selfish patterns started helping me see them so I would leave to avoid drama. The way she started living around me drew us more and more apart.

The stud Day-day ended up telling someone she stole my phone. She started making threats that she was going to "come beat my ass." Niki told me not to worry, letting me know she had my back. One day she was playing around with Niki but taking it to far. Somehow we ended up in Niki's apartment and the big, huge stud girl who looked just like a man got a hold of me, trying to rip off my clothes.

I was really uncomfortable trying to fight her off. Niki kept saying, "Get her, Cali, get her!" I was thinking at first the girl was playing, but after a while, I panicked because she wasn't playing. Something came over her.

The stud had this crazy look in her eyes and wouldn't stop trying to attack me, grabbing my clothes, throwing me around. I punched her a couple times in her stomach, telling her to back off. I wasn't trying to play fight. Prior that day earlier, she told me that she didn't steal my phone and that the only reason she wasn't going to fight me was because Niki was her nigga, which meant she was her friend.

I ended up having to run from the stud, cutting the back of my ankle on a piece of glass. I was still frightened the huge stud wasn't going to leave me alone so I ended up hiding out for a while. Niki had my back through all of these situations I had been going through. We ended up arguing over stupid things, but mainly, we argued because I wanted more from her than wanted to offer me. I wanted a different life with her. I wanted her to give up being in the people's lives she was in to think about the kid's future. A part of her just wasn't ready to give things up. She was still trying to understand who she was and what she wanted. One night it was cold and rainy and we had already been arguing because I chose to hang out with some of the black community. Niki didn't want me to hang out with them because she already knew their intentions for me. She then told me her baby daddy was going to come over and that I would have to leave. I asked her where would I go and she told me, "Go where you have been going." I had been going in the four-family flat but really didn't want to even be in the same building there because I felt unwanted. That night I walked down Six Mile headed to Goulburn to see if I could go sleep over there for the night even though I hadn't been going over there.

That's when I met a white girl with blonde hair who didn't look like a drug addict at all. She told me that she was visiting one of her home boys and his name was Country. I felt comfortable enough to go inside the house with the girl because I had limited options. I went in the house and noticed it was a crack house. I saw the girl hold a pipe up to her mouth, smoking crack. I knew I wasn't going to do any drugs because I had been strong minded enough this far not to ever turn into my own nightmare. Two men ran the house named Country and Black.

Country was a very good-looking brown-skinned man with long dreads who had a nice smile. He had found an attraction in me but treated me with utmost respect. He claimed to me he could tell that I wasn't a drug addict. He had different drug addicts working for him who people called out there in the city phones. I had nowhere to sleep and thought, wow how could I actually fall asleep in a place like that? The smell of the drugs almost made me sick. I asked him to air it out for me, and he had one of the woman on drugs who he called a phone do so.

I was extremely tired and told Country my situation. By the time it stopped raining and we walked to the store so that I could grab some snack to eat. He bought me some snacks as we flirted holding hands down the street. I never really had any interest in any men, but when I met him, he sparked a charm of security and safety in my eyes. I was desperate, wanting someone that wasn't trying to harm me to care about me. I knew that I would return back to Niki's and this situation would soon be over.

That night I made a terrible decision. I felt that because he had allowed me to stay in his dope house with him, I felt I had to have sex with him, not wanting to be thrown on the streets if he approached me. I wasn't smart about my decisions.

That night he never came on to me until it was some time the next day. He had one of his workers hook up one of the back bedrooms for me, trying to say he wanted me to stick around to be his girlfriend. I went along with it, having little interest in him but not trusting him based on what I've already been through in my lifetime. I was woken up that morning to one of his woman phones coming into the room asking me if I needed anything such as clothes or etc. I told her I was fine. The man who called himself Country laid next to me, cuddling with me, comforting me.

I than agreed to have sex with him, feeling myself somewhat attracted to him. As we had sex, my body was very tight and small from being unexperienced and only having sex with a man a couple times in my whole life. His penis was extremely wide and long. I started to feel my body in pain. After some time of trying to please this man, I told him I couldn't go any longer. I started to get out of position, telling him my body was hurting. He ignored what I was saying still thrusting his penis inside of me. I was crying by that time from the pain, telling him to stop. He wouldn't stop. I remember my face being in the pillow while he was doing this. I remember his hand grabbing my hips very tight, not letting them go. It felt like this was lasting forever, but I think he might have done this for about fifteen minutes.

When it was all finished, I wiped the tears off my face. I was confused if I made the man mad by not letting him cum. It seemed that when I hopped off him telling him to stop, it made him angry. The worst part about the situation was we didn't use safe sex. I really felt stupid for not knowing if the man did or didn't. I was a rookie at sex and needed some guidance. I put my clothes on. The man who called himself Country then went to the store. I left quickly from the house and headed back to Niki's.

I felt disgusting and knew I needed a shower. When she let me in her apartment, I never told her what had happened to me. I went directly into her bathroom and washed my body up, scrubbing the filth off my body. I felt so terrible it had felt like I had gotten rapped even though I agreed at first to have sex with him. Niki asked me where I had been since she had a clue I wasn't in the four-family flat because she went looking for me. I told her that I went to a friend's house because she told me to leave.

A slang way of saying she told me to leave I learned in the city was "she put me out." The next couple days, I noticed I had bumps filled with puss all over my body. I knew that the atmosphere I had been in wasn't the cleanest. I figured I had a reaction from dirty clothes and staying from place to place. I knew that something was terribly wrong with my body. I decided to go to the emergency room right away at the hospital. She told me that she wanted to see my results when I came back.

When I went there, I knew my body was shutting down. My stomach was having pains. When the doctor tested me, it came out that I had caught chlamydia, which is an STD. I was disgusted and very embarrassed. I hadn't been having sex with Niki at all since the incident with the man named Country, ashamed of what had happened.

I was then treated for all STDs that could have been related. I felt like a piece of dirt. I knew that I had caught the STD from Country because he was the only other person besides Niki I was involved with.

When I got back to Niki's house, I hid half of the paperwork in my purse, ashamed, not wanting to tell her where I caught the sickness from. Showing her only part of the papers for the bumps that I found out that were actually called boils. It was my first time having any of those medical issues. I was very disappointed in myself for letting my life get out of control like that. The girl CC that was living in one of the apartments across the hall from Niki's apartment connected to the four-family flat went inside my purse when I was on the porch talking to Niki. The girl CC grabbed the other half of my paperwork, reading my results out loud. I was so embarrassed. By that time, I had no chance to explain and Niki flipped out saying that I could have given the STD to her because I wasn't going to say anything.

She just didn't understand I was ashamed of what had happened to me and I did not want to tell her. I never had intentions of having intercourse with her at all after I left the hospital. I just wanted it to go away. Around this time, all the neighbors were outside on their porches watching everything that was happening. Niki then started getting loud, yelling, swearing, throwing all of my belongings on the front lawn that was mainly dirt and dead grass. I felt like a fool, crying. I felt like a child very lost. I was hurt.

The neighbors next door let me come to their house until things cooled off. They then told me that I could move into the four-family flat empty apartment next door to them. I had nowhere to go so I decided to do that. I took what stuff I had and moved into the abandoned apartment that had no electricity or water.

I knew that I didn't want to live like this any longer. I didn't want anything to do with Niki and she didn't want anything to do with me. That next week up, my boils and STD cleared up. I slept on some couch cushions on the cold hard wood floors of the apartment. I was still disgusted and she was still mad I didn't tell her. Being so distant from Niki and the kids made me sick. It was tearing my heart apart that everything turned out like this. I knew school was starting soon, and I had to get myself enrolled. Even after everything we had been through, I knew our love was stronger.

One night Niki brought me some food but still didn't want to forgive me. She knew I wasn't eating because I was homeless. She was still my girl even though she was hurt. In all reality, there was stupid reasons why we couldn't be together. I knew that if I didn't love her, I would have traveled a long time ago for good down Gratiot Avenue on the 560 bus headed to what I knew was civilization across Eight Mile. In the suburbs, the laws were strict. Most of the police officers drove chargers.

Chapter Seventeen

This whole other world on the West Coast seemed challenging and very scary. The main goal for many and most was to make a living. Money seemed to be many people's motivation as the days went on. Niki and I didn't want to be together. We both knew the drama we would have if we tried. From that point on, I took every day very seriously. I never knew what the future held for me. Survival came to me quicker than it would have for most. More and more I realized I was blessed. Yes, it was true the Lord was looking out for me, keeping me alive.

My problems seemed to be all the same like many light-skinned girls in Detroit. The women were jealous because I was lighter than them. Jealousy rose to its finest as each day went by and I lived. Everyone around me expected me to be a drug addict, but because I wasn't, I got respected. Some people failed to realize I wasn't one. Then again the ones who did understand I wasn't understood me. Many who knew me understood I stayed for Niki and the kids.

Many African American men approached me; the women hated me for that. It seemed that black women looked at it like I was white and felt that I belonged being with only a white man. They looked at me as if my race of woman were coming and stealing all their race of men. I wasn't interested in men really at all. That could be a reason some women didn't pay much attention to me at all. For that, I was happy to be labeled as a gay.

Changing into a woman wasn't easy especially in a city of foolishness and poverty. The day came down when I left the streets of Detroit. It was a normal day of staying in the abandoned apartment.

The difference of any other day than that day was when I woke up the first thing I thought about was getting ready to go back across Eight Mile and sign up for school. The woman who allowed me to stay in the lower part of the flat of the apartment left earlier that day to go register her son for school. She was a cocky woman who could have been perceived as not the nicest woman. With a grin on her face that made me have an instinct not to trust her, I kept my eyes wide open. I always knew she wasn't all nice and she had two sides to her character.

The day was passing slowly. I then put on my shoes and walked to the corner gas station. Most the time when I walked to the gas station I stood tall, walking with courage ready for anything. Once I reached the gas station I went inside to the back of the store to get something to drink. I usually had few money so I would get two juices for a dollar. A few people were always in the store in the morning's either getting gas or loose cigarettes that people called "loosies" that were fifty cents a figurate. Once I grabbed my juice I paid for it in a rush. I was aware still of my surroundings. Before I went outside I watched a red van pull up. A boy went inside and paid for the gas. I waited a couple minutes before I started walking home. As I walked a couple steps outside, I saw this woman in her mid-twenties driving the van looking at me. I was looking at her too. By this time, I was getting nervous, wondering what was going to happen next. The young woman driving smiled, calling me over to the van. It may have been a sign from God, so I walked over to the van.

At that instant, I told the young woman my story about being from California. She wanted to instantly help me. I knew she could tell as a black woman from the city that I wasn't a drug addict.

God sent the woman named Neddy to help me. God sent Neddy to help me get away from that area. God sent her to save my life. Who knows what would have happened to me if I wouldn't have made eye contact that day with her. There was a feud going on between Niki and I for all the reasons of what we had been through. It was mainly because we were broken up living on the same street, in the same hood. The hood was broken into two or more sections of Six Mile.

CALI GIRL, HOW DID I MAKE IT IN THE TREACHEROUS STREETS OF DETROIT?

The gas station was extremely ghetto. Most people who knew me called me Cali because I was from California. Every day someone who spoke to me either had a motive to sell me their hustle or their dream. No matter who tried approaching, me I always smiled and walked away saying no thank you. It didn't matter how things were. I stayed to myself when walking to the store or anywhere at that matter. Neddy was different though with her intentions for me. She was different from the average person I spoke to from the city. She had every intention of positive actions.

That day I was down and out from everything I had been dealing with. When Neddy told me I could hang out with her and her family, I was thankful for being able to get away from there. I needed to get away from Six Mile. I felt that now that Niki and I had problems there wasn't nothing there for me. More and more, I was being dragged down with everyone around me who really weren't doing anything positive with themselves.

I jumped in Neddy's van with her. She was familiar with the area and wanted to see where I had been staying. As her family and I packed into the van, we rode down Six Mile to where I had been staying. Neddy's aunt who was with us had her CCW strapped to the side of her hip. I really didn't pay much attention to the fact that she had a gun.

When we pulled up to where I had been staying, her whole family jumped out. Of course by that time everyone had been sitting on their porches. Niki was outside on her porch. I didn't want any problems based on the fact that I knew the circumstances of the situation I was in with her. I showed them the apartment. I was happy Neddy took an interest in helping me get away for the day. Neddy's auntie was already a Detroit homeowner. After I showed them the apartment, the woman and her mom said, "I don't know why you are bringing people here when this isn't your apartment." The building was an abandoned building. Neddy's aunt wasn't playing games with them. You could tell she was a strong African American woman who was there for her family and friends.

I was glad the Lord sent them to get me away from this situation I didn't know how to leave alone. When Neddy's auntie asked the woman and her mother who owned the apartment building, the woman Lanae got smart with her, saying she was the owner. Her aunt knew better than that and they started exchanging words. The woman claiming she was the owner was threatening to call her cousins over there and that's when Neddy's auntie let her know she wasn't playing any games. She had her CCW right there in her purse along with her licensed weapon. Everything happened so fast and I wasn't paying much attention to their conversation because I was trying to get some of my things together.

The woman and her mother told me right then and there in front of Neddy and her family not to come back to that apartment building or there would be problems. The old woman said, "Lock the apartment doors so that she can't get back in there to get her things." When Neddy heard that, she told me to get all my stuff together. I didn't have a key and neither did the loud mouth neighbors. The back door was busted, and even if they locked it, they lived upstairs and could get in from their apartment if they really wanted to get inside.

Niki saw this happening and started getting smart with Neddy's auntie. They helped me get my things, not wanting to see a young girl like me struggling in an area they knew all about. They knew I didn't belong there, and so did I. I was really upset I had to leave the boys and Niki, but knew I couldn't stay around there any longer. In a sense, I was very relieved that I ran into the right people who could help me.

When I looked out the window, all I could see was how upset Niki looked that I was leaving. I was ready to leave, but loved her and knew I always would. Once we were further and further away, I didn't know what to say. I explained to them that I didn't have any family in Michigan and stayed around Six Mile because of Niki, and her sons. I then told Neddy the incident that happened to me that caused me to catch an STD. The girl Neddy was weary because she didn't know me. She thought I might have been a run away and wanted me to call my dad so she could talk to him. I called him telling him some craziness went down and this woman was here helping me wanting to speak to him to make sure I was who I said I was. He told her I wasn't a runaway and she told him about me catching an STD. I was really embarrassed not wanting him to know what I had gone through.

Chapter Eighteen

I knew that I wouldn't be able to go back to those apartments to speak with Niki again for a while, and if I did go back, it would have to be at night when no one was outside. I knew if I would return during the day, there would be trouble waiting for me. I later on heard from talking with Neddy and her family that Niki ran over there starting some drama with their family while I was inside showing Neddy the apartment. Neddy's auntie said she would have used her gun if she needed to for protection. I wasn't aware of how gun play played a huge role in Detroit. I didn't want Niki to get hurt no matter what was going on.

I knew that all this happened because the people who were allowing me to stay in the abandoned apartment were jealous of the people I was with. It was a typical thing that happened around there. People in the community were jealous of how each other were doing. The community focused on how better or worse people were, instead of coming together as a whole to conquer defeat.

It seemed that everyone was trying to be the best in Detroit, but mainly, people who weren't doing well wanted to see other people that were from their city fall. It was a shame to see a community that didn't always pull together. Later that night, Niki's cousin who was a drug dealer, slash gangster was upset because Niki could have gotten shot. He told her that he was going to put a hit out for me for putting her in danger and didn't want me back over her house. Niki told him that it wasn't necessary and told him to relax.

Earlier that evening, for the Fourth of July, I met some of her family in the hood at her aunt's house, met her cousin. I had no idea that any of this had occurred until later on when I called Niki and she told me what was going on. When we left from that four-family flat, we stopped at a tire shop in the hood off Eight Mile so Neddy could get a tire for her van. A white man then came up to the van asking for a cigarette. The man went from asking for a cigarette to not knowing who he was in an instant.

This family I was blessed to meet seemed like a really real and laidback family who was down to help anyone they could. I felt alone again not knowing what to do next. I was blessed to have someone looking after me though. When I told Neddy that Niki's cousin was claiming he was going to put a hit out on me, she showed me a tattoo on her arm that said "lucky." Supposedly, he was her ex-boyfriend and she had his number. She called him up, leaving me at her apartment to go and meet him. There at his house was Niki and that's when everything started coming together more.

Neddy came back and told me that he didn't want me to go back over to Niki's house, but if I did, then he would try and get rid of me. The power of my love for Niki was too strong and I still wanted to keep her in my life. Neddy allowed me to stay at her house for the next couple days, allowing me to keep my things there. I went the next day and hung out with her niece and aunt who lived a couple blocks away from Niki's family's house. I was a bit nervous and knew that it would be easy for someone to point me out in the hood because I was a rare look. I ended up somehow waiting until it was late at night when I took the bus to Niki's apartment. I was in luck. No one was around to spot me in the area.

Niki pulled me in her apartment and apologize I didn't have any idea what was going on. I told her I was sorry about not telling her about the STD, telling her how I caught it. She hugged me and we told each other we loved each other. The neighbors started calling for her and she was buzzing from drinking. Niki told her child's father's cousins to look after the boys so she and I walked to the gas station for a cigarette and to say good-bye.

She told me it wasn't safe for me to be around anymore, and she would try and contact me when she moved from that area. I told her I would come at night in the future to visit but, didn't know when.

She and I ran before the neighbors saw us but, I saw one of them at the gas station. Niki went into a shock fell out on the cement and started having a seizure. I was so scared and didn't know what to do.

Thank God just in time another one of her child's father's cousins pulled up and asked if that was Niki and I said yes. By that time, she got up, still frightened to get me to safety. She asked the cousin to drop me at the Eight Mile and Gratiot bus stop so no one would be able to catch me for seeing her. We gave each other a hug and a kiss. We felt as if we weren't going to see each other again but knew this wasn't our last good-bye. The next couple days I spent across Eight Mile to stay with a friend in the suburbs. I made sure to keep contact with Neddy.

The first place I went to retrace my steps was Sixteen and Harper. I went back to the twins' apartment where my friends had once allowed me to stay with them and their family. They were holding most of my clothes for me that I had left. The first month that I was dating Niki, I was visiting the twins and met a girl named Mimi and her boyfriend who called himself Smoke.

When I met Mimi, she told me I looked familiar. She then realized she met me at Marty's house. I slightly remembered her coming by Marty's house. It was true she was her first cousin.

I had never seen a chick from the hood with so much class. Her cousin was different from any other black girl in the hood. She kept herself up with the best brand clothes. Her ears and fingers were covered in gold jewelry. People could tell she wasn't a hood rat type of female even though she was from the hood.

Her cousin's hair stayed done. Appearances said a lot about a person. It was proving to me that she was a classy chick that still didn't mess around and would fight for herself and the people she loved.

Mimi never wanted me to stay in the hood with Niki. She knew I didn't belong there and had so much potential to be all right. Her skin complexion was dark but her skin was smooth and clear. Many women were jealous of her because she was pretty enough to be a model. She lived in the same apartment complex as the twin's family.

A lot of girls when they met Mimi were intimidated by her by the way she spoke and carried herself. Mimi was an upfront person that would fight you if she had a problem with you. Our friendship seemed to be growing now that I was finally back from staying out in the city. Even though I was bisexual and she was straight or the fact that she was dark and I looked white, she never judged me or shied me away as a friend.

My life was scary at this time. I didn't know what was going to happen next. I couldn't stay with Mimi and her boyfriend because her boyfriend would act as if I owed them for them helping me allowing me to stay with them for a week back when Niki and I were fighting.

I always thought they were kind people but just didn't appreciate the extra negativity that her boyfriend brought along with his attitude. I chose to stay on Six Mile, not wanting to feel as if I owed the world something for staying with them and tried to stay put there until I couldn't take it anymore.

Since I was back in the area I focused on trying to get money so that I would have a way to feed myself. My main focus was that and making sure I had a safe, warm place to sleep. I gathered all my clothes from the twin's uncle that I had left at their family's house and what I had been carrying. I put it right next to Mimi's apartment in the inside hallway of the complex in the storage room that was blocked off with a door. Some nights I found places to go and sometimes I didn't.

When I didn't have places to go, I would sleep in Mimi's storage room that had a mattress. I would lay down and put it back standing it up when I was done using it the next morning. Mimi would give me a blanket. The doors to come into the complex stayed open all night and it was a bit scary not to know who could come in there. Some nights I would stay up with Mimi until two or three in the morning and then fall asleep in there. I was very cautious when I spent my nights in that cold, creepy storage room. Being so close to Sixteen Mile made me have memories of Megz and the adventure that led me to where I was at that point in my life. I thrived to understand why everything was changing for me. I sat there asking God to guide me but still was prideful not to give up and go home to my father and family.

It seemed that everything in that area reminded me of the girl I had once thought I seen having beautiful laughter and a shy smile.

I never wanted to completely let go of her spirit that was captured in my heart. So much time was passing by, and it seemed as if time was running out for me to get enrolled back in the adult education classes for school. I needed to get stable and find somewhere to live so I could at least try and finish go to school. I left my clothes that I wore in the streets at Neddy's house, in a dollar store checkered bag that was blue and white. She offered for me to stay at her house so that I could attend a school down the street from her apartment.

For two weeks straight, I would take the bus and go back to Neddy's area, put in job applications all around by her house. I put in a few over near Mimi's house as well. From hanging out with Mimi, a girl named Lyisa found an interest in me right when she met me. She was a beautiful white thin girl with huge blue eyes and blondish brown hair. She was two years younger than me.

What captured me to gravitate to Lyisa was the fact that she had so much ambition and hyper positive energy that showed she was ready to take over the world. We smiled when meeting each other, laughed a little, and from that moment on, we were intrigued but didn't exchange numbers. I asked Mimi and her boyfriend Smoke for her number but they didn't give me her number back when it was around for the summer time, when I was living on Six Mile. That's when I wanted her number when I first saw her. Some people would have labeled her as a preppy white girl around this time who like old-school rock music and who drove an old blue fire bird. I was very intrigued to learn more about this girl from Michigan.

When I finally got Lyisa's phone number, we started hanging out but we didn't hang out alone too much. She came with a package and his name was Winston.

Winston was a gay boy who was friends with her and always spent the night and confined in her for love. Even though things were cool with Lyisa, I seemed to start liking her. I was still hurt from Niki so it was hard for me to trust her. I just took every day in that situation day to day not put all my eggs in one basket. Winston was nice and polite to me. Winston and I ended up having a cool bond.

For a few weeks Lyisa and I were inseparable, practically doing everything together. She would come and pick me up and sometimes let me sleep at her house. Even though she had a job, she had enough time to spend with Winston and I. She wasn't stuck up for having a nice car and a job. I was treated no different from how she viewed her own life.

At times there would be little arguments over jealousy issues between her and I and some of the people around us. We really moved to fast in our first meetings anyways. I figured we moved quick because I needed someone that would care about me. Lyisa and I still had our hearts belonging to our exes, which caused another reason for us to fall into arguments.

I started making sure I called my dad a round this time to let him know I was all right. I wanted him to understand that the little I had already struggled I was going to make it through and come home with my high school diploma. Every day seemed like a new adventure. I was constantly singing and rapping every day, working on music to put my heart into that instead of worrying about a chick. I would put most of my emotions into my rhymes.

Chapter Nineteen

The love I progressed started flowing out my mouth, expressing my struggle to many putting something behind the name "Cali Girl" wherever I went to hang out with someone. The days I spent with Winston and Lysia were fun. I went and signed up at another school because on Six Mile, I had got wind that the woman and her mom with the loud mouth that caused all those issues when I went with Neddy to the four-family flat to get all my things was trying to have kids from my original school find me, feeling they wanted something bad to happen to me because of Neddy's auntie saying she would use her CCW licensed weapon if they kept it up stepping any further. They were intimidated by that weapon that could have lost their lives and blamed me for their stupidity for opening their mouth trying to start a route between them and people they didn't even know.

I heard through kids at the school that were attending there a woman would drive up by the school offering the kids twenty dollars to reveal where to find me. She should have known twenty dollars wasn't enough. That was little money, and she should have never been doing that anyways. Lex's mother never contacted me. His mother tried to get me to sign a papers before moving out saying I owed her ten thousand dollars. I never signed the papers.

I was so upset by the situation, which caused me to move out, staying away from her by any means. She was also bribing kids at my school to tell her where I was. I didn't care much. I just knew I didn't want any problems to catch any cases that would mess up my record.

When I was hanging out with Lyisa, she started doing shady stuff to me when she noticed I met and started hanging out with a girl named Tina.

When I met Tina, I was hanging out with a crowd of kids at a bowling alley on Twenty-Three Mile when this boy took me with him to hang out at some more kids at a party that was being held. It ended up being her little brother's crowd of friends. I was blessed that God gave me a chance to know her. She looked at me as if she also knew I had great potential to be successful and all right. I was happy to have met her because she started helping me when I needed a ride and it was important.

Tina started allowing me to stay in her old bedroom at her dad's house where I had met her. I was just happy that she came from a hard-working upscale family that treated me like I was part of their family. Tina was a very good person who was trying to survive by staying with an aunt and going to cosmetology school at Paul Mitchelles.

When I told her my story, she helped me see I wasn't the only one struggling to survive, but it was possible with strong focus that anyone could survive it with God's help. I was happy with staying at Tina's dad's house so that I could have a fresh new start. Lyisa and I were growing apart because we started hanging out with other people. We decided we wanted to stay in each other's lives, so we decided to go to a "Puddle of Mudd" concert in Pontiac, a city a half hour away with a boy that Tina introduced to us that was very nice named Dustin. Dustin was a nice single white male who was very work orientated, who had gone to Michigan State University, and who graduated with a degree that helped him own his own house at twenty-four.

At the concert, I could tell that Lysia was flirting with this chick that met us up at the concert who we had met prior at a party earlier in the week.

I was a little jealous, but then again I wasn't. I noticed she was also flirting with Dustin. I was paying more attention to the band because it was amazing watching them live. I started feeling uncomfortable, but since I really didn't have anywhere stable to live, Dustin said I could live in the upstairs part of his house.

I didn't care that she was flirting with him as much as I started to care she was flirting with this girl we just met. At the concert Lysia and I were sitting on some speakers close up to the stage when the guitarist gave her friend she was flirting with a pic and then went to hand me a pic and she felt that he was reaching out to give her the pic, but in all reality, he gave me the guitar pic. Since her friend had gotten a guitar pic, she wanted a guitar pic as well. I felt really good that he gave it to me even though she wanted one. It wasn't even about the guitar pic. She came at me at the concert all disrespectful as if I intercepted the pic and it belonged to her. I knew that it wasn't true. He had meant to give it to me, but it just made me furious the way I was getting treated terribly more and more as the concert went on. She was claiming to me that she liked me but then was all over the girl she had meet at the concert.

At the concert she hardly gave me any attention. The attention she gave me was negative. I was trying to avoid drama all night and wanted to fix how things were already going for Lysia and I. The way I handled it ended up turning out bad. We argued all the way through the parking lot trying to find the car as soon as possible so that we could get back in to our town. We wanted to get away from each other.

Finally, we found the car and arrived back at Dustin's house thirty minutes later. When we got there, Winston got poor piss drunk. The whole time Lysia kept asking me if she could have the guitar pic that said "Puddle of Mudd" on it.

I told her I threw it out the window on the way home. She didn't believe me but played along as if she did believe me. At the house my feelings were a bit hurt. Dustin was a recovering drug addict that wasn't supposed to be drinking, but he had a couple brews at the concert. We encouraged him to drink, not knowing his situation and by the end of the night we regretted it.

Winston ended up acting a fool on the second story of the house drunk talking smack to Lysia. That's when she locked him in the room because she was driving him home and wasn't ready to go yet. Since the door was locked and he was locked in the room, that didn't stop him from hopping out the bedroom window and jumping down to the lower level of the house to the back yard. After he did that we put him back in the house and he was still talking smack to Lysia so belligerently drunk by this time. He ended up getting kicked down the stairs by Lysia because she was mad he was disrespecting her. Dustin's house was a two-story house with a basement.

By the time that Dustin got up from laying down in his room relaxing when he realized Winston was wasted asked Lysia to take him home. Lysia started spazzing out being rude to me because Winston tried to kiss me when I was drunk. I always got along with her friend since the day we met.

It wasn't the fact that he was gay and tried to kiss me that made her, mad it was the fact that he considered her best friend sitting there trying to kiss the girl, she had some feelings for. In Dustin's garage right before she decided to take Winston home I told her I would wait there because I was going to spend the night there. That's when Lysia and I started pulling each other's hair in the garage taking all our anger out on each other. She had provoked me to retaliate but had started the fight originally.

Finally, we broke it up and I pulled out the guitar pic and asked her to be my girlfriend we went inside and sat down and talked. We stopped fighting but, knew we weren't going to make it in a relationship long. She took Winston home and after that I felt that I had made a terrible mistake by bringing Lysia over there to show her how blessed I was getting by having someone say I could stay somewhere permanently for a while in their home.

In all reality she had Dustin's number and started becoming really close to him sabotaging mine and his plan of letting me stay at his house by manipulating him to like her and start buying her gifts which made her words of manipulation get to him to change his mind of letting me stay at his home. Things now were moving in a couple different directions for me. I didn't have a stable home and needed to feel secure. I had been feeling as if someone was after me but, in a reality they weren't.

People just wanted me to stay out of Niki's life. I had seen a couple people who were around the Six Mile area and had heard the same rumors that I had heard. It made me get spooked and I decided to go back to the one person I thought could really help me and that was Megz the girl who brought me out here. Megs had once been able to take my breath away but now as I walked up to her apartment I grasped for air scared not knowing what to do with myself. I had written a letter and carried it in my hand that said basically that some guys were after me and I needed some where to stay. I was also asking her to forgive me for everything that had happened between us.

I blamed her for being in Michigan, waiting on her to grow up and realize how much she loved me. It was similar to the fact that I loved Niki and the boys staying on Six-Mile for them as well as staying in Michigan for Megz.

I ran the buzzer three zero five outside because, the building was locked from the outside. There was no response to my buzz. I didn't want to stay there long so I saw a lady and her child walking in the building so I asked her to please give the letter to door three zero five. I left right away with hope of having her call me willing to help me. She did call me a couple days later on my cell phone but, just question what was going on in my life. She couldn't help me because, she was living up north.

My outlook on life started changing. I noticed that I was really home less out in Michigan and knew that No one was going to just give me anything. I walked a lot of places at times and used the bus. If I really wanted to get out of an area fast because, I was paranoid of someone after me I would ask strangers which way they were heading and hitch ride a couple miles up the street with them.

It came to be a small world where I was at. It seemed that everyone pretty much knew everyone or had family that knew somebody that knew somebody that may have knew somebody. I was starting to be pretty known just based on my story alone and the area's I started to gravitate too that I had once had friends in those areas.

Come to find out the two women who let me live in their lower flat of their abandoned building were cousins with the guy who I had pick pocketed for sixty dollars so I was already feeling as if I was in danger once everything came to play out. It wasn't until later when I met a guy with dreads who took me to his block on the east side called Alma when there was a block party where I knew the guy who was cousins with the two woman and their cousin who I had pick pocketed would be there. The young man who was helping me called himself Wayne and he use to hustle and work for my old acquaintance who I figured was mad at me for what I had did to his cousin.

He came and spoke to me telling me what I had did was petty and there was no hit out for me but, when I get a chance I owed them sixty dollars. My friend told them I would repay them and as we smiled with kind words from both sides finishing our drinks we looked around at the old school cars that were decked out. The paint jobs and rims of the rental cars were different colors. I spent one more day in the city and then hopped on that familiar transportation which for me was the five sixty bus line. The bus helped me make my way back across Eight-Mile to the suburbs. I had relief that I didn't have a hit out on me or anyone after me.

I started to hangout in Mt. Clemens, and Clinton township more. I knew I had to stay out of the cold streets of Detroit because, I had already experienced what type of life I would have out there if I was to continue to live out there. I knew what the cold streets of Detroit held beneath them from the cracks and crevasses of poverty that laid on its people. Many people's souls were cold and hungry with no baring of a change. Megs would call my cell phone a lot on restricted, and she told me in our last real conversation when I had left the letter at her mom's that her mother didn't want another visit from me and called the police, letting them know as well Megz even started having girls call me and prank my phone. I was done with her games and accepted the fact that she couldn't help me. She did tell me to go to the department of human resources to get on food stamps. I was still really prideful and didn't want to get on welfare. The last time I saw Megz was when we somehow ended up at the same place at the same time. I was surprised she was there and didn't know she was coming there with another friend.

I had picked this girl from Flint earlier in the week and had her with me hanging out and she happened to be there with me when Megz showed up with the boy named Nole. She saw me attending to the other girl so she went outside. She heard me call the girl babe and flipped out. I didn't want to fight her and she was talking smack. She came towards me throwing her hands out I restrained her wrapping all my arms around her so she couldn't hit me. It was a lovers quarrel right in front of all of our white community in the trailer park. She screamed mad I had called this girl babe. I started saying baby stop baby stop as I clinched down hard her to restrain her. I kept telling her in front of everyone to calm down.

Holding her close to me made my heart start beating fast so I dropped her, pushing her away from me once I seen her calmed down. She still was upset so she pulled out her nice-sized pocket blade leaning down trying to stab my tires. I got mad and I pushed her. Yelling at her more and more, I said "What is wrong with you!" She started screaming at me. I didn't want to fight her, so she told me to leave the mutual friend's house in the trailer park. I knew in her mind she loved me and what I had said in front of the other girl must have made her go crazy. It was an immature move on my part, but it was being more naive than anything for not catching myself. Nole who she came with grabbed her and put her in his car.

The whole time he was holding her back, she was cussing out the girl from Flint, threatening her. I told the girl from flint to get in my car and we drove off after everyone told Nole to take Megz wherever she was going once she was in his car. Everyone left. Later that night she called me apologizing saying she would never hurt me because we had been together for two years.

I didn't know how to feel. I loved her still but knew she was sick to the point where we couldn't be in a serious relationship. Her emotions were everywhere, and she refused to take her bi polar medication. Refusing to take her medication our contact ended.

I decided we had to let each other go, but, around the same time frame before the last day I hung out with Megz I had introduced her to a boy named willie who I paid gas money to pick her up and bring her to my house. She ended up getting his number and pursuing a boyfriend-girlfriend relationship with him knowing that we all hung out with the same crowd of friends. I still hung with the same crowd which made Megz and I close even though we were not technically in each other's lives.

It was very irritating at that point. I avoided her every chance I could. I was still mad my acquaintance and Megz played me like that. Mad I had to still see them around the same parties I kept my calm. Thank God I never saw them around even though at the time it was my biggest fear if I did because, I didn't want to get me feeling's hurt. It seemed that the love I had with Megz was a different then the love I had with Niki. The difference in the two different love affairs was that with Niki we shared love that matured into a grown up experience that was hands on for me.

My experience with Megz was a younger love experience that wasn't much hands on. Our relationship had always been a love that was based on a long distant. The two people were always nine years in age difference. I started attending school again going to receive my high school diploma. I went two times a week to school. I was really trying to achieve my goals by proving to everyone back in California that I could finish what I had started.

Chapter Twenty

My heart was strong as I started allowing God. I knew that following my heart so far didn't get me far but, knew that the Lord made me a lover. I wouldn't be myself if I stopped being positive loving the world for what it was. I didn't talk to my father or family back in California much.

Most the time when I would talk to my grandmother or my father they didn't have anything nice to say. I knew I could prove my strength and God was going to lead my path for me. Usually my father and I would clash heads because he always wanted to be right about everything and I spent my time trying to prove him wrong. I started hanging out more in Mt. Clemens which was were my school was located.

Mt. Clemens was a small city where mostly everyone knew everyone or most people were related to each other especially in the black community. While I was hanging out with Winston, I met him through Lysia we found a lot in common.

The first time we hung out was at a house where he was staying with this older man and his boyfriend. Winston never claimed the boy as his boyfriend and at the time I could see why. Winston's so-called boyfriend was infatuated with him, and it was very possessive and annoying for Winston. I was making a sandwich, just ignoring them. The night seemed to ease and wind down. Winston and I parked his car in Mt. Clemens over by Grospect in these apartments. He didn't have a license and ended up taking everything that he had in his car. It was just a crazy night for us. I would never forget.

Some guy ended up talking to Winston outside the apartment. He then invited us to his apartment to hang out. I was familiar with the area already from a guy friend who took me in that area when he lived over in the same complex.

I also had a home girl who lived on the other side of the Clem from school.

I wasn't scared of being in that area. Winston was lost not knowing where he wanted to go in life. He was confused as I watched him looking for what I had been looking for and that was love. I felt that if the devil came over and tampered in his life that night. That night he tried crack at a person's apartment that we didn't even know who we had just met made me pray hard.

Winston was a tall and white gay male with confidence. I didn't think anything of going in the man's home but maybe he was gay and they would have liked each other. The man offered us both crack. I said hell no very defensively. I knew already from my mother being a drug addict that I never wanted to even try it.

My dad educated me on the world as a child. My dad made it clear how that if you tried hard drugs one time you would get hooked to it. He was always in the back of my mind.

I told them to get that shit out of my face!

Winston pulled me in the room and kept saying, "Try it with me. It will only be one time." I said, "Fuck no, my mom's a drug addict." I told him not to do it but just let him do what he wanted. I left him in the room alone and waited in this man's kitchen. I was upset and tried to barge in the room saying if he tried it I wouldn't be his friend anymore. I was so pissed off that this boy I was cool with was doing crack. It was so disgusting and I wanted to smack the shit out of him.

By the third flicker from the lighter, it made me gag in my mouth and I ran out of the room, rushing into the bathroom. Looking in the mirror all I could see was my mother's face. I knew I never wanted to be like her. I was done being nice.

I splashed cold water on my face. Right after that, I walked outside the man's front door of his apartment getting some fresh air, staring at the stars off his balcony. I was grossed out but knew Winston had nowhere to go.

This boy named Chico who lived next door to the man who allowed us to come in his house said that we could spend the night at his house. He had found an interest in my friend Winston and they had their own conversation going on. I knew that I had no control now over what Winston was going to do next but held his keys in my pocket for safety. I was totally clueless to Winston and Chico's connection.

After thinking about the whole situation it was random to me for the thought but I felt my thoughts must have been God trying to talk to me, because we didn't have anywhere to go.

Chico was a bisexual man who was an artist, but he was more labeled as an artist then labeled as a bisexual man. We spent the night there and the apartment wasn't too bad. It was full of furniture with a computer with a lot of RNB music on it.

The next day, Winston and he ended up hooking up in the bedroom when I was asleep. Winston told me the details later on. Chico was an optimistic dreamer. He was one of the first people that seemed creative to me. The night that Winston did crack hurt me seeing him betray his soul like that. I knew that once he did that there was no going back. After he hit the pipe, he had the nerve to put the crack pipe in my face. All it did was piss me off, making me madder and madder after I told him no.

The fact that he did it anyways trying to test me irritated me to run out of patience with him. I lost a lot of respect for Winston that night. The feeling of anger and regret of wanting to be there in that moment made me feel in disgust.

I saw for the first time what my mother had left me for. It was right there, and it was taking Winston just like it took her. I also told Winston before he did it that if he did it, I would never be his friend again, and he didn't take my feelings into consideration, doing it anyways.

That night when we spent the night is when I met a young slim African American woman standing in Chico's apartment, drunk. The woman's name was slim and she was Chico's cousin. I saw how good and in shape she looked and didn't even pay much attention to her name. I asked Chico right away if she liked women. He replied that, "she needs to be alone right now". I had never had something said to me before. The he told me to just ask her further questions. In the morning I woke up and went to walk around the streets of Mt. Clemens wondering what I was going to do.

I walked over to a cemetery by a McDonald's praying looking at the cemetery as a place to get quite and peace so that I could speak directly to God for answers. I started praying to go for love. I prayed for some to come love me. I then prayed for someone to come help provide a home for me. After that, I prayed for change! I took a deep breath and made conversation with the guys in the oil place. I ended up hanging out with the people who worked at the oil place. It was also right next to the cemetery. I used the bathroom there and wanted to apply.

After I left there, I went back over to the familiar area where I had just left. I found myself sitting on Winston's car daydreaming. He was still hanging out upstairs with Chico for the day. There she was when she walked by a super thick working chick with a slim body. We spoke and exchanged words of thought. It sparked an attraction between her and I, but I really didn't know how to read her.

The woman told me that she was also was from California and her family had stayed out there. I wasn't surprised that she was pretty because, in California, there was a lot of pretty people. She became most entertaining as a friend and a close friend. We then stopped hanging out. I ran into the girl I was much familiar with from school who lived on the other side of the apartment building. She was the first black girl to try to date me in Michigan. One day in class, a year prior, I was passed a note to her, when I was living with Lex and his mother. The note had told me I was cute and sparked up a conversation. I was too scared to talk to the girl at the time, so I really acted shy. I had never dated a black girl back when I was first out in Michigan. I wasn't racist because I was black I just didn't know how to take all the outgoing realness of a black woman.

A black woman had at first intimidated me when I was freshly new to Detroit. After being in Detroit it was how some black classy woman carried their selves started attracting to me more than what I was use too. I walked Rihanna to the beauty supply with her older sister. She said, "look at you Cali you were acting all brand new and look at you out here hanging out with a girl over here." I guess she meant in a black community area. I wasn't sure at the time what that comment had meant.

I laughed though when Rihanna said the comment because a part of me loved the flirting between us. Rihanna was a cute girl that stood out, making sure people knew she liked girls with the style of rainbow belts and bright colors that she wore. I was interested in meeting more bisexual girls because I hadn't really met many in the area since I had been in Michigan so it intrigued my young heart.

The next few days I got to hang out with Rihanna and her friends I got to see them hip roll, and do ground work and dance. The dances that they did wasn't familiar with but, I liked how their hips would roll. The dace was different then how people from California danced. I learned that many African American people danced like that in our community. I felt that everything had happened for a reason and around that time I had nowhere to stay again.

Somehow in some way I had managed to survive that summer. The summer would end at some point soon. The cold breeze in the morning started making my body shiver. All the hairs on the back of my neck started to stand up, making me feel angry.

My eyes would feel itchy and irritated from lack of sleep as I would force myself to stay up long nights in Rihanna and slims apartment complex. The complex was built as an outside stair way leading you to an upstairs row of apartments or a downstairs row of apartments. I managed to talk with someone throughout the time of being there until a time where my acquaintances were home to allow me to shower or sleep.

The night that I had nowhere to sleep made me sick from walking around all night. All I could do at that point was turn to God for help to provide shelter, food and love for me.

One day this boy from Florida that lived in Mt. Clemens half his life messaged me on Facebook. We decided to hangout taking some interest in each other even though I never spent my time interested in guys. We ended up meeting up and walking around Mt. Clemens looking for something to do.

We walked right by a movie scene that was being recorded in his neighborhood. That was very interesting to me based on the fact that I used to model and act.

Walking by the movie scene, I wondered what my life would have been like if I would have stayed in California to pursue my acting and modeling career. After we couldn't find much to do, we ended up going to his house so that I could take a shower. His family was there, and they were nice to me, allowing me to take a shower at their house. He lived with his mother, aunt, cousins, and siblings.

We walked to downtown Mt. Clemens, and by that time it was 11:00 p.m. I didn't have anywhere to spend the night. We walked around for a while and then this short man who was as tall as me at five two was staring at me while he crossed the street. He spoke to me, asking me if I had a cigarette. I was still a bit guarded because it was late. I still was tired from previous night.

I had nowhere to go but the boy Que who I was hanging out with from Florida stuck by my side. He even said if I had to he would sleep in his shed with me because his family wouldn't have allowed me to spend the night because there was no room for me to sleep. I appreciated the gesture even though I didn't want to do that. When the short man named Chet asked me if I had a cigarette and I said no, he struck a conversation with us. I told him the truth that I had nowhere to go and I was from California. Que and I were both tired and new we had to do something.

We knew we couldn't walk around forever. He told the short man how he had been walking around with me for three hours and was tired. We both were hoping that the man would help us. He told us to come hang out at his mother's house and he would try and figure something out. We all started walking to his mother's house from downtown Mt. Clemens sort headed back toward Que's house. We walked a couple blocks to the left and then another couple to the right when we reached his house.

His mother answered the door. She was a very nice short woman with a loud voice scolding her son for being out so late since he was on parole and just came home from doing time. He reminded me of a short Italian man. He had an absent as if he lived in Philly or New Jersey. Once we started speaking to him, I could tell he had a good heart and I started having a little bit more faith in him to keep me safe and help as much as he could. I didn't expect too much from this stranger. I could tell his personality he was trying to stay young and stay paid in the streets. Everyone knew it was a recession!

Many people did what they had to do to make money. He was only good at three things! Convincing people into his idea's, raping to his music, and selling dope I seemed to connect with him a little bit because, we were both artists.

I loved what he had to say in his music. I felt that the way his flow would come off and rip that he had so much potential to go far in the music industry if he could stay out of trouble.

The short thug allowed me to sleep in his living room floor until the next day when he called his older friend Jerry to come over. He told me briefly about his friend saying he was a funny man. He insisted for me to meet him because, he might be able to help me with a place to stay.

When Jerry came inside the house, I was hardly paying any attention.

Chet was talking to Jerry, explaining to him how he wanted to go out. Jerry was a retired man from Chrysler who had plenty of free time on his hands. He wasn't married and all his sons were adults except one that was seventeen in high school. Chet said that I could stay with him on one condition and that was for me to go back to school. I couldn't have a stable life style so I stopped going prior to meeting him.

My friend's mother made it clear she couldn't have anyone else live there based on the fact that there was only one bedroom. Jerry overheard all I was going through, offering me to come stay at his house on Twenty-Three Mile.

Que stayed with me at Chet's house until he heard Jerry say I could stay with him. After that he ran back to his house to grab his family's car to drop off my stuff I left in his shed. I was grateful for my friend sticking by me as long as he did. I was also glad I was able to meet someone who was giving me a life-changing opportunity of possible security and shelter.

Que reminded me of myself of a loyal female who was an entrepreneur. He then told me to be safe. He left after returning my purse back to my hands.

Jerry, Chet, and myself got into Jerry's 2009 black Charger RT with tinted windows and sport packaged tires. Chet was turning the music up really loud, acting crazy while Jerry was speeding fast and faster down the freeway. I was very frightened because I still didn't know them too well. By the time we got to Twenty-Three Mile road it was far from Mt. Clemens. It was my first time being on twenty-three-mile road.

When we finally arrived to Jerry's house, the front yard of the house's appearance was set up really cute to me. The inside was furnished and even better than the outside because it was comfortable. The first night staying the night there was very uncomfortable for me. It was always hard for me to sleep anywhere new. It was especially hard for me to fall asleep with complete strangers around me. I had to work the situation I had. It was better than walking around all night till I was sick and tired. I was running out of options for myself.

The next step that I had to take was to get myself enrolled in school. I hoped that Jerry was safe and would allow me to stay at his house with the understanding of me not doing anything with him sexually or misleading him.

The next couple weeks seem to go by all right. Jerry and I were two totally different people with not many interests in common. We spent most of our time together having some drinks and smoking weed. The weed would calm me down to deal with him for saying out of wild type absurd things to me.

As time grew on more, I learned that he only spoke to me like that when he was drunk. At the time in my life I had no one but Jerry helping support me. He drove me around trying to lead me in the right path even though we both partied. He let me use his phone and then later on bought me my own phone so that people wouldn't call his phone back. It seemed that he was a good guy helping me as much as he could. He was a French Canadian who was a United States resident.

When I first met he was taking life for what it was just trying to enjoy himself. He was somewhat depressed but chose to have a hobby in guitar to put his time into. Everywhere we went he would bring his guitar. I've learned that this world can break you down but if you have some kind of love, which is mainly going to come from God no matter what kind it is you will survive.

I learned that if you have some kind of faith and love for yourself then you can make it through any tough times. Having faith with love helps you start having something to live for especially when you're at low times in your life or feeling all alone.

Jerry and I began to establish that nothing was going to happen sexually with us because, he was originally looking for a hot young chick to come and shake up his world. I wasn't looking for that and he soon learned that it was only going to be one way with me. I felt as if God sent him to save me but, I also felt he was falling into a pit chasing bad woman who would do hard drugs dragging him down.

It seemed that he had an addictive personality with a head on his shoulders that reminded him he had a seventeen-year-old son at home he felt he had to take care of. We then established a father daughter relationship and I started calling him dad. I mainly did t to remind him yes I might be hot and young, but, I would not mess up a blessing that I felt the Lord had sent me. We soon established a best friendship too confining in each other about any and everyone around us. I stayed hanging out with him as a father or friend because I wanted to stay out of trouble.

It seemed that every time I would go stay at a friend's house and need to be picked up there, Jerry was coming to rescue me out of nowhere in a black 2009 Charger, smiling, reminding me of Johnny Cash's lyric of "A Burning Ring of Fire." That was who I called my adopted dad perfectly. He played his guitar even though he really was a work in progress. In his house he had a lot of equipment that would help a new artist try and proceed to follow their dreams.

At that point in my life I never wanted to go back to California. Jerry my new dad spoiled me making sure I was taken care of. We ate at you could eat Chinese buffet and a sandwhich joint often where I would always order an Italian sub every time we went there.

The first thing I did when I was first around was helping Jerry's son who was living there going to high school clean the house. After cleaning I went and signed up for school. Things weren't as I hard as I thought they were going to be.

Jerry treated me as if I was daughter. Finally, after a few months of living with and going to church when we often did I realized that love comes at you through all different directions.

God can save you from any bad situation by sending you love through human beings. My new dad Jerry bought me a beat up car and got me on my feet. He helped me a lot but, had a down fall that he was too friendly to strangers and drank too much around this time. I loved having my own car again and was glad he bought me one. It turned into a lot of freedom for me. I felt as if a car was freedom that could take me on my way to my next adventure. I was legal too with all fines covered. I kept the house clean and took myself to school the days I had school. In school, it was hands on! I was in the adult education school in the course of getting my credits for my high school diploma.

School work wasn't hard for me. My mind was focused trying to succeed in all my classes. I only attended school a couple hours a day. I need one and a half credits now to graduate high school.

Chapter Twenty-One

I met this boy on Twenty-Three Mile Road in November who worked at a restaurant my dad had taken us to by our house. The boy and I started hanging out often. After a while, he then introduced me to his two half-sisters that had their own studio apartment in Mt. Clemens. No one had called me in Michigan.

When my friend started, it made me feel a sense of remembrance when I was a child and was called that from my grandfather. We never did anything sexual but at times, I could see myself dating him. I noticed that my friend's two sisters were pretty and nice.

I started hanging out with the two sisters for a couple weeks straight without their brother. Sometimes I would spend some nights over at their apartment. It was nice having girl time as we all would get ready together to go out to downtown Mt. Clemens to club hop.

This guy who was involved in the local rap industry around our city helping with local artists' promotions downtown at the clubs wanted us to hang out with him.

After having him come smoke with us it happened to be a small world because he already knew the older sister.

Around the fifth time, he came to hang out with us he brought a friend with him that was my father in California's age in his early forties named Dough. Dough could tell I liked girls. He was an older cat that took care of his responsibilities and kept hustling to do so. He sparked up a conversation with me about me being gay.

Dough told me that he had a daughter that was gay as well. I was dying to meet a gay young woman who would care about me.

CALI GIRL, HOW DID I MAKE IT IN THE TREACHEROUS STREETS OF DETROIT?

I took my chances by telling him to show me a picture of his daughter! He told me he would call her and that's exactly what he did. I was still upset from earlier because, right when I first started hanging out with my dad Jerry I took him to Detroit that morning. He allowed me to drive, showed me is car. His help showed me how drastically my life had changed.

I didn't think that the neighbor Lenae who had problems with me for bringing people over to see the apartment was going to come inside after me throwing blows at me. She told me that she was going to whoop my ass for putting her and her kids in danger because Neddy's auntie claimed she had her CCW. Niki was in the room, saying, "Fight back, Cali, fight back." She was mad because I still was intimidated by color. She told me after the lady hit me a couple times if you could hit me back then you could hit her back Cali I know you're not that week. I told her I didn't hit her back because, she was my elder. She didn't want to hear it. I waited in the car as she got her and the kids things together.

After they all came over my dad Jerry's house for a couple days and then got dropped off to the boy's family's house. She didn't want to stay on Six Mile anymore and the apartment building was being condemned. She and I kept in contact. There was then a time where she had nowhere to go but except her baby daddy's family house so they could look over the boys. My friend told me she was going to Atlanta to visit family soon so she could get away and get to live differently.

I wanted her to come back to Detroit, knowing I still loved her with every intent of her being a big part of my heart. I wanted her to always have a part of me, so I told her I would write her something interesting for her to read on the bus there.

I then opened up a pink notebook and started writing. Coming up at first with something for her to read to better understand what went through. The idea then turned into a book, I decided to write to explain to the world who I was, not just her. She told me that she needed somewhere to stay until she went to Atlanta. It was only two weeks until she was going there so I asked my dad if she could stay with us. We drove over to the hood by Seven Mile where we were staying with the boys at her baby daddy's family's house.

I popped the trunk and put her suit case in the trunk. When we got to my house on Twenty-Three Mile, I washed her clothes for her. We spent a lot of time just talking about the kids and the past experiences we had went through. We also spent our time having passionate sex in my room that was in the basement and the guest room she stayed in. We also hung out with my dad Jerry Going to some of his different friends' houses for drinks even though I wasn't old enough to drink I still did.

Most of my experiences with Niki when she was living with me were good besides when we drank together we would get into arguments that would lead to us making up later that night. If we didn't make up the night, we would make up that morning while we ate breakfast and let each other sleep alone. Our passion was still there, but we just didn't know which direction we both were going in. Niki and I went with my dad Jerry to have some drinks at a friend's house. I was stupid and had her in a room full of woman that all were pretty much interested in me but one.

It put her in awkward predicament. Which I didn't see at the time. We were both drunk and she then snatched my phone out of my hand breaking it. I was so angry I cussed at her telling her we would go back to Jerry's and then talk about it the next day. When we got there, we ended up arguing and I told her not meaning it that I didn't love her nor did I want to be with her.

By saying those things to Niki, I made her feel like shit. She and I were at a rough spot in our lives. I always expected people to be more than what they could be for me. I expected more from her. I wanted her to change her ways and settle down so we could all be a family. I felt hurt inside for saying all those things that I said to hurt Niki when I was drunk, but it was too late I couldn't take anything back. I came into the spare room where she was laying and spoke to her telling her I did love her and I did want to be with her, but couldn't because neither of us were ready to deal with each other's worlds.

I wore the matching bracelet that was green that she had on her wrist that I gave her as well to wear so that she would think of me when I wasn't around her. We laid down beside each other. She started kissing me, not letting me up, going lower by that time sucking on my body below. All of what we were arguing about didn't matter. After we had sex, we both laid there holding each other, but the next day, she was still mad at me and wanted to go back with our boys to stay with them. I didn't want her to leave.

I gave her all I had which was ten dollars and dropped her off in Mt. Clemens at the Gratiot bus stop because, my dad already felt that he made a wasteful trip by picking her up and she wasn't staying. I felt bad but, knew she had to go. She told me she would call Jerry's phone number to check on me but months went by and I never heard from her.

I started to think in the back of my mind I hope her and the boys are okay. Back to when I met dough and he called his daughter on the phone for me and I spoke to her. She sounded nice but I didn't know what to expect from her based on myself not having the best of luck with the ladies. I convinced him to give me his daughter's phone number. I had a feeling since I wasn't looking for this girl and she was sent to me through God out of the blue through someone that it may have been meant to be. I would just have to find out and see. I felt as if God knew when someone needed love in their lives.

I felt that he wanted my heart to grow more and be touched at the same time as well. A week after phone conversations, we decided to meet. A girl named Tish told me she had a baby boy named Jordan who was around one years old. We decided to meet each other at the family dollar up the street from her house. She walked up there and met me. I was at another girl and her boyfriend's house down the street from there earlier after school. When I met Tish, she was so much taller than me. I immediately liked her butt because it was big and round. She was also a pretty brown-skinned girl with straight white teeth. I was intrigued by her beauty, and every time she asked me a question, I couldn't stop smiling. We walked back to her mom's house where she allowed me to spend the night with her in the living room. I told her the house looked familiar, that it looked like my friend Rante's house. She told me that I was her brother. I used to hang out with him when I first was going to school at riverside. Sometimes I would drop him off there after school. She asked me when have I ever been over to her house because she had never seen me before. I told her I had been over there one time.

The moment I met her son Jordan, I fell in love. He was so cute with the nicest smile. I played with him for two days straight, not ever wanting to leave their house. The way Tish and I were connecting was so cool. She was a sweet girl who seemed to like me as well. I really liked her and we slept in the living room until she cleaned her room out. We didn't do anything sexual right away with each other because we really liked each other and wanted to see how much we liked each other without having sex like typical people do.

That month I never went home but still stayed with my dad Jerry. I did call my dad and check in with him. She was clearly not talking to Jordan's dad. He didn't start popping up till that next month. Even though he was popping up, she still showed the interest she had in me. I was finding ways to come up with money because, my life style became expensive with the smoking and eating fast food habits.

Tish and I ended up going through a couple situations where it just made us want each other more. I had no idea I was going to end up falling out of love with Niki, putting that part of my heart to rest and start falling in love with Tish. Everything that she had to say had put a smile on my face.

The days were cold as the weather changed and the nights I spent lying next to my queen. In my eyes, she was the most beautiful girl in the Clem with a nice booty. No one could tell me any different about her. She carried herself well as a high school graduate and a strong single mother. Tish's mother and brothers spoke to me often. Any time Tish and I would get into an argument I would just go fall asleep in her brother's room if he wasn't home.

The times we spent arguing over dumb stupid stuff, I wish now later in the future that we could have spent those times coming to an equal understanding of the love we shared for each other. We knew that the feelings we started having for each other were strong but, we didn't know how to apply those feelings to be strong for each other. In my mind, I wanted and needed Jordy and Tish. I wanted someone to love me and found myself containing my time with them.

When I started to realize that you cannot love someone without loving yourself first was later on. I don't regret meeting her or loving her. I just regret not loving myself around the time we were seeing each other. I regretted not spending all the money I spent on people around us on myself and not the society we lived around. Her world was different from mine, and her neighborhood was basically the projects of the suburbs that mainly was filled with a black community. Where she lived wasn't as bad as across town. There was something about her that caught us in stares and glares.

When she finally brushed her body against mine, I felt the lust that made my heart race. From that moment on, I really didn't know anyone but Kimmy over in that area plus a couple local bi-sexual girls. I had a passion for my new situation. Every day seemed to be more and more of a struggle for us because no one wanted to see us together outside of her home. Even till this day she would never know how much she truly meant to me because we were living in the moment.

Thanksgiving was nice with her family. I slowed a lot of my lifestyle down when I met Tish and her son. I felt that it was the right thing to do. I felt that everything happened for a reason and I was supposed to be in their lives. I mainly stayed in the house with her and the baby unless I left outside to smoke with her brother.

She didn't think it was cute at all. I am always asked now in present tense if I miss her and her son. I always said yes when I talk about my experience with her. I then sometimes pick up the phone and call her to check on them. I am grateful every experience has only made me stronger.

Around December, I met a man from Detroit on her street who was intrigued with me before I even knew who he was. He told my girl's brother to have me talk to him because he was interested. He told me about it but I didn't know who the guy was until he rushed to help me jump my car, that was parked in front of her house. I felt that Tish's eyes beaming on my back as I saw her glancing from her kitchen window watching me.

Anything I did I would be straightforward and tell her the truth about it even if I thought it could hurt her. I never wanted to be labeled as a fake individual. Some things I learned later on are never supposed to be said. The man and I became friends.

A couple weeks later, I got a call from his baby mama and her cousin. I clearly explained my situation to them about him approaching me. I told them how I was at my girlfriend's house, already in a relationship.

A wall started to grow between me and Tish. It started growing higher and higher and higher. I noticed other people started to get in between our relationship. Her baby daddy started coming around frequently, which caused us to argue, which then started causing us to fall apart.

The cousin I spoke to on the phone wanted me to come down to Detroit to hang out with her. I wasn't able to at the time still wrapped up with Tish so I didn't even try. I was starting to get jealous that I wasn't a man.

I started feeling that I didn't know what this young woman wanted from me. I hung out with her cousin at her house down in the city off Moran and Gratiot, one of the deadest, dangerous areas on the east side of Detroit. We only hung out once and then she moved back to Arizona with her ex-girlfriend. The young female would travel back and forth whenever they got into it. Tish and I started trying to make it work but the more people who got involved in our relationship the more our love started fading.

I still questioned my ex's true feelings for me. I knew she had love for me, but it was so easy for her to give up trying to make it work.

I've always felt that if you loved someone, you would stay and fight for the love. Love should be preserved for as long as you can preserve it for. I don't know how Tish and I lasted for as long as we did. We both ended up putting up with each other to the fullest disrespect at one point of time. My heart wanted her. The more I saw a change in us I chose to break up with her. I still came around her house hanging with her brother more than I hung out with her. It still felt as if we were together because the feelings were there. Kimmy started hanging out with Rante at Tish's mom's house. I longed to chill with her even though we stopped talking to each other over petty reasons of dis loyalty in our friendship back when I hung out with Nini. Kimmy and Tish were not friend at all. I started to talk about my feeling for Tish to Kimmy. She made it clear she didn't want me to date her.

It never ended to seem like there was things Tish did to make me turned off from trying to work it out with her. I still came over to her house noticing that she was obviously now messing with her baby daddy. Her child's father would come over more and more at the same time I would.

I didn't care about the reason at all. I just knew it made me very uncomfortable to keep seeing this dude. To me, he was crazy and uneducated. I didn't see him striving for a better life. He was abusive toward my ex. Her child's father was known for having had sex with her friends and people she knew. He even came on to me at one point of time and I talked shit brushing him off my shoulders ignoring him like he was a little piece of lint. He hardly did anything for his child and the way she had once loved this looser made me bitter she still had him around.

Even though all of this was going on, I never stopped doing little things for her and her son. The first time we got in a physical altercation was when I allowed her best friend Jaz to drive us down to the gay club. I allowed her friend to drive my car because my license was suspended.

The club's called Passion's in Detroit off Seven Mile on the east side was popular. I was so excited until the minute I walked in and they wanted to leave right away.

Tish ended up getting drunk off a little bottle of Grey Goose I had bought for her. As I watched her sit in the back seat with this light skinned girl named T who was Jaz's friend. I was getting jealous and irritated over hearing what was going on in my back seat. I ended up calling Tish a foul name! she freaked out on me pulling my hair and scratching my face all up at the same time.

I was drunk by that time and all I could feel is the cold snow outside.

We parked at the local cosmetic store by her house. I grabbed my car keys quick out of the ignition before anyone else could. I was so drunk I ran all the way down Gratiot to Harper which was about a three mile walk.

I ran so hard not looking back, crying with tears all over my face from being affected that I just got attacked by the girl I loved. She was trying to show off in front of the other girls. I figured I was outnumbered so I was doing the right thing.

I went to Mimi and Smoke's house. Mimi was at the time still my best friend and had my back. I called her crying telling her I was coming over. I told her how Tish had scratched my face all up. When I got there I was drunk balling my eyes out.

My best friend asked me what had happened. I told her how we went down to the gay club. I was still trying to make it work with Tish and she was showing out in front of her friends by putting her hands on me.

I started yelling at Tish over the phone, crying and screaming louder. Mimi was trying to get a fill of what had happened so she asked her. She was too drunk to really talk. She was walking distance from her house. Her friend Jaz and other friend lived across town. I didn't care anyways where they stayed and decided to stay the night at Mimi's house. When I looked at the clock it was two something in the morning.

When I got back to my car the next day, I was worried about losing my notebook that I had started writing my story in for Niki originally to help her have something to read on the bus to Atlanta.

My notebook I was scared of losing became a powerful autobiography about my life. I was told by many people that if a person was able to make a living in Detroit successfully off having nothing, then they could make it anywhere in the world doing the same thing!

I got back to Tish's house the next day, knocking on the door. When Rante, her brother, opened the door as he usually did for me, I hid back my tears.

I was so upset that his sister got drunk and put her hands on me.

I was spending my precious time with her while she was sitting there wasting my time for her own selfish reasons. Love was hard to come by in my jurisdiction.

Our spoken whispers seemed to finally come to an end. I walked straight into her room while she was awake. It was the moment when I made eye contact with her that I couldn't hold back the tears any longer!

I burst out crying, telling her don't ever put your hands on me again. She pretended to be shocked to see me at her house, but we both knew we were in love with each other. Of course I was going to be there after that.

As time started passing, I tried my hardest to stay away from her. Harder than ever I would try to not look at her house on car rides across Gratiot, once I crossed the bridge.

Through out what we had been going through, I still always thought about her son caring, for him. I felt that he was basically my baby too. I loved her little boy and our problems would never change that.

A week passed by and I couldn't hold off from seeing her any longer. I stopped by her house hoping to feel less pain. I really was embarrassed but still went inside with her brother. Whenever Tish would come into his room, we usually would ignore her. I couldn't help not to ignore her. I felt hurt that she would do something like that to me. When it came time for us to be face to face, all that came out of her mouth was a kiss. Our kiss proved our truth was pure when our eyes locked into a stare knowing we both loved each other.

My mind was starting to say one thing but my heart was saying another.

My opinion of love at that point made me feel as if love was distorted. I had the worse perception in my mind of love. I thought that in order to make Tish happy, I would end up have to give her whatever she wanted in return seeking closure from knowing she was happy. I realized that it was my fault that our relationship failed. I knew I had spoiled her too much. I didn't care about spending my cash on her. I was hustling all the time and we had it!

I let things get past love at that point and didn't know what I had created. She never even asked me for much I always use to offer to do good things for her. I longed for something more. Much more of anything seemed better than nothing at the time. A couple days later we experienced a good sexual connection between each other. It embraced my feelings for her even more.

Our two bodies together proposed love that it could have been real lust. Our love then was a steady feeling in both of our hearts. The feelings became stronger for her and baby Jordan. I felt that even though we weren't together it still felt like they were mine. Since Niki chose to take her sons a different path I felt a piece of my heart still belong to them.

I knew God had separated us at that time so that Niki and I could get our lives in order. There wasn't a day that went by that I didn't wear that matching bracelet that Niki wore too. We both had a copy of each other's hearts even though we were living two different lives with different people. I started to feel as if Tish felt I was weak because I loved her so much. It was around Christmas time and her baby daddy ended up actually buying his son a power wheel jeep that cost three hundred dollars.

Chapter Twenty-Two

Everyone was shocked, including me, because he wasn't a big financial help to her for his son. I was a little jealous because I loved that little boy, and it was too late. I bought him some black diamond earrings and Tish some diamond earrings that were fake diamonds but real silver but they were under the tree. I was happy though that her baby daddy did buy his son a nice gift. I had a couple more gifts at my dad's house on twenty-three-mile road. I was staying at home more often since my latest break up. I invited everyone over to my dad's for dinner.

Kimmy's child's father, my ex-girlfriend, her son, Kimmy and her new baby all came for dinner.

When Kimmy and I didn't have any contact with each other, I would pray to God that one day we would be in each other's lives again. I used to have a copy of her baby Jay's ultrasounds on the dashboard of my car. I never let anyone drive my car except Kimmy around the time we were in school together. I clutched on to my friend her like sponge as her ears soaked up my stories for her entertainment.

I realized later on that in the situation I was in, people aren't always what you want them to be. I had been hanging with a woman named Trina at the time and Tish really didn't approve of that. Everyone showed up for dinner but, it was a disaster because, nothing was cooked.

Tish started bringing up little things to start arguments with me. She was changing her son downstairs on my bed while Kimmy and her baby daddy started to cook dinner. Whatever my friend's child's father made wasn't done all the way.

Everyone ate and then Tish and I were back at the arguments. She said another smartass remark and I told her it was time for her to leave. I had been trying so hard to cater to everyone else and everything seemed to go wrong at that time.

My dad was drunk and complaining about a lot that was going on. I ended up having to ask them to leave. I felt used but not necessarily by Tish. Christmas came quick and surprisingly I got a call at eight a clock in the morning from Tish saying in the softest nicest voice to come over because, there was a present for me under her tree. I was happy she called even though I was still mad at her. I got all the presents under my tree that I had to give out and put them in my car. I went over to her house exchanging gifts.

I opened my gift from her and her family and thanked them not knowing what I wanted to do next because, I had no blood relatives in Michigan. Not having any family made my decisions hard for me. I talked to Tish's mom, asking her if I could stay and eat with her. I asked her if she could make some greens, baked mac and cheese with some other southern food. Her mom said she would cook me something. I really felt good about having her mother like me and respect me being in her children's lives.

Tish got her son ready as her baby daddy came over with his present. I chilled for an hour after that and then left. When he was over she was acting fake so I just left.

I came back over later, when everyone was gone and visited with her mom and ate. A couple nights prior to Christmas, I came into her house and she was in the bathroom with her baby daddy. I didn't know what they were doing. I was irritated and ignored the fact that her ex was in a bathroom with her. He was not loud in her mama's house. Her mama didn't care for him much based on how he treated her daughter and grandson. What seemed like what had once been mine was not mine any longer.

A few days later was New Year's. I was mad that I hadn't been able to spend much time with Tish even though we weren't together. I decided to throw a hotel party off Thirteen Mile and Ninety-Four freeway. Kimmy, her child's father, his sister, and their friend came to my party.

I also had met this older woman a week prior who was in her early thirties who had I flagged down telling her she was fine as hell. She later gave me her number. She ended up telling me she was a nurse, but I later found out when I was spending the night in her home after knowing her a year I had seen a cup on her dresser that said, the Detroit police. I felt so award because I knew my life's style was fast. I didn't want to get into trouble as well as it made me feel awkward because she lied to me telling me that she was a nurse.

It felt even more awkward that her five-or six-year-old told me that she was a police officer. I asked her about it and we joked around. She smiled with that. I smiled, and then we dropped the subject. I figured she kept her life a secret because she wanted to protect her children. I knew why she protected her family at the same time her country.

Detroit was a rough setup, and it would suck for her to be foolish and give her identity away. I didn't blame her but felt she should have kept it real with me. Much secrecy had motivation and determination behind it. Everyone in life has a reason behind the things they did. I was so far away from home. Everyone showed up except Tish.

My aquatinted Toya showed up so we went out to I hop with everyone. In the middle of eating around the time when the ball dropped I called my family to tell them Happy New Year's. I could tell when it was time for me to speak to my father he was extremely upset, clearing his throat a few times throughout our conversation. I knew he loved me and was upset I was eight states away on every holiday since two thousand and eight.

Tears started to flow down my face right along with my conversation as I immediately tried getting off the phone. I was extremely embarrassed that I started tearing up in front of everyone I was with. I felt so embarrassed for the rest of the night. I tried holding the tears back when my father was chocking up, but I couldn't hold it any longer.

At the restaurant at that moment of me breaking down, all I could remember was Kimmy's voice telling me it was going to be all right as she and everyone there could see it all over my face what I was going through. The only friend I knew for a while was Kimmy.

Even though we went through some things in our past time since knowing each other, there was also good times we shared having fun laughing away. The experiences we shared was imaginable for me.

Toya was very kind, paying for my food at the restaurant. I was very grateful after having such experiences that someone could help me out as well as me helping out other people.

Kimmy's child's father tried walking out without paying for his food. Kimmy was embarrassed and sent him back in to pay for the food. We all went back to the hotel room after that and hung out for a little while and then everyone left. Rante, my girl's brother, ended up having to spend the night.

I had two queen-sized beds so I didn't care. The family. He was basically like my brother. The next day we woke up and I drove him home. The next month I had continued to go over to Tish's house. I started realizing that she didn't really want a friendship from me. It was a different relationship than before.

Not many exes had continued to be friends most the time.

All I could do was accept it. I started coming around and still cleaning up the house when I was there hanging out with Rante. I would mainly come around her house still because, I cared for her and little man.

My hopes for patching up my relationship with her was very unstable. After watching the seasons change, I realized that I had to slowly let go.

I started hanging out with Nini again around that time. I knew Tish was against it because she knew Nini's background from knowing the same people who knew them.

Even though Tish and I had been through a lot of drama, I was still loyal to her. I didn't know who to really hangout with so I kept going back to Nini one of the only people I had known for so long. Nini and I didn't hang out with each other often and continued to stay our distance from each other both having different lives.

Times were hard in Michigan for a lot of people including myself. The world was going through different stages when it came to the economy. I was never the person who would look at my life and feel sorry for myself, even though at times I feel that I had ever right to feel the way I did towards people around me for what I was put through.

What I didn't realize was there was people who had more to wake up and deal with than myself. I wanted to help as many people as I could but, had no funds to do so. I wanted to help pretty much any one I met. Trying to give the people of Michigan encouragement.

My father used to tell me this too shall pass. I would try and remind the people I met that the saying my father once told me was true. The only way of survival is to flow with the positive core of energy.

God spoke to me through people telling me that it was his job to save his people, but it was my job to deliver his message. Some people really don't know how to take in all of that message so I just try and let it sit on their brains, instead of shoving my opinion down their throat. I wish that I could say money is the only issue Michigan's community is going through but, it's not.

Money is about a fifty to seventy-five percent of the issues of the everyday person in Michigan, but it also has a lot to do with the way people treat each other. I started to find myself living fast in the moment with no educational goal except being a dental hygienist. At the rate I was going I would never be able to see the days of my career expanding.

My adopted dad Jerry thank goodness had bought me a little red car. I started hanging out with this boy they called Lee-boy from Mt. Clemens. He told me that he had a friend that robbed his grandparents of his credit cards and jewelry from a guy he claimed was his best friend. He introduced me to his friend Bill who felt bad for me that I didn't have anywhere to go. I guess he didn't have anywhere to go that night either.

He offered for me to spend the night in the hotel with him that was up the street from Tish's house. I didn't know him very well but took his offer up. That night he told me that I was a nice person and that he would introduce me to his girlfriend to see if she could help me. I agreed and that night tried to stay far away from her boyfriend.

There was only one bed and I was tired. I left all my clothes on and slept right next to the boy trying to stay completely away from him so he didn't get the wrong impression of me. In the middle of my sleep, I found myself cuddled up to him and woke up immediately jumping off him angrily immediately apologizing.

He told me everything was good and we went the next day to his girlfriend's house. I kept it one hundred percent real with the girl when I met her. She was a pretty girl but was a couple years younger than me.

I was nineteen at the time. I told her how I had never messed around with her boyfriend. Telling her that the night before I found myself too close to him so I jumped away from him. I told her that I didn't have anywhere to go and needed a place to stay. I told her my story. We found interest in each other but never really spoke on it. She talked to her mom and they allowed me to stay.

All together I think I stayed with them in Warren for about a month. At the time I dressed like a stud but would put on make-up.

The girl Riss and I ended up getting super close, ignoring the fact that Bill had even been around. I ended up letting them use my car a couple times. Bill had locked my keys in the car and had to bust the window to get my keys out because it was late and raining. When they came back from going to his mom's, he explained it to me, saying that they would pay for it.

One night Riss and I stayed up late talking having a heart-to-heart about our lives and the different life styles that we had. She opened up to me that night as we both laid on her bathroom floor crying about the torture and abuse we had both been through.

I knew after talking with her and getting close with her that I never wanted to lose contact with her. I was in a young state of mind but knew that one day she was going to look up to me and I was going to be something great.

I knew that we were both from two different parts of the world but went through a lot of the same things as growing up. I started to catch feelings for her but, knew she was never going to leave Bill. She introduced me to a girl named Ash who had the biggest booty ever.

She was a pretty classier African American chick who kept herself up well. She and I hung out some time before Riss and I had our heart to heart.

A couple of days before we had our heart to heart early in the morning I hung out with the girl she was trying to hook me up with. We went out to eat and then went by her friend's house to grab some for her stuff.

After that she and I parked to talk in front of the house.

We had high wedge bushes so they couldn't see who was ever parked in front of their house. She climbed into my backseat, telling me to jump in the back with her. I was really shy not realizing that she wanted to have sex with me. I then looked like a little boy. I hopped in the backseat with super confidence. I messed around with her. She started moaning and all I could think about was dang the neighbors are going to hear her because I had a busted out window on the passenger side. I covered her mouth up, and once we both finished, we went inside the house to use the bathroom and then I went to drop her off at home.

I felt that I really couldn't change the fact of how Riss and I met so I went along with what I thought she wanted me to do and that was to hook up with her friend. After never seeing her friend again but admitted to Riss that I had sex with her friend in front of the house. She made jokes that her neighbors new my name, which made me smile.

Even though I thought that she wanted me to hook up with her friend, the look on her face said otherwise when I told her. Her mother by that time had brain-washed her trying to put it in her head I wanted Bill.

I didn't want Bill. I really was interested in her! Her mom ended up saying I had to move out of there. I was fine with the decision but a little bit hurt because here I was once again getting close to someone I barely knew hoping that they were going to be someone deep and futuristic in my life. I never saw Riss again after that for about two or almost three years later. I later heard through Lee-boy that she had a son with Bill a year later after I left her house. I always thought about her but never wanted to look back because my mind was very confused about her intentions for me around that time.

Back in Mt. Clemens Lee-boy told me that he wanted me to get close to his best friend so his best friend so his best friend Smelly would give me some money.

Nelly who I called my little sister, her boyfriend, and Lee-boy had re-thought this plan out to get Smelly boy back for what he had put Lee-boy's family through while he was living with them.

The story I heard from Lee-boy was that Smelly boy had robbed Lee-boy's father's watch and his grandmother's jewelry along with her credit cards.

He wanted to pay back so then he came up with the idea of robbing him but, just didn't know how. I really didn't want to do it but, it was a recession for every one and I was young minded.

I decided I didn't want to rob him after the first couple times of hanging out with him. I felt bad for even the thought and new that karma was nothing to play around with. The more I hung out with him, the more he disrespected me. I used to do him favors all the time by driving him around for gas money.

Finally, the last straw hit me when he took me to a party with him. At the part he downed a whole pint of vodka and took a bar. I was really annoyed with him. By the time we got to the gas station, he gave me ten dollars for gas. He had already slipped up calling me out of my name trying to be cheap but kept trying to stunt on everyone at the party with his money he had from selling herb.

When I got back to the car, he was passed out. I was angry by now because I really didn't want to go through with the whole idea of stealing from him. Lee boy was back at the party wanting me to come get him.

I immediately called Nelly's boyfriend, asking them what should I do. He told me to drive to his house. I drove apologizing to God for what I was about to do. I needed the money and knew I had some things fast to take care of the things I needed to take care of.

When I pulled up, Smelly was still passed out. I went inside leaving this grown African American young-minded man who was almost thirty years old in my car passed out from drugs and alcohol.

Nelly's boyfriend and his brother decided to go outside to go through his pockets. I went with them still weary if they were going to give me anything out of this situation. I went through his one pocket that had twelve hundred. He was still passed out.

Nell's boyfriend's brother went through his other pocket, and then her boyfriend snatched the duffel bag off the floor. I never got to see all that was in the bag but, gave six hundred dollars to Nelly and then him and his brother kept the rest of all that they had grabbed off him.

I was really scared because I had never done anything like that before. I knew I had made a terrible mistake with God but knew that I would pay through karma eventually.

The police then came and removed Smelly boy from the parking lot. The police then came and looked inside pleased with not finding anything suspicious so they left. I was so relieved that they were gone but, wanted to get the hell out of there. I left and then came back the next day getting my car to return back to Nelly's family's house.

When I went back, I met up with Nelly. She was literally like my younger sister. She was younger than me who acted as if she was grown. She made a poor choice with the boy she had been dating.

Even though he had his own place, he really didn't treat her all that well at times. She came back crying saying that all she had to show for from the six hundred dollars was a hundred-dollar phone. She said her boyfriend took the rest of her money. I told her that I had my own bills and told her that I couldn't give her any more money. She got mad at me and ended up leaving the house for a minute to go meet up with a friend of hers I didn't like. I left not knowing what was going to happen next.

My car wasn't there it had been at a friend's house. I ran six blocks trying to get away from the house, feeling that when my little sister returned she was going to try and set me up for the few hundred dollars I did have.

When I finally got to Gratiot Avenue, I could see my little sister walking up the street with two other girls. They were looking as if they were looking for me. I was so heated that she would turn on me. I felt then as if she was going to try and jump me for the money.

I called an old friend named Dave to come and pick me up to drive and drop me off to my car. When my friend picked me up, I headed to Niki's house down in the city but hadn't seen Niki or the boys since the time she was staying with me at my adopted dads.

When I got to my friend's house, I kept quiet about my money. I got re-familiar with Niki as I took her to pick the boys up from their elementary school. I was so happy to see the boys.

When I finally saw, them I gave them hugs and kisses. After school we went to get something to eat at a fast-food place. When we got back Niki and I smoked our herb to keep calm.

I enjoyed that we ended up having time to just look into each other eyes as we remembered and reminisce on what we had once shared with each other. In my dearest loves life, she seemed as if she was doing a lot better.

I was very proud of how good she was at taking care of the boys, alone. She was still single and didn't have a man. Regardless, I always knew that we couldn't be together.

While I was around, I needed to tell Niki the truth of what I was going through. We always were close enough to talk about pretty much anything so I pulled her aside and told her what I had did.

I then pulled out the money and told her how I had something to do with robbing the boy. She happened to know someone who had been living on twenty-three from our old six-mile neighborhood. They told her what I had did. She was disappointed in me!

I knew the only way I could get less karma was to right things with the money. I knew I couldn't just give the money back. I told Niki that I would stay around and drive the boys back and forth to school.

I stayed there about four days and ended up spending money on the kids while I picked them up and got up early to take them to school. I ended up giving Niki two hundred dollars and spending about two hundred dollars in that four days I was around.

I knew that she had to take care of the boys and trusted that she was going to get them some school clothes and food. She had already so far, bought them some clothes while I had been around. I was so proud of the boys for being good in school. It seemed that they were growing so fast, getting taller and bigger. I had gotten a call from Nelly's dad telling me we all needed to have a sit down and not to feel uncomfortable to come get my clothes because everything was going to be okay.

Niki said that she would come with me to have my back. I told her how the girls were looking for as I ran six blocks up the street and then got picked up and dropped off to my car. I knew that everything was going to be alright and new that I had gotten myself into the trouble.

I didn't want anyone else to fight my battles. I knew that Niki was down for me so I told her to stay and take care of the boys. I picked the boys up from school, telling them I had to go handle some business back out where I lived. I kissed the boy and hugged Niki, kissing her for the last time listening to her words of comfort telling me if I needed her to call her.

After I went down to visit with T, we realized that she wasn't going to do my hair based on the fact that we didn't have much time since I had plans to go get my clothes.

Everything turned out completely different then I had expected. When I got to the house her father called everyone in the living room to talk about what Nelly and I were involved in. We told him what we had done and I told him I had already gave Nelly six hundred dollars.

I told him that I spent all my money, which was true. I offered Nelly fifty dollars because I felt bad for her that she allowed her boyfriend to just buy her a phone and then take the rest of her money.

Beyond everything we were going through, she and her family allowed me to live with them as if I were part of the family. When everything was said and done, I put all my clothes in the car but, decided to spend the night. With them for one last night. Part of me had planned to go return back to California, but the other part of me wanted to stay and deal with my problems because I knew one day if I ever wanted to return to the area that I may have some problems.

Nelly and her sisters all hugged me and we said we were sorry to each other. I still told her I knew she was looking for me and could tell she was going to try and jump me for the money.

I told her how I felt that even though I had made a mistake with God by stealing, by me giving it back to God's children I felt that maybe the Lord was going to give me a chance not to have terrible karma. I didn't know what to expect next.

Tish drove by and called my cell phone, honking, waving, saying good-bye after an hour of me telling her I was going to go back to California. It was really sweet of her, but we both knew we couldn't be together. Something got into me and I decided not to go back to Cali.

When the boy Smelly confronted me about what had happened, I told him the truth about his best friend wanting to set him up.

He really didn't believe me and his best friend sat up in his face scared and mad because he didn't get anything out of setting his best friend up, denying the whole thing.

It was like the revenge lee-boy had for the man didn't do him any justice because he felt as if he didn't benefit from setting him up because he didn't get any money. I never had any problems when I see smelly places in Mt. Clemens but never had to worry about him trying to set me up.

The fact that I did rob him carried strongly throughout the streets that a white girl had robbed him. It was crazy because it seemed like he knew so many people and when I would meet someone and they would hear my name people knew I was the girl who robbed him first and then after me he kept getting robbed from so many different crowds of people allowing himself to get close to the wrong types of people.

Even though I made myself a legend, I always felt so bad when people would ask me, "You're the one who robbed Smelly?" I left a note one day on Niki's new house. It had looked as if she hadn't been there in weeks. I prayed that we could have been able to get in touch again.

When I left there, I had been hanging out in Mt. Clemens a lot with the same old crowd. I ended up getting into it with this stud girl. How it all started was I was on shady side and I was in my car with my black heels on. She was trying to show out for the two girls she would drive around.

I was familiar with one of the girls. The same girl from the apartments that was interested in me back when I was in school. The same girl who passed me that note and I was too scared to talk to her. Life was so crazy, but I guess the girl was trying to act or threaten me. I went straight to the city and grabbed my home girl T, really mad that these girls were trying to play me like this. I then went by Nini's sisters house.

Her stud sister ended up being there. I was happy I at least had two people there who would have my back if someone else tried to jump in against me, gaining up on me. When we got there, they had been calling me all day to come and fight. I showed up and took all my jewelry off putting my white gold hundred-dollar chain with my middle initial letter attached to it in my glove compartment.

I didn't feel like fighting, but T told me, "Girl, you brought me all the way from the city if you don't beat her ass I'm going to beat your ass."

She was serious and I knew it! She was from the hood but didn't play any games about her respect or friend's family. I got out of the car quick.

I saw the girl her name looking for her trying to fight her because she felt as if she was going to try and jump in. I started laughing hard as hell but got straight to my business. Neecy then drew the first punch and then I just started repeatedly punching her in the face. We were squared up with each other for a good twenty minutes fighting.

I never ended up getting hit in the face. By the third round, I knew self-consciously that I was the winner. I got crazier and cockier jumping up and down.

All I could remember is blacking out, hearing the crowd of people watching us fight instigating us letting us do what we felt we had to do for our respect. We went two rounds and after that I screamed for another round.

My opponent finally gave in as we both felt the feeling of being tired. She went back to her crowd of friends and I went back to mine. Immediately we all rushed to our destinations. Our destination was to get back to Detroit City.

Time had passed and I felt a feeling of confusion. I then started to feel like I didn't know where I belonged or who I belonged to hang out with. Times started to get harder and harder. The summer was coming up and I felt as if the past had to lay to rest. That's exactly then what I decided to do. I went back to live with my adopted dad Jerry once again. I still had my car that my adopted dad bought me. I had a suspended license but, needed my car.

My car was the only transportation that I had. One day my dad Jerry had allowed me to go to Detroit with his friend Erica. She had to go to a friend's house and it happened that when we drove off Eight Mile a mile away from where She ended up having to go, we ended up at a street called Hamburg off Eight Mile. I was sitting in the passenger seat dressed with a red fitted hat that covered my black Remi sew in that I had just got put in. I was dressed in a white plain t-shirt and a pair of blue skinny jeans.

My birthday was coming up and I was excited, but it made me realize that time was passing by so quickly and I missed out on a lot of time with my family when lived out of state.

The first time we drove down the block, Niki saw me and was dressed in a white tight dress. She had lost a lot of weight and looked very slimmer but still had a nice thick booty. It was warm outside, which meant she was outside with a group of people. I heard her scream my name Cali, as we drove by showing she had recognized me. I recognized her as well. I asked Erica to turn around so I could see if it was Niki, since we had lost contact with each other. She did so and we went back to that street. It happened to be her.

Erica slowed the car down and I talked to Niki, telling her that She was my dad Jerry's friend. She gave me her number and we drove off right away. I then came back to the same block on my own time taking the bus.

Niki looked beautiful with her hair put in tiny little braids. Her hair was pinned up. I had never seen her so happy and beautiful. She shared the news with me of her current relationship with the young man who lived across the street from her house right where we were on the street Hamburg. He was eighteen and she was twenty-three. She was happy having some short of support. Niki's baby daddy wasn't around because he was in a relationship with another one of his baby's mama. He also had a few children with a few different women. Willing to put up with the hood I decided to stay in the hoover hood off of eight-mile.

I decided to start searching for a house of my own. Seeing Niki's sons ended up being a beautiful experience for me and them. I missed them so much. I hadn't seen them in a while. The boys and I had a bond that would never break. I know it was wrong for me to pop in and out of their lives but knew I couldn't continue to deal with just any bull crap. I wanted a home of my own where I could relax and have the boys over to escape the negative life style they had no choice to be involved in.

I found a house that was abandoned a couple of blocks away from Niki's house on a street called Bradford. The street looked familiar when I realized the house that I walked around to find was across the street from the house I had once hung out in with Marty. The only difference was the house was now burnt down. I was really shocked but felt a sense of comfort that I knew the area I was in a little bit from once being over there. I decided to start fixing up the two-bedroom house that I had found. It had a small kitchen, living room, and basement area that was already remodeled. The house still needed work done to it based on the fact that there was no back door and the front lawn needed to be cleaned up.

I went to Mt. Clemens was staying in between this guy Melo's house and my dad Jerry's house. Earlier in the summer, I had spent most of my days in Mt. Clemens. I was happy that I had met some generous people along my journey who helped me by letting me stay with them when I was in hardship of trying to survive in a state I still had so much to learn about.

I decided I would rather stay in the abandoned house closer to Niki and the boys rather than stay in Mt. Clemens. He helped me buy locks to put on the front door of the abandoned house. He came over to the house to help me cut the lock off the front door and then replace the new door locks with a fresh set of keys.

Melo had respected that I was trying to do something for myself instead of staying at his house. He even gave me my own room there at his house that he didn't stay in that he was g remodeling. He had been living with his mom at the time he was remodeling.

Even though he gave me that option to stay with him, I wanted to stay in Detroit to strive for something better. I wanted a place I could call my own. I was happy to finally be getting things going in order for me to get a secure place I could call home.

A guy that I had once met in my past named Bryan helped me put everything in the house. He was just a friend but didn't want me staying in the abandoned house that had no back door alone. It was still a rough area especially for anyone who wasn't from there. He didn't want to stay in the hood but did so for a little while with me. He was the type of guy who drank beer every day. He didn't end up lasting long staying in the hood with me.

My dad Jerry ended up bringing his weed whacker, push broom, tree trimmers so I could clean up the front yard. He even helped me clean. The next thing that happened next was really terrible. I was peeing in the backyard because the plumbing wasn't working.

The water and electricity was off. We had to use the bathroom in the backyard outside. I ended up losing my dad's keys to the car and his house in the backyard. He was upset with me but ended up staying the night in the house with me because he didn't have anyone he wanted to call to come and get him. He also didn't want to leave his Malibu-model vehicle in the hood. He wasn't mad at me for long and forgave me the next day.

Although he forgave me, he was very irritated when I came back from hanging out with Niki on her block when I ended up coming back to the abandoned house drunk irritated because, one of Niki's sisters had pushed me down when Niki went to the store.

My knee hit the cement, cutting it leaving a bruise. I was going through a rough time and prayed to God for a more positive future. I prayed for a better life and hoped that there would be some type of door opening for me to be able to change some negativity I couldn't control that was going on in my life.

In the morning, I woke up with my shorts covered in blood from starting my period in my sleep. It was really gross, but my dad always tells that story to people of how heavy it was. I was really embarrassed. My dad's friend who owned a tow yard came and picked us up.

He towed my dad Jerry's car to his house. I went there and took a shower resting up able to think of my choices of if I wanted to continue to be around the hood. Even though I wasn't dating Niki, she and I were sexual once again with each other when the boys weren't there in her home.

I wanted her all to myself and had the thought in my mind that she was ready for a mature relationship, but I was wrong. I was proud of her for having a vehicle and getting out of the old hood she was in, but all she did was put herself in a different part of the hood.

After dealing with late night parting on her current block and hearing guns being shot off all the time made me realize I didn't want to stay in that situation for long. My car was parked in the drive way of the house I was claiming was mine. I finally ran into an old friend that I once had known named Jazzy and her sister Princess. Her sister was younger than her but they both had the same things in common and that was dancing. goofing around, and doing hair. I met her prior in the same hood when I was first hanging out with Marty. They were really good at doing hair they knew how to do quick weaves and sew ins.

Jazzy's mom told me I could come stay with them because, there was no electricity or running water and especially a back door. I felt that by her mom allowing me to come stay with them a few blocks away. God was trying to tell me something. I felt as if God was reaching out to me to make sure that I continued to be safe.

I had been staying away from Nikis because of the past drama that had been occurring with her sister hating on me and the fact that I knew it was never going to be anything between her and I because, she was messing around and seeing the young man across the street from her house. I didn't feel like dealing with all the extra drama but really didn't want to leave the kids there.

When times get hard and Niki really needed an extra helping hand I was there for those kids helping with toilet paper, snacks, and food. I loved those boys so I felt responsible for them. I had the neighbor who lived across the street from Niki recognized me from when I went to the Detroit county jail a year or so being tight with me. She was really cool.

I would go over to her house to chill with her on her porch, just to have someone to talk to when things would get all rough between Niki's people and I.

I guess she and Niki didn't care to much for each other, especially after seeing how Niki was treating me, made her dislike my friend even more.

Nini use to tell me how great it was of me for being down for Niki's children. I loved hearing her tell me that she was proud of me for sticking by the kids because they weren't my actual blood children.

I made sure when I was around them that I gave everything I had to contribute to them. It seemed that even if things are all bad with people that didn't want me in Niki's life I would always manage to find her some way somehow and try to help her. She always wanted the best for me. She saw so much potential in me and didn't want to see me struggle. I chose to stay around a bad area for the love that I had for them.

One day I was walking down the street, a block away from Niki's when I was hanging out with a neighborhood kid when all of a sudden when I wasn't paying any attention a tall girl had snuck me from behind pulling my hair.

All I remember was she was kneeing me and another girl jumped in. I couldn't see anything but felt the girl and saw another girl jumping in. I didn't even know these girls but knew that this occurred based on jealously. At the time I was dressed up looking good with a blue name brand outfit.

I was really angry that this had happened to me.

I was able to pick myself up off the ground. I was able to drag myself back to Jazzy where I was staying. I wasn't able to really see what the girls had looked like who had jumped me. I remember being kneed in my eyes, so I couldn't see.

One thing was certain and that was I wasn't going to let those girls get away with jumping me. Sitting on Jazzy and Princess's porch gave me plenty of time to calm down and think.

Niki drove by and asked me what had happened to my face.

I told my friend nothing, brushing her off as she repeatedly asked me.

I finally told her that I had got jumped over off Strasburg but couldn't see who the girls were. I knew if I found out then I would go back to fight. I needed to stand up for myself.

So angry I saw something come over Niki's face as she drove off speeding. My friend was headed over to the area where she knew people to find out who jumped me.

The next day Jazzy and Princess walked with me around the corner to Niki's house. Her mom kept trying to tell us to let it go. We were too angry to just let that go so we ended up going over anyways.

Across the street was Nini's house. When I told her what happened she had told me what she had heard. She told me that she knew of a girl named Mercedes who had claimed she had snuck me on her own.

I also heard through the grapevine that some guys that sold drugs on that corner apartment complex had told the girl to jump on me. I knew that the guy I had kicked it with wanted to mess around with me, but I let everyone know I didn't roll like that. I wasn't about to have sex with anyone just for the heck of it.

I never knew the truth of the matter about why this random tall chick I even didn't know would just jumped on me like that for no reason.

Niki ended up telling me the same name of the girl everyone heard had jumped on me. There was witnesses of what had happened. The hood wasn't that big. It seemed that someone, knew someone, that knew someone, who would have known you.

The neighborhood was in an uproar between whatever drama Niki and Nini had with each other. They argued on the fact that Nini had owned her home. She was there for quite some time before Niki.

My friend would party with the dude across the street. Niki was seen till all odd late hours of the night. I know it would piss off Nini because, she would always tell me how irritated she was. She was more of a rough chick, who described herself as a dog!

My friend expressed herself in a manner that would come off ready to beat someone if they messed with her or her family. I started to look up to her in a sense because she was married with a home that she owned. She was around my dad's age. It seemed like the more I hung out with Nini, the more it would anger Niki.

Well, the day finally came a couple days later when I decided to drink a pint of dark liquor. I went around the corner to get my revenge on this random girl I didn't even know.

It was simple! I had to prove in the hood that I wasn't a push over.

If one chick jumped me then another one would next time as well if I didn't prove myself in the neighborhood. Niki drove me around the corner to the girl's house who jumped me as Nini walked over there through the alley off of her street to have my back.

I wanted justice and was still kind of nervous but knew what I had to do if I wanted to survive in this area.

Chapter Twenty-Three

When I got in front of the house, I screamed, "Bitch, come out!" Immediately she opened the door with a dirty grin on her face. She came out with another girl behind her.

Everyone let her know it was a one-on-one fight. We instantly started fighting, throwing all punches. We looked like two lions in a lion's den fighting.

I knew she had gotten the best of me the first time we fought, when she jumped me from behind. I had to use this ignorant female as an example for everyone who was watching! I didn't want to ever be picked on in my own living area.

I figured if she didn't know me, she could have just jumped on me because I was mixed and looked more white than anything. I would never know the truth on why the girl attacked me but, never cared as long as she knew I wasn't a punk. I chose to be in the hood and acted as if it was my home and I knew that another ignorant female like her would come along and try the same crap.

Throughout the fight, I never even got punched in my face. Even though I had been intimidated by African American females in my past, it was the last straw to where I let all mental thoughts go and just whooped on her bad in front of the whole neighborhood.

The female this time didn't even come close to getting the best of me!

I did get tired in the middle of our fight. I was able to show her what I was about! Then I walked away fine, jumping back in the car, yelling, "If you don't understand, we could always fight again." She went in her house fast as we drove off. All I could do now is watch myself and the areas I chose to put myself in. I was finally able to show Niki that I wasn't no punk and I could protect myself. I know she was proud of me for handling myself well!

A couple days later, on the same block a couple houses from the corner where I had been hanging out with some dope dealers in their trap house, trying to find ways to make money when all of a sudden the same female I fought had appeared sitting down on the couch.

I could see that her jaw had looked misplaced. I honestly think her jaw was broken because, it had been a while since then for it to look the way it did.

I didn't feel bad for her jaw being dislocated because, she jumped on me which started the whole fight.

When I was in the trap she never said a word to me.

At that moment on, I knew that I had did what I needed to do and that was survive to earn my respect. I asked the girl why did she attacked me in the first place? She had nothing to say. She was in there with another girl and I was waiting for them to jump stupid.

Surprisingly the two females stayed still. I knew I had gotten my point across to her not to mess with me ever again. I showed her that it didn't matter what race you were anyone could be able to fight. I taught myself not be afraid of woman based on their race or their loud mouths.

Niki came pulling up in front of the house hearing that I was inside. She started screaming for me to get in her car.

When we pulled off she explained to me that that trap house was no place for me to be hanging out. She told me no guys from the hood were going to give me any money or pay a decent amount of money for anything I had to offer. I was really relieved when I had seen her pull up.

I knew that I was making a few mistakes but God was standing by my side so I feared none. It wasn't until I continued to stay in the hood area that I was able to figure out my beautiful talent which God had given me.

Next door to Niki's house she had befriended a woman. I ended up going to her house to meet her through another neighbor prior to the fighting incident.

I ended up feeling a sense of heat come over my hands that allowed me to feel the woman's situation with her man that she was with. It was crazy because I didn't expect for God to send me a message to send to them. I told the woman how I could feel a sense of lacking from her child's father.

Her man sat in the living room with us while I read her hands. I laid her hands upon mine as I felt a little nervous to feel warm heat come over my hands onto her hands. I was also nervous to tell this bigger hood chick that I didn't know very well the truth about what I was reading from her situation.

Finally told them about how I had felt a sense of absence from her man that was sitting right with us. They didn't judge me, but then they both started agreeing with me. Everything that started flowing out of my mouth ended up being truth. She told me that it was weird based on it being very true.

It was my first time meeting the woman I had just read. I went over there from being affiliated with a friend who knew her child's father.

That's when I came out saying how my ex-girlfriend Niki lived two doors down from them. That was one of my first out-of-body experience as an adult that would help me understand right away not to be afraid but, to embrace my Lords gift he had given me.

This was the first spiritual experience I had ever had. From that point on, I would always prayed to God to give me the power to read people with my hands. I went back to the house that was abandoned off and on just to get away.

When I slept alone in the abandoned house I would sleep with a big wrench for protection. I would pray to God to be my ultimate protection. I knew I wanted to leave the hood because, I was struggling.

Niki and I hooked up one last time when we had been drinking. We hooked up and after we went next door to her friend's house who was the only white girl around besides me in the hood. Something terrible happened next.

Niki then had a seizure at friend's house! I was so scared and it was only my second time seeing her health go into that type of situation. I was terrified! I loved her so much. I started kissing her, scared for her life, holding her close to me. I felt a shiver come over my body of what would felt like the end of what could have been her life and mine.

I forgot who was around and blocked out the world. The reality of the matter was that we were two totally different people who were looked down upon in the hood for such as strong friendship. People knew who I was too her in her life but never wanted to except who I was to her in her life.

They told me to back away still sounding them out it took me a minute to comprehend. I knew that they would tell her sisters about me being all over her. They told me to leave right away as her sisters were on their way to help her.

I left running back to my house feeling the night pressed against my face. All I could see was pitch dark black streets. I kept running faster and faster. I started to cry and worry. I couldn't help but, to be angry of the fact that I couldn't be there to help her.

I knew that if I would have stayed in the hood, then I was putting myself in danger in the night with people who didn't think things through when they were partying on the block till early hours of the morning.

When I got to the house, I unlocked the front door and went inside. I immediately searched the whole house except the basement. By that time I had took a board and nailed down a big thick sheet of wood that I measured that could fit in the back door way. I was the only person then who could get into this house that I was trying to save and wanted to build as my own.

In Detroit, they have a law where you could squat in a house. Squatting in a house meant staying in a house without paying any bills with in a time frame based. As long as the squatter took care of the house, paid for electricity and water the house could become their's!

Also the squatters would have to get their mail sent to the address with their name on the address to get the process going.

I wasn't even at that step yet! I had big dreams and I kept dreaming of a future of something to call my own.

My birthday was coming up soon and turning twenty. I really wanted to have a good transition for my birthday because the previous year was pretty rough. I had to go to the hospital because my skin was breaking out from staying in that abandoned house from the carpet. I was keeping the place clean and it was a nice house. The carpets needed to be shampooed and I didn't have any electricity or water. I used a broom to sweep the house clean.

I didn't know what would happen next would take such a drastic twist to my fate.

Chapter Twenty-Four

At the hospital I ended up meeting an EMT student who was interning.

He was a polite young white man around my age who was really husky. I asked him if he could give me a ride back to the hood area because, I was tired of taking buses all week feeling very exhausted. He agreed to give me a ride.

I was still very cautious because I didn't know him. He made a stop in the hood for me so I could meet up with the neighbors across the street from my abandoned house that I had befriended who was a young female our age.

He was scared to come inside the female's boyfriend house. I think he was scared because we were in an area. I was only down the way from the hospital. It was weird on how he was acting to me but, really I knew it was a racism thing.

He was scared and intimidated by the hood. I just came to check on her and say what's up and after that I got back in his car and we traveled down Chalmers.

We kept traveling until we got to the fast-food place, so I could stop and get my little boys some ice cream and some food before we stopped to Niki's to see if she was okay. I finally got there a couple days had passed.

When I got there we pulled up in front of Niki's house. One of her sisters was sitting on the porch. I asked her sister if Niki was there. She said no she was at the doctors. I asked her if the boys wanted something to eat. She said yes as she started coming up to the door.

CALI GIRL, HOW DID I MAKE IT IN THE TREACHEROUS STREETS OF DETROIT?

I thought one of Niki's sisters might have still be on some craziness, so I just rolled the windows down. She started acting a fool thinking that I did something to cause her sister to have a seizure. I then went to hand her the frosty as she snatched it out of my hand squeezing it, I watched it smash all over the side of his car window. She punched the window after all of that

The young man pulled off fast. When he pulled off swerving to the right onto Eight Mile, the turn was sharp. As we made a right, we got flagged by the police to pull over. He did the Michigan turn around. We ended up in Warren on the white area. It was crazy how segregated one mile or across the street could change things.

He finally pulled over. Warren was pretty much the divided line to where mainly whites lived but, it was still a low income society.

When we finally pulled over, I was looking a bit rough from living over in that hood area. I looked so gross from taking the bus all day. The officer asked the young man to get out of the car. He then asked who was driving me around questions of how he knew me. I listened as the driver told the officer that he really didn't know me.

The officer was racist and told him not to be picking up girls he didn't know. When he ran my name, I had a good record to where I didn't have any warrants. I was relieved, but angry because the police officer told me to get out of his car to walk.

The officer asked me what we were doing in that area and I told him the truth that we were visiting my ex-girlfriend because, she had just had a seizure. I told him the truth how when we got there she wasn't home.

I knew who really was there was the devil waiting for me. Her sister who caused a bunch of unnecessary drama never should have based on the dramatic neighbors, telling them about what had occurred between Niki and I prior that night before she had her seizure.

Everything caused a spiral of anger come out of me on the walk home. I was angry that young man treated me like that when the cop had pulled us over. I was mad because he was friendly.

I walked away with my head held high really, shook up and angry from the whole situation so far. All I intended to do was check on Niki and bring the kids ice cream because, it was literally in the ninety degrees weather around that time. As I walked in the strange ghetto of Warren I didn't know what to do next to keep myself safe. I didn't want to just abandoned the kids and Niki by going back to my dad Jerry's house. I knew that I had to find a way to return to check on her.

I got really uncomfortable as I started trying to walk through Warren to try to find a safe place to go since everyone affiliated with the hood area we knew had known where my abandoned house had been. I needed to shower and get something to eat but, had no way.

I then saw some nice people sitting on their porch when I asked them if I could use their phone. They allowed me to use their phone, greeting me with such kindness. I told them what had happened to me and they told me I could stay for dinner.

The woman and her grandson were very kind to me, allowing me to charge my cell phone because it was dead at the time.

Before I met them, I had been walking around exhausted, needing sleep for at least four hours till it was in the evening. I had an inclination that Niki's sisters would be driving around looking for me.

Something happened then that I didn't expect. I knew her sisters would be drunk if they weren't already besides one sister who didn't put herself in Niki's problems. I then sat on the family's porch hearing Niki's sister zoom past me down a side road.

I recognized her car and knew that they would jump me on sight if they caught me all because they were assuming I did something to their sister the night she had a seizure. I knew they wouldn't listen to me because they never really liked me in the first place. I then started to wait inside until my phone was finally charged up with enough juice.

I called my best friend who lived with her mom and sister off Eight Mile.

She was disappointed with me because she originally never wanted me to continue to stay around Niki or her ghetto lifestyle. I didn't listen to anyone but continued to follow my heart.

My best friend had her sister call one of her best friends to come pick me up. I had met him a different day and he had dropped me off before in Niki's area. The nice family protected! The son and father who had been conversing with me walked me three blocks away from their house to an auto part store so that I could get picked up by the young man who was best friends with my best friend's sister.

Right before I left the nice family's house, I exchanged phone numbers with them, thanking them for giving me dinner and keeping me safe. I was feeling very blessed for these strangers to be helping me out of what was a traumatizing situation.

Once I met up with the young man, I told him the truth about my situation. I told him that I had nowhere to stay.

The only place I could go was across Eight Mile. I told him that I really needed somewhere to sleep for the night. He then took me to his brother and his new wife's house down Eight Mile on the west side of Detroit. I knew I was safe from that moment on once I met D. Her husband was away in the air enforcement. She was a new wife but was pregnant. She was five months.

Her husband had been away in Iraq at the time. This young woman was very respectable, beautiful, and nice. We ended up talking and being able to relate in some ways. We talked more and more and ended up staying up until 5:00 a.m. talking. It was really cool and I could tell we had a bind from then on.

That next day was my birthday. Come to find out her sister's birthday was the day after mine. That night, D and her sister invited me to go with them on a party bus. I knew that I needed to go out to get my mind off all the chaotic drama I had been going through just to hold on to loving Niki and the boys in the hood. I had never been on a party bus before and was extremely excited to go on.

Both sister knew the promotors of the party bus well and had known them for years. Since they knew the people throwing the bus we were able to get on the bus for free. I was grateful and glad I had met them. I could read people pretty well! I read that they were good hearted people who only wanted to see me successful.

Because my new friend D was pregnant, she didn't smoke nor drink. She went on the party bus gracefully and classily, staying completely sober the entire night. She was holding her pregnancy very gracefully.

The party bus was big with plenty of room. There was a stripper pole in the back of the bus. All I could look at was the lights that were very colorful that lit up the inside of the party bus and the huge plush cushions with plenty of room around to stand. It was packed though with a nice sized amount of people, which made the party even better. It was an experience that I had never gotten to experience before.

All the ladies on the bus were looking beautiful. My new friend was a beautiful African American woman with a gracious smile that showed how responsible she was. I decided not to drink on the party bus either but chose to smoke so that I could sit back and observe everything that was going on around me. I was pleased watching different types of people come together drinking some of the most expensive bottles after bottle. I was pleased with how my birthday went and knew that we definitely "Stunted hard," which is slang term for having a nice birthday while looking good, respectful, and having a great time.

The party bus drove us downtown and passed a lot of nice points of Detroit city. I enjoyed the beautiful tour of the city as I took pictures of the scenery. I was blessed that my birthday hadn't been ruined, but if I would had stayed in the hood where Niki was, it probably would have been ruined by her sisters for some drama that could have occurred based on race or the fact that someone didn't like I was bisexual.

By the time we went back to D's house, I slept in the living room exhausted, barely able to walk in the door from being so tired. I was so grateful for her hospitality but knew that I could stay there forever.

The next day I called my dad Jerry to tell him I wanted to come out there to stay for a little while. I told him I was tired of being in the hood and constantly fighting and struggling. He always usually would come to my rescue and that's exactly what he did by allowing me to come stay at his house. I had this man who I had recently just met come and pick me up driving me to my dad Jerry's house.

My dad was always happy to see me. There were still clothes and boxes of mine in my room in the remodeled basement. I was happy that even though I hadn't been there I still had all the things I left untouched there. My dad was aware of the house on Bradford and told me that it was too dangerous for me to continue to live in the area.

The summer was almost over when I started to hang out with Lisia who introduced me to a boy named Tommie. Tommie was a white boy who had a positive energy to him. He would come to my dad's house on the weekends and pick me up. We decided summer was almost over so we went to Marine City, which was right off the lake for some fun with another guy friend of his.

We found a slide that connected itself to the lake. When I dared Tommie to go down the slide without knowing if it was safe or not, he agreed.

Watching Tommie the dare devil slide down the slide a few times made me nervous. The slide slid all the way into the lake.

He was trying to show off so he went down the slide, but I just preferred to lure myself in the lake using houses that laid along the road that connected them to the lake. It was a very beautiful site. The population was fair but, it wasn't a huge city.

My new friend was ready for an adventure. I then told Tommie let's see if him or I would be able to touch the bottom of the lake near shore first. We then held hands pushing each other farther and farther down to the bottom of the lake. We then came back up and counted again and again pull ourselves under the lake trying to see who would come up for air first. We got out of the water and I felt a sense of bravery come over my lungs from holding my breath for as long as I could in the lake.

When we got back to Tommie's car, we traveled a couple miles back toward my dad Jerry's house when we found a property that had a huge tall pole that was built in the lake for launching our body's into the water. I was trying to have a good time by challenging myself by grabbing the rope and swinging myself high, throwing myself into the lake.

Tommie was done after a while. He then had to go soon because he had his friend had to work. I asked him to use his phone because mine was dead. I then accidently slipped and dropped Tommie's cell phone in the lake. I was upset with myself for ruining his time right before he had to be at work. He wasn't mad at me because he had insurance on his phone. He then dropped me off at my dad's house, rushing to get to the phone store before work.

When I got to my dad's, we watched a movie in the living room. Usually my dad was strumming away on his guitar so it was cool to spend time with him. The next day my dad Jerry and I went to his friend's marina down the street. My dad Jerry's friend's dad owned the marina so we could go over there any time. They called my dad's buddy Marina John.

He was a nice older man who followed his life ways as living as he was full-blooded Indian. He would talk to birds by doing a bird call with his hands. He would also carry around big knives and tall sticks. I was really intrigued when we went over to his house to see what he was going to do next.

My dad Jerry bought a boat for five hundred dollars. We got invited to Marina John's dad's boat that wasn't in the water but being stored very closely in the space where they would store and put away peoples boats indoor for the winter that would be coming along soon. I had remembered that summer was great for adventures. The new Internet site that everyone was using was Facebook. I had started using the site to meet search for old friends. I used the site keeping contact with friends and family. It seemed like many people had stopped that year using the other online site that many people used to communicate.

I searched for the girl who had lied to me about who she was for so long to check on her and see if maybe she grew up. When I put her name in the search bar, another girl with her same name popped up, except they had different last names. I thought the girl was pretty so I added her not knowing if she was bisexual or gay or anything at that matter. I really should have learned my lesson from meeting people online since I was in that actual state from acting upon it a couple years prior. I messaged the girl and we started up a conversation.

Come to find out the girl Megz lived with her mother a mile away from my adopted dad's house so we planned to hangout. I was quite lonely and over my break up with Tish.

Tommie and I were at his friend's house in Shelby Township, which was a more of an upscale class of people who financially were above middle class. We went next door to his friend's house for a graduation party. We ate and took a couple beers back to his friend's house feeling a little uncomfortable that we didn't really know the girl next door to his friend's house who was graduating.

I used his friend's computer when I told him that I wanted to go pick up Megz, the girl who had the same name but looked completely different from the girl Megz that I had come to Michigan to meet. He was one of my only friends who drove at the time so he agreed to drive me to go pick her up from some apartments called the Farms that most African American people from the city would move to to try and have a better life away from the hood.

What started becoming bad about the apartment complex is that people from the hood started turning it into a drug zone. When we picked up this mysterious girl that I didn't know too much about, she had her hair in a bun. She had a red hoodie on with a pair of jogging pants on. She was a white girl with freckles and long brown hair. She was beautiful and barely wore any makeup. When we pulled up she said hello and got in the car.

Tommie thought it was weird to pick someone up that we barely knew he put his trust in me and continued to be his friendly toward her. When we got to my dad Jerry's house, she introduced herself very sweet like, and then Tommie and Megz went to hang out with me in the area I had been staying and that was the basement.

At first she acted very hesitant because we still didn't know each other. It took a little while for her to open up to me, but once she did, everything seemed to fall into place. Tommie was tired so I pulled out the couch futon for him and gave him blankets and pillows. This new acquaintance decided she wanted to spend the night and the truth came out that she was bisexual and preferred girls. I was excited but didn't pressure her to do anything with me.

The next few days we started getting closer and closer. We ended up getting so close that she never ended up going home. My dad Jerry didn't mind her being around at all because she had been different from other girls that I usually dated. She was different from friends as well that I had brought around. She didn't have any children and was the first Caucasian girl that I ended up having a connection with then dating other than the girl with her same name I had come to Michigan originally to meet.

The more I hung out with her and Tommie, I realized that I started to feel complete. Having two people that I started to care for to feel the void of loneliness felt like an adrenalin rush to my heart. With my new girlfriend by my side and my adopted dad and one good friend, I knew at that point that I didn't need to give my heart to a bunch of people. The summer was almost to the end and I had some legal issues.

Over time I had got caught driving on a suspended license and had to go through the motions with the government for breaking the law. Most of my fines were paid, but I still had a few more fines left to pay.

The connection I had with Megz started growing stronger and stronger. The summer passion we had gained with each other reminded me of the passion between Noah and Aly in the movie the *Notebook*. This young woman and I amazingly became a love story of my own that was full of passion and desire

My dad and Megz wanted to go out by the lake to hang out, so that's exactly what we did before the summer was over. We hung out at the marina, but the water was dirty so we never got in.

Megz and I would play my dad's car radio loud as we danced in the summer's heat, feeling the passion of each other. The more we spent understanding each other's hearts, the more she and I opened ourselves up being honest about our lives and the people who were in our lives. Even though we were young we only had each other at the time.

The summer was beautiful but then it came to an end. Just as the summer came to an end slowly, so did Megz's and our relationship. We started arguing and having trust issues with each other. We found ourselves getting into petty arguments.

It started to seem like the type of love we had wasn't enough to stop repeating our past lifestyles. I felt as if my love was slipping away back to her old patterns of hanging out with a bunch of people partying all the time. All of a sudden one day she had been telling me she was going to come over and then tried to play me to drink with this guy.

My dad let me take his car to go pick her up. She knew I was coming, but on the way there, she stopped answering the phone, and right when I got there, my phone had died. Right in front of her house a couple doors down was this young man walking. I didn't want to waste my dad's time by letting me use his car because I knew that once I returned it, he wasn't going to let me use it again. I asked the young man if I could use his cell phone to call my girlfriend.

Prior off and on to this situation, my girlfriend had been trying to act like she could dominate me and beat me up if we ever fought each other. It made me angry, but I would always ignore her comments. I asked the boy if he knew my girlfriend. It happened he said he was on his way to her house because she wanted to drink with him.

I was so angry with her feeling like she was trying to play me, or what another way to put it was she was lying and cheating on me. I told the young man that I was about to pick her up and did he want to come to my house to drink over there. He said yes and got in the car with me. He had known her for a couple years so I wasn't worried at all about him pulling anything stupid.

By this time, it was midnight and she wasn't answering her phone. She called back twenty minutes later, asking me to come back and pick her up. I had already gone to pick her up and she was acting funny when I called her to come out to the car by not answering her phone. I was upset by this time and felt like she was up to no good.

Once I got home, I told my dad my phone died and she wanted to be picked up. He didn't want to waste gas but had to go to the liquor store so he agreed to pick her up, but told me make sure she answers or were not driving over there. I was twenty years old at the time. I shouldn't have been drinking but, once we got to my dad's house her and I started to drink.

We both drank a lot together when we did drink with each other. I felt as if the devil took over the situation between us because, here we were arguing once again. I felt like I loved her so much that my feelings would be hurt feeling like a knife was stabbing me in the back when she would lie to me or keep things from me. Next thing I started fist fighting in the kitchen.

We went from fighting in the kitchen to fighting in the driveway. She pleaded for us to go inside and go to sleep. The devil came inside my body somehow and we started fist-fighting outside. At that point, I blacked out and started beating her like we never loved each other at all. There was a little bit of blood in my driveway.

My mind was so clouded at this moment. She ended up busting my lip a bit. I can't believe we were actually fighting each other. The neighbor said he was going to call the police.

The boy took off down the street because he didn't want any police contact. The police were on their way, and when she went walking with the boy, I got extremely jealous. I was hurting inside and had no idea what damage had been caused. I ran after her with my white shirt ripped hanging half off my body. Rite when I caught up with them the police had pulled up.

At that instant we all ran from the cops. The boy couldn't escape the police and the dog followed him. They put him in the back of the police car because he had a warrant. The police put the dog in the back of the cop car as well. I ran and rolled instantly under a neighbor's truck.

Two cop cars drove by fast toward my adopted dad's house. When the coast was clear, I ran back to the house. When I got inside all I could do is cry and cry. My adopted dad held me tight in his arms. The police came right up to the door hearing my crying because, the living room window was open.

My adopted dad yelled at me to shut up. The officer then told him through the window that my girlfriend wasn't going to press charges. I was glad I wasn't going to jail but I was upset the more I sobered up. I fe

It stupid for blacking out because, I hurt someone I was in love with.

My heart was broken. I wouldn't even come out of my bedroom. Around nine in the morning the next day, the girl I had fought the night before came to clean my adopted dads down stairs bathroom for ten dollars. When she came into my bedroom, I hid under my covers in shame. I was ashamed that I had let assumptions and alcohol fight her as if she was a stranger. When she came into my room her whole right eye was puffed out and swollen.

I didn't recall doing that to her, but could see her eye was blood shot with veins from me poking her eye with my finger. The first thing that came out of her mouth was "See what you did to your girlfriend!" She then said if you love someone, you don't do that to them. I started crying and told her I did love her. I grabbed her trying to hold her close.

I felt as if I was going to lose her behind this. She sat on my bed. I told her I was sorry. I knew in my heart that sorry was not good enough for what had occurred. I wished I could have taken that night back. She laid down with me on my bed and we both cried. We both were holding each tight crying. I showed her my scratches and my lip. Her face was extremely messed up where I hit her in her eye.

The guilt inside me hurt my heart badly. I told her I didn't want to lose her. We started kissing and she wiped my tears off my face. She continued to finish cleaning the bathroom and then left. I didn't come out of my room for two days. I couldn't eat nor sleep. I laid in total silence in the dark.

We were both very broken hearted. We started texting each other again. Her mother was mad, and her friends were angry. At that point no one wanted to see us together. I knew in my heart that she had loved me or she would have pressed charges on me. It seemed that after that situation we decided to stay together but, it took a lot of trust from her to believe my promise to her that I had made to her to never put my hands on her again. I kept my promise to her ever since then.

There came a time a few months later and we broke up again. This time when we broke up, we did not get back together. I got myself evicted out of my adopted dad's house after that in January.

Through this guy I knew who called himself Forty, I met a girl from Ohio that was living with her mom in Detroit. She was a stripper who I later on found out was addicted to cocaine. The girl told me that she wasn't addicted to drugs. She explained to me that her choice of drug was smoking or drinking. I still was in love with Megz and didn't want anyone else. Even though she was the type of female who would run through other woman with no emotions connected she gave me more respect then she gave other girls.

The night I met the thick girl Jeneuve, my friend Forty had called her over to his house in Detroit to dance for me. I had never had a stripper dance for me before so I was extremely excited. She danced for me and when it was over she called a cab. She wanted me to come to her hotel with her. I was still quite nervous. My friend told me she was a nice young woman and to go with her. He reassured me that I would be safe with her and that she would look after me. When the cab arrived we both hopped in, not knowing a thing about each other. The one thing we did establish that night was that we were both seeking someone to be a good friend to us, so we took the risk to see what would happen. We got to one of the motels off of Eight Mile. We then chilled getting to know each other. We didn't do anything sexual with each other that night. I wasn't an easy girl like that especially when my heart belonged to someone else. We knew that at that point that we were going to be close.

The female I met worked at a bar slash strip club that had their own menu for serving food. The club was called "Back Streets" located off of Six Mile and Van Dyke.

From the outside of the club, it was known as a hole in the wall but was maintained inside with a nice variety of women. Most of the women who worked there were African American though.

There was a great chef there who cooked the best lamb chops and green onion with rice. The club was cleaned by the waitresses and employees. The bar always stocked with different variety of liquor as well. I would wait for my new friend at the motel until she would get off work. She never asked me to do anything she was affiliated with. I really appreciated the fact that she never tried pressuring me into anything. I wasn't working and really had nowhere to stay besides with my new friend. I didn't want to be homeless so I agreed to work at the club as a waitress.

My friend was going through a bad break up with a girl who also was a dancer. In the state of Michigan, you have to have a dance license, which is only legal for just that, and it cost my friend two hundred and fifty dollars. She had experience at dancing at other bars as well. I never met her ex-girlfriend but wasn't too fond of her because, of the way she treated my friend. I decided though not to get involved with her past.

After a week, the female friend got me a waitressing job at the club. I worked at the club and was getting paid under the table, being able to keep only my tips. I was the only light skinned, mixed chick there.

The people who worked at the bar didn't want me to work as a waitress. Many people wanted to see me dance as a stripper but I didn't want to dance there. I didn't like some of the customers who came up to the bar with a selective amount of money. That was the main reason I decided not to dance there. As a waitress, I took home more money than I would have compared to if I was to dance there.

It wasn't like I had never danced before. I just knew if I was to dance, I would want to make the money I deserved. I had danced at two clubs in Detroit before so it wasn't a big deal but I had only worked at each club one night.

At the club's most dressing rooms would require the dancer to pay a woman who was called "The House Mom" to help the girls get ready for their shifts.

Usually the management wouldn't let any employee's hangout in the dressing room unless they were supposed to be back there. I would just hang out in the chef's kitchen usually with him watching him prepare the meals for the customers. I would also hang around other parts of the bar when I needed a break.

I met a decent amount of employees at the club. I felt a lot of negative verses positive attention from customers and employees.

One time a customer had tipped me forty-five dollars off of a five-dollar drink. A lot of women were jealous of me for being light skinned or what some people called me "high yellow."

My friend and I stopped getting motel rooms. I remember we started staying at her mother's house in the city. At her mother's house, I had befriended her younger brother. She started getting jealous of our friendship and assumed I was sleeping with her brother. Even though he was handsome with a personality who knew how to treat a woman, I never crossed the lines with her by doing anything sexual with him.

I wasn't looking for a man anyways. Truthfully I started liking my friend more than as a friend and I knew that if I was to start talking to her brother in more than a friendly way that it would have been disrespectful. I couldn't help what was going on because, my friend and I were living two different lives.

By me befriending her brother, I needed someone to talk to when she was using drugs it started tearing us apart as friends. I was afraid of getting sucked into her life style, so I got away from what was going on.

Toward the end of my experience working at the club, I was working one night when I tipped a female named Monte. After I looked out financially that day, we started getting to a friendship point after we hung out a few times.

Monte reminded me of one of my ex-girlfriends. While Monte was dancing on stage I thought that it was my ex-girlfriend.

Chapter Twenty-Five

After a while, I didn't have anywhere to live. My adopted dad allowed me to store my things at his house. Jenueve was getting jealous that I was hanging out with Monte. Monte had a dance license that would give her the ability to dance at different clubs.

The police would come into different strip clubs to check to see if females had there dance licenses, which would make them legal. The females who didn't have a dance license would end up going to jail if they were caught.

Monte lived on the east side of Detroit with her son and her girlfriend who was a transit bus driver. I was blessed that my friend and her girlfriend allowed me to stay at their house for a while. We all got along great. I slept on their couch in the living room that pulled out into a bed.

I would meet up with Jenueve when I went to work. She started going back and forth with her psycho ex-girlfriend who had mistreated her before we met. I went to her mom's house to hang with her and her family.

Her mother had finally told me the tragic story about her daughter's ex-girlfriend cutting her daughter's face with a razor blade in a few different areas and very deep.

I was so upset hearing about the situation when they had to rush her to the hospital not knowing if she was going to make it out alive. I was frustrated and angry as I listened to her mother talk! I felt that my friend deserved much more than that from people.

In my mind at the time, I questioned my friend's ability to love. Who was I to question when I had my own problems! I also questioned if she had just gotten out of abusive relationship then how would she have ended treating me. She started acting funny towards me, but I knew she cared for me. I stopped working at the bar due to the fact that it was turning into a mess I was getting hated on by people based on my skin color.

The staff had also told me there was too many waitresses. It seemed that they didn't want to put me on the payroll. I figured it was because the club wanted me to dance and was waiting for me to change my mind. Monte said she wasn't making any money in that bar so she wanted to try to go to a different one. Some chicks would do extra things with customers to make up for the fact of the low money that they were making for slow nights.

The more I saw my friend get sucked into her lifestyle, the more I realized I didn't want to get sucked into the game she did. For a minute, Monte and her girlfriend had separated.

They ended up getting back together as the time passed. I spent most my time at her apartment practicing my cooking skills. The holidays were coming up and it made me miss my family in California.

My adopted dad Jerry allowed me to bring him Thanksgiving dinner. I had bought all the food myself and brought a friend with me to prepare all the meals. We cooked up a little bit of everything.

Something I loved making was stuffed mushrooms with hamburger and shredded cheese. For some reason, all I could think about was Niki and the boys.

I was wondering if they were okay while staying off Eight Mile. I couldn't help but to wonder if the boy she was seeing across the street was treating her right. I missed them so much More knowing I loved them.

When I wasn't with them, I met a man who was crippled in a wheel chair from being shot when he was younger. I had befriended him by starting to stay with him and his son on Sixteen Mile in Clinton township.

I still didn't have a stable home so I was happy he allowed me to stay with them. I felt that the man was lucky to be alive after being shot in Detroit.

Even though he was paralyzed from his waist down, he still kept a smile on his face. The good man who was looking out for me was named Faheem.

I ended up bringing Thanksgiving dinner to a few different places including his house. I felt that everyone needed a little love in their lives. He wasn't married nor did he have a woman to help him around the house. Even though he ended up going to his mother's home for Thanksgiving, I cooked big to show him how much I appreciated him being there for me. I would travel back and forth from Twenty-Three Miles, Sixteen Mile, and Detroit where Monte had also let me stay with her. I traveled so much to continue some of my friendships.

The next day I hung out with a guy named Rick. Rick acted as he cared for me, but when I asked him to take me to the store, he decided to impatiently leave the parking lot. He could not even wait until I was done shopping. How rude! I was trying to buy a holiday outfit. Instead of calling my cell phone to tell me that he had to leave, he just left. Instead of like a normal person would do, he did the opposite. A normal person would have come inside the store to give me my purse. This jerk dumped my purse in the parking lot and drove off.

When I came outside the store, I called him over and over again to see if I could get my purse out of his car. I walked to the bus stop getting ready to head to the suburbs, when something told me to walk back.

I walked back and by luck I saw my purse in the parking lot laying there. I was very happy that something inside of me told me to go back. I then met a nice man who went into the grocery store with me and his mother and he allowed me to cook some dishes that I wanted to pass out to some people at his house. It was such a blessing for me to meet such a kind souls.

Even though I had already cooked I wanted to prepare some more meals for other people who I cared for, who may have not had any Thanksgiving dinner. I felt that God had sent this man to me that day to be able to deliver food to God's people. That night after me and the man had dropped off a few plates to some people he dropped me off to a friend from Detroit's house. I found myself wanting to make one more stop. It seemed I was going backward in time. I knew the hood was dangerous after all that I had been through there.

The last time I was there, I had my two friends with me and got a gun cocked out on us by Niki's boyfriend, telling us to leave because she wasn't home. I knew that I had to deliver this last plate of food to Niki and the boys. I felt it was a risk but I had to anyways. By the time it was dark outside around ten a clock at night.

My guy friend from Detroit and I pulled up off Eight Mile and Hamburg in the hood. I was lucky because Niki's brother was sitting on her porch and asked me if I was looking for her. I replied to him yes and that I wanted to drop off some food for the boys.

Her brother ran across the street to the house of the guy she was dating. She came outside in decent clothes looking as if she lost some weight. She looked as if she was happy in her new situation. I got out of the car and gave her the food.

I asked her if she still loved me and she replied, "Yes, Cali!" Then she said find me everywhere I go with a huge smile on her face, which made me smile along with her. She then told me the boys were sleeping. I told her instantly that I wanted to see them and she replied that they had been asking about me.

The last time I actually got a chance to see them was on Niki's birthday. I had pulled up on the block and gave her a gift with two new outfits for them. They last thing that they had told me was "Cali, don't go, but I had no choice but to leave them because I was in a bad situation staying in the hood." I knew I had to better my life, and one day when they were old enough, they would understand that I always loved them and wanted the best for them.

I knew that the little things I did weren't good enough in my eyes because I wanted to do much more for them and could barely do for myself at the time. I then made a promise to myself that I wouldn't come back to the hood until I was financially stable to do more for them. I was mad at myself that I couldn't give the boys the world. I wanted to give them the world that my grandmother had once given me as a child. Niki had once made a promise to me that she would never let anything ever happen to me.

Our life on Six Mile had been rough when her sisters jumped her and then jumped me right after because they could not accept the fact that she and I were more than just friends. Her and I went through so much together in such a short amount of time when I was in her life. The next day I stayed off eight-mile in a motel with Jenueve right around the corner from Niki's block.

From that day forward, I knew that I couldn't keep going back. I knew that Niki resented me for popping in and out of her and the boy's lives, but she knew as well as I did that we truly could never be happy living in the hood, living a fast life style. I wanted so much more for all them. I always in my heart wanted them to move out of the hood with me and have a better life but, that was all Niki had ever known so it wasn't going to happen like I wanted. I started to then realize that she would be angry and worried about me if I stayed away too long. I knew that when the day came and I was stronger I would return to let them know I still loved them.

The last thing she and I spoke on was our love for each other. I prayed that she would never forget about our special love that we shared. I prayed all the time that she would never forget about me. I had hoped that if someone we both knew had seen me somewhere that they would reinsure her that I was still alive and all right.

The guilt of being away from them took over me each day. Christmas was now the next holiday coming up. The hurt inside my heart from never coming back to see Niki and the boys started haunting me in my dreams. Christmas was another holiday that really made me miss my family in California. Christmas has brought back a lot of childhood memories for me, of my sister's and little brother.

I started wondering how my siblings were. I had lost contact with them ever since their mother had turned to meth which was a hard drug. She sent them away to go live with her brother in another state while she ran the California streets. My father kept contact with her family. I knew his heart was breaking. He later told me about how she chooses her path in life and it wasn't being in our lives. I didn't understand why she would do anything in the sort that would damage herself, let alone my brother and sister. I never gave up my faith that God would take care of my family even though we were all separate in different areas. The abandoned house that I had been fixing up around the corner from Niki's house stayed abandoned. I left my car in the driveway as I went back across eight-mile to the suburbs.

When I was gone, someone ended up stealing my car. Most of my things were at my adopted dad's and Monte's house in Detroit. I decided to go out to Ohio to meet Jenueves family with her younger brother. I picked a few outfits, letting Monte know that I was going to be away for Christmas. Her brother and I jumped on the Greyhound and traveled for about three to four hours until we arrived there. When we got there, we had gone to his aunt's house. I ended up not paying my phone bill at the time and it got shut off. I was told that Jenueve would possibly come there to meet us. She never ended up coming to spend her holidays with her cousins and us. Monte and her girlfriend were very worried about me because, my phone was off. I knew other people who cared for me was worried as well. Jenueves brother gave me some gift cards to do some Christmas shopping for people. I ended up shopping for all my friends who had children.

Cincinnati was different from Detroit in my eyes. It seemed to me that it was more of a ghost town. The area I was in was mostly black people. It was finally Christmas and I started feeling as if I didn't belong there with people I didn't know. I was feeling uncomfortable with her brother because he was trying to pursue more than a friendship with me. We ended up getting into an argument because I wasn't putting out. I felt stupid because I didn't know anyone in Ohio and felt stupid for leaving. I was so mad I told him not to worry about me.

I told him I would get back to the Greyhound on my own. I was angry and walked away from him. Walking up the street with my luggage in my hand. I asked this guy who was walking the same way I was.

CALI GIRL, HOW DID I MAKE IT IN THE TREACHEROUS STREETS OF DETROIT?

The guy's name was Damano. He was around my age how to get to the Greyhound. He told me it was quite far from where we were. He could tell I was close to tears. He asked me how my Christmas was going and I told him terrible. I told him it was terrible because I was eight states away from my family who loved me and away from Michigan where I had built my new life at. We sat and talked and talked I told him about a week before I had left I started talking to this light skinned boy named Greg whose family had known some people I knew in Mt. Clemens.

I told him how prior to the holidays in July, I was living with this guy in Mt. Clemens who actually lived with his mother because his house was under construction, but he still allowed me to have my ore. I told him how I had a blast around that time going to John B New, which is an island party that's held every summer. People would have to take a boat to the island that everyone was partying on. Basically how to explain it is it's just like Mardi Gras in the lake and people would hop from boat to boat drinking, partying, and listening to music. Some people took a jet ski or a canoe to the island close by. I told him about when you actually got to the island how girls were walking around flashing their boobs, enjoying themselves collecting necklace beads.

This was one of the funniest events that I had ever been to. He told me as we talked more how he had never been but wanted to after hearing about what was going on there. Damano was at his mother's house where we were for the holidays. He didn't want my Christmas to be ruined as we sat at his mother house a block away from where I had been visiting with Jenueves family he looked up directions to help me get too the Greyhound. His sister and her two children showed up and his brother was there. His mother insisted that I stay for Christmas dinner.

They had the biggest Christmas tree I had ever seen decorated with the most beautiful ornaments. They had many presents under the tree for each other. In my heart, I felt sad that I was spending my Christmas with strangers and not my own family. I fought back the tears as we prayed together celebrating the birth of Jesus Christ. I prayed to God, thanking him that I was safe with a family that was godly. I ate an original Christmas dinner with his family that was different then I was use to but, I enjoyed it very much.

Even though I kept fighting the tears his family had made me feel very comfortable. They drank lots of eggnog and started doing a gift exchange with each other. I was very surprised that there was a gift wrapped under their tree with my name on it. I knew that God wanted me to be there for a reason. His mother was a single mother who was very nice. She asked me a lot of questions, and I answered them very politely and respectfully. When we were done enjoying each other's company, I thanked his family and gave them hugs.

Damano and I walked down the street where I said my goodbyes to the Jenueves family, reassuring them that I appreciated their hospitality and thanked them for having me over even though me and their nephew fell out. Damano then walked me to the bus stop and showed me which bus to get on. The bus I got on took me straight to downtown Cincinnati. I knew nothing about the city I was in. I just knew one thing and that was I needed to get home back to Michigan.

When I got on the bus I asked the bus driver where would I get off at to get to the Greyhound. He was polite and told me exactly when my stop came up. I had too many bags to carry, but I had someone who go off at my stop help me get two blocks away to the Greyhound. I ended up missing my bus that I needed to be on.

The next bus wasn't for six hours. The downtown of the city looked muggy and small. It wasn't different than the places I had been to. It seemed more dead and colder. The bus station was packed with lots of people. I grabbed something to eat and patiently waited on a bench for my next bus. It felt as if I was going to be there forever. Sitting there I met two guys who were polite to me. The two guys were from two different parts of the world. One guy was coming into town and another guy was leaving out of town. One of the guys had lived in Cincinnati The other guy was a white guy on his way to Tennessee. There were so many different types of people there.

As people would walk passed me and sit down near me, I would wonder about their lives and who they were. I knew in my heart that

CALI GIRL, HOW DID I MAKE IT IN THE TREACHEROUS STREETS OF DETROIT?

I would write about my experiences in my book that I was writing about my struggles.

The luggage I had carrying all the Christmas presents in was breaking. My zipper from my luggage was ripping. The two nice guys I was talking to carried my luggage to the front. The front desk handed me some duct tape so we tapped my bag up. I decided I wanted to see what Cincinnati was all about. The young boy my age said I could spend the night at his house. I reinsured him that I wasn't going to hook up with him, I was just curious for a friend in his city.

The young man's name was Chris. He told me how he had gotten into it with his girlfriend and she left him on the Greyhound back to her parents' house. He also told me his sister like girls like I did. I could tell there was something genuine about him. He was kind and I could tell he just wanted to help me. Feeling as if we met for a reason, I changed my ticket for two days prior than when I was originally going to leave. We said our good-byes to the guy we had been talking to.

As we walked the cold empty streets of Cincinnati, we talked about our lives. When we finally got to his mother's house, she was an African American woman whose mother owned a bar across the street that many older people would attend. When we got to the house, his mother and he offered me something to eat. I had already eaten so I wasn't hungry. Two hours had passed by and his sister had walked in the door. She was a little bit tilted from drinking. She had really pretty big brown eyes that I couldn't help but to stare into. She also was a mother of two, but her children weren't there at the time. The bar that his grandmother owned across the street from his mother's loft had been there for centuries and had mostly regulars attending.

The bar was called Clocks. I only went to the bar with him once and didn't stay inside because I wasn't twenty-one yet. I didn't find any interest in drinking. We originally only went over there so that he could talk to his grandmother. Since his grandmother was upstairs above the bar in her loft, we walked around the right side of the building throwing rocks at her window, trying to get her attention so he could speak with her. She never came out so I never got a chance to meet her. It was cold that night, and since nothing was going on, I told him that we should go back to his house.

    Later that night, it started pouring as he and I chilled with his sister. We all decided to walk up to a karaoke bar across town once it stopped raining. It was exciting for me because, at the time, I was rapping and singing for fun and felt that I had great talent. The bar was kind of small. Around their town it was known as a hole in the wall but was known for its great customer service. The bartender was a sweet older lady.

    Most the community knew that it was the hood. Mostly there was a lot of crack heads, dope addicts, or tricks driving around trying to score a date. I sang one of my favorite Alicia Keys songs. After that, I wanted to rap but it didn't happen like that. The crowd actually like my singing and wanted me to continue on. At the time I had been smoking tree's and wanted to find some. I wasn't a fool though and wouldn't smoke just anyone's trees.

    The bar tender gave me two shots of whiskey. One shot was on the house and the other I ended up paying for. I enjoyed the holiday and was interested in the background of their town. Some guy pulled up that his sister knew and we hopped in the car with him to go to a drive through burger joint. When we got there, the guy paid for our food and drove us across this bridge back to their house. When we got back to their loft, his sister and I went upstairs and he went to sleep downstairs.

    His sister's bedroom had the biggest windows I had ever seen. I could see the top of the roof of the building across the way and inside the building windows. To me it was very epic and a form of art of their city because the buildings were old.

    All I could remember was how beautiful it was when the rain hit. The last day I was there, we ended up walking a few blocks to one of their friend's house, which was an area known as the projects that was near a school by a bunch of low income apartments. I was nervous to be walking around even though I was with them. They had told me how rough the area was which made me even more nervous.

    I immediately had my street smarts on and watched all my surrounding the farther we got. When we ended up at their friends house the inside was quite nice with a well-respected family that had been staying there. We didn't stay long because I had to make my way back to the Greyhound to get back to Michigan and my bus was leaving soon. I knew that Monte and her girlfriend were going to be very worried about me because I didn't have a phone to call them on.

The last thing we did before I made my way to the Greyhound was take some kids that were over her friend's house next door to buy candy from this woman who had a whole cart of candy she sold to the community. I thought it was such a nice thing to do for the kids. It was quite interesting. I really respected the woman to the fullest for doing something for the kids like that. I said my good-byes and added the young woman online on my website whose house we were at.

The Greyhound was further blocks away downtown. I had such an interesting time there and learned how Detroit was not the only city that was struggling. There were many more cities all over the United States that had been struggling just like that. The Greyhound ride seemed short too me. On the way back to Michigan I thought about my friend Greg who was from Pontiac who was in Toledo at the time which was a city in Ohio.

I pictured getting off there and having another adventure as I looked out the window from the bus. I knew that I wouldn't be able to do that and it wasn't a good idea. Another hour and a half passed by and I knew I was finally getting closer to my stop in the city.

Finally, before I knew it, I was in Detroit City downtown at the Greyhound station. I felt a relief that I was finally home. It was really late at night by this time. I had no ride and not much money left. I asked a lady if she could tell me where Gratiot was, and she told me that it was very far from where I was.

The buses had stopped running and I was very afraid to walk in the dark. My phone was still off and no one was answering my calls because they were sleeping or working. I got more afraid as the time was passing by. I asked a cab how much it would cost to drive me home. The cab driver replied it would be twenty dollars. I didn't have twenty dollars.

Finally, I asked a woman if she was going in the direction that I needed to go in and she said no. I couldn't understand how this woman saw me in tears walking in the dark could turn me away being the fact that I was also a woman. I almost panicked. I knew I had to do something fast or I would be in danger.

A guy was stopped at the light and I asked him if he could drop me off. I pleaded with fear in my voice that I would give him any money I had on me left if he would just get me home. Out of the kindness of the man's heart, he agreed to do so. On the way there, I gave him the money and told him about my crazy experience I had for my Christmas holiday.

The man was an older respectable black man who told me he had a wonderful daughter and would hate for her to be in a situation like mine. He ended up going the wrong way on the freeway and it startled me. He then turned around and headed the direction of Montes house on the east side. I didn't know who would let me in at that time of the night or if the two lovers were home. I also knew they were going to be mad because I didn't call them so I knew they were worried about me.

As we pulled up in front of their apartment complex, I thanked the man and told him that God would bless him. I buzzed the buzzer really nervous because I knew I was in big trouble with my friend and her girlfriend. Monte then said, "Who is it?" That's when I replied, "Cali!" On my way to the second floor, Monte's girlfriend rushed me in the door, saying, "Get in here now!" I was so happy to be there and started crying with tears of fear and joy.

Once I started crying they knew something wasn't right. They went from mad to worried, and from worried to understanding once I started telling them my phone was off and the whole story. I took all the Christmas presents out and put them under the tree. They both hugged me and was glad I was safe. I told them I loved them and that I was so glad to be there. I had gotten Monte's son a blue jump suit. I didn't go anywhere for two days after that. I was so happy to see them all, so very happy.

I was grateful they had left their Christmas tree up as well. After that trip, I was very selective on who I hung out with. There was finally snow on the ground outside. It was very cold that winter. All the gifts I had gotten people and their kids I had passed out. I managed to give everyone their gifts except Niki and the boys. Part of the reason was I didn't want to deal with any drama in the hood. I felt that I had been through way too much drama as it was.

My intuition told me not to go back to that hood where they were living. I knew in my heart something wasn't right about that area. I knew it especially after the dealing with the people who were in her life that it would bring nothing good.

I knew one day that we would all meet again, but it wasn't going to be any time soon. Some time had passed and I started hanging out on Twenty-Three Mile Road and on the shady side in Mt. Clemens more often. I would say hello to people but eventually ended up just staying to myself. I would take the bus back and forth to Monte's house to visit with her family. New Year's hit and I was finally spending more time with my adopted dad Jerry on Twenty-Three Mile Road. I started hanging out in some apartments on Twenty-Three Mile that they had called the Farms. I ended up meeting this guy with lots of ambition who was from the west side of Detroit who was living in the apartments with his child's mother and his son.

Chip was his name and he introduced me to a chick named Ange. I asked her if she minded if I could cook at her house for New Year's. I was able to get a ride up to the grocery store to get what I needed to prepare the food. It seemed that every holiday, I would make cream cheese and salsa dip and stuffed mushrooms. Most the people who came, I barely knew. I just wanted to start off my new year on a good foot.

Eventually Chip and I started hanging out more till we ended up becoming good friends. That New Year's, I ended meeting an old man named Old School. Old School introduced me to his daughter. We all started hanging out all the time. I went over to Old School and his daughter Cece's apartment not knowing where I was going to be staying next.

The closer I got with them, the more they wanted me around. They decided that if I needed somewhere to stay, that I could stay with them at their apartment in the Farms.

Cece was in college to become a lawyer. Old School didn't have any other daughters but her. Chip and this boy who called himself Stunner would rap across the hall in Stunner's father's apartment.

Stunner was younger than me but had graduated high school and had the opportunity to go to college in Los Angeles, California. According to him, he was supposed to leave to go to college in May. Throughout the next couple months, Old School and Cece allowed me to stay with them as long as I helped out providing food in the apartment. I spent most of my time writing and rapping across the hall. I had such a strong passion for music.

Stunner and I started recording with other people that we would hang with. Stunner's roommate J digital owned all the beat and recording equipment. He would allow Stunner to use it whenever he wanted because he had experience. Stunner would use the equipment to make beats and sounds that would fit everyone's music. Their music was so different and unique. Between chip, Stunner, and I we all had our own different sounds, which ended up making us a strong team. I wrote a lot of my stuff and was still trying to find my right sound by experimenting.

Everyone who was around us had their own ideas and projects they were working on. Everyone wanted different studio time and many different time slots were filled by the guys. I didn't focus on having them record me so much. I knew that one day my music was going to be founded by someone who would be able to make the proper beats for me and help me find my true sound. Some people said I was a better rapper, and others said I was a better singer.

Even though I had a lot of different criticism, I still continued to push my dreams by focusing more on writing my music rather than recording it. I continued to write the book that I wanted to release, expressing my feelings of my struggles. I knew that the experience of being there on Twenty-Three Mile deserved a part in my story because, I watched other people push their dreams.

I made a couple friends in the apartment complex that would allow me to come over to their house, wash my clothes, and even wash up if I needed to. Even though it seemed that drama followed me the more I was friendly to people I still kept my head up thinking I could find one loyal friend. The only song I had recorded with Stunner was a song called "Liar" that I used my own lyrics to when it was my turn to show my performances. That was my actual first studio experience, and even though it wasn't a real studio, I still felt the positive vibe that could have come from it. It was an interesting experience to share with people who supported each other's dreams

Everyone had their hopes and dreams that one day they would have their music out in the industry. Our hopes and dreams day of being inspirational for people kept us together trying to make a better future for ourselves. Stunner and chips dedication grew stronger dealing with the music as I started to separate myself to continue my dreams in getting my book finished. We all would come together though no matter what and try to form some type of music even though we all had our own lives.

Telling my story was my main dream I wanted to follow. I wanted to help people just like me who had chosen their own path in life, and people who needed to express their life struggles. Old School was very supportive to me. I never had so much support in my dreams then when I was living at him and Cece's apartment.

Old School and I had an understanding that I was not interested in him, not in the slightest way besides a father figure. Even though he was always making slight remarks hitting on me, he knew where his boundaries were with me. He would have rather had me as a friend than nothing at all. I used to appreciate the way he believed in me.

Other guys that I had hung with found me attractive to, but I was like one of the guys so I was respected as one. Sometimes I wouldn't realize my true beauty and the person I was growing into. I had never thought of myself to be better than anyone else. I was always happy just to be alive especially being in May is that God gave me a powerful heart for love. My heart given to me gave me the strength to love people who had hurt me. I had skill not like many people but, my skills were held with me mainly in my writing.

Even though I wasn't the strongest artist in the music industry, it didn't bother me much because I had the strive to follow my dreams as a writer. There was another rapper that we had hung out with that was a strong solo artist that called himself a.m. He was fairly good and reminded me of a rapper from Atlanta.

In life I had learned that everyone their own story to tell. After some time, it felt that we were all pretty much a family, even though we hadn't known each other too long. It seemed that we would hang out from the time that we all woke up, meeting each other at either Old School's apartment or Stunner's dad's apartment to work on music. When we all would meet up in the mornings the first thing we would do is smoke together, putting pressure on each other to get our individual music projects done.

Chip and I ended up being close. I could see the pain running through his eyes. As we continued to make music together and hangout he turned into one of the only men I would confine in about my personal business. I know that the crew we were hanging with, including him, didn't understand why every time something happened between us, it would cause me to stay at other people's houses and leave the area. I knew they resented me for it but would never quite understand it.

Chapter Twenty-Six

I was used to running away from my problems and didn't know another way of expressing myself after arguing or getting into it with the guys. One some occasions, when I would leave to stay at other friends' houses, I always found myself returning where I had belonged, right there with old school and my crew of inspiring artists. I would always let them know that us getting into petty arguments didn't matter because, one day, we would all make it together. Sometimes they made me feel that if they got successful in their careers before I did, they would leave me. I started to think that possibly they thought exactly what I had been thinking. The more time progressed we all started going our separate ways.

Chip started focusing on other things that no one could be mad at him for. Cece was still going to school, and Old School was always I knew I wanted to finish my dreams but also had to get an education. I knew that couldn't get an education until I got a stable home.

Kimmy, my friend from Mt. Clemens, came over to meet Old School and Cece one day as well as Jerry my adopted dad. It seemed that they were all my family in different ways. I felt as if I had built something that was all mine. I had brought so many different people together who had so many different stories about themselves and what they had been through. It seemed that everyone I cared for had so much pain in their eyes from being mistreated from other people in their lives. Even though we all had pain built up in our hearts it seemed that when I was in their lives the pain would vanish.

Looking back at everything I had been through in Michigan, I felt as if it was all God's plan to make me a better and stronger person. I felt as if I wouldn't exchange the struggles I put myself through for anything in this world. Feeling that I got an opportunity to see the differences in what love was and wasn't, it made me open my eyes to the world out there. When people are young, they think they know everything, but in reality, people of all ages think they know everything.

Experiences and time are what builds people to find out their true foundations of their hearts giving them some wisdom to know how to start protecting it. Over time, I have realized many things. The number one thing I had realized is as much pain as I had gone through I still wasn't a miserable person. I had a light in me that others could see before I even got the chance too.

After being hurt so much, I knew I was blessed that God gave me a heart to never give up on my dreams or knowing how to love even without it in return. I waited for a change to occur in my life but started to understand that in order for that change to come I was the only person who could change the good, bad, and ugly of myself being my own worst enemy to get the total amount of success I had asked for.

Always what stayed on my mind was putting my passion into music by writing how I felt or expressing my true enter beauty which was my strongest points. I would never be able to forget how free my music liquors were or that would shoot out of my voice when I would perform in front of someone. I took in the criticism very well knowing that weather it was good or bad it was enough to help me become a better artist.

Even though I was living in the same area as my ex-girlfriend Megz, she would come and see her friend's only. We never hangout with each other because, our life styles were very different. I would always have love for her but never could understand why her heart grew so cruel. I felt that her heart grew cruel because of our fight or because it already was cruel, and by me being in her life before the fight, I had the potential in changing her heart for the better.

Every time I heard the song lyrics on the radio come on, saying, "Just going stand there and watch me burn, that's all right because I love the way it hurts. Just going stand there and hear me cry, that's all right because, I love the way you lie, I love the way you lie," I would always think about my ex-girlfriend who I loved. It seemed that it didn't matter how much time was passing between her and I. My heart was still lingering on the love I had for her and nothing could erase that.

Old School and Cece had been planning to move since their lease was about to end. I didn't know where I was going to go next or what type of adventure were coming. Kimmy's child's father's sister was staying in a nice hotel that had a kitchen built in the hotel room. The room cost eight hundred dollars a month. She allowed me to stay with her in the room. I tried to keep myself happy by being around people who I felt that I could relate too. Trying to cope with the face that I was homeless and not with family I found myself with a major problem and that was alcohol. Everyone I surrounded myself around drank and smoked as well as I did. I thought the alcohol would help me forget things, but in all reality, all it did was make my situation worse. I knew I had an issue with liquor because, a few months prior I went to the hospital on Twenty-Three Mile road where I had been staying close by.

The doctors there had told me that I had hepatitis A caused by drinking so much alcohol that made me felt that the more I drank the less I would feel the pain in my heart of everything I was bottling in. When the doctor told me the news, I was scared. He told me that all I would have to do is stop drinking and it would go away.

I tried to change my life around by leaving the drinks alone but it didn't work. One minute I would stop and the next minute because of who I surrounded myself around I found myself right back doing the same old things that were holding me down from being successful. Around that same time period when I went to the doctors I gave the ring that Megz gave me when we were together back to her. The ring stayed on my finger for months and months even when we were not together. The ring's sharp slits were starting to cut me deep just like the pain from being away from her. I didn't want something that symbolic on my finger any longer. I wanted to forget her the love that her and I shared.

I realized that after I gave her the ring back that it meant I was finally letting her go. I didn't know how to take in those deep feelings. I just knew that by me letting her go, it made her grow cold towards me scarring her heart forever. I knew that she did love me and I would always have a part of her heart, and vice versa me as well. Knowing that things would never be the same between us, we both went in different directions. Later she told me that she threw the ring out and didn't want to hold onto it any longer. I had always regretted giving it back to her but knew it was for the best.

Flame, Kimmy's child's father's sister had many gay guys coming over to the hotel to drink and party with us. I was finding out around this time that she had new Megz because they dated the same girl at one point of time. It was a small world. The stud dated my other ex-girlfriend Tish too. It seemed as if the gay community was small and everyone knew everyone or dated the same people.

I hadn't seen Megz for a while but somehow we got into contact. She decided to come up to the hotel with her two friends to smoke and visit with me for a minute. I didn't know how the visit was going to be. I immediately jumped in the shower, getting ready to see the last person who held my heart.

When she and her friends got there, we smoked then she took two shots. Fifteen minutes they left! I was really hurt feeling as if she used me just to smoke my herb. When she left, I went back inside to face the people I had called friends. I was extremely embarrassed and blew it off like it was no big deal.

I encouraged my so-called friends to drink with me. I was so hurt I started drinking as if the drinks were going to numb my pain. I drank twelve shots of vodka back to back, with a mixed drink as well. At the end of the night I was so drunk I locked myself in the bathroom running a bath for myself.

The next day when I woke up I was lying in a tub of water with cake all over me. Basically the people I thought were my friends somehow got into the bathroom and someone threw cake all over me as I lay there in a tub full of water with alcohol poisoning. Luckily God let me live through that.

I stood up and washed my body off praying, "thanking the Lord for being alive as the hot water ran across my body washing away all the cake and dirt from the night before". The experience I had reminded me of when I was living in California when I was seventeen years old. When I was in California I had drunk almost a whole fifth of rum with one other girl.

My father came home to tragically, find my eyes rolling in the back of my head laying in our empty bath tub with all my clothes on. He immediately turned on the cold water scared trying to wake me up. I was coherent but sick and couldn't move. It felt as if my body was paralyzed.

My father took me out of the tub, holding me, drying my face off. He repeatedly called my name over and over again. I was young, feeling so stupid. At the time I felt that everything that I wasn't able to experience in high school because, of my father being so strict on me was important. In all reality he was just trying to protect me from ruining my life. That was the first time I had ever gotten alcohol poisoning.

I remember my father being very angry with me after that, but if anything he was scared of losing me. After my experience at the hotel with the people I had been surrounding myself around, I decided to go back to Old School and Cece's apartment in the farms on Twenty-Three Mile road. There was still white beautiful snow on the ground, less than half a foot high.

As I traveled back to where I had been greeted by two familiar faces, I felt a sense of relief come over me. It seemed that every time I had disappeared, Old School always welcomed me back with open arms, reminding me that I needed to stay focuses on my future and my dreams.

Chapter Twenty-Seven

The girl whose hotel I was staying at ended up moving to another hotel. Even though I wouldn't be seeing Kimmy any time soon, I knew we would continue to stay friends even though I chose to stay my distance based on what happened at that hotel room. The studio at Stunner's house is where I took most of my anger and aggression out. The music would help me relieve a lot of my feelings that I couldn't express any other healthy way besides my writing.

In January, my adopted dad had this crazy woman in her late thirties move in with him. I figured it was because he was lonely and half the time I couldn't deal with all his emotional issues so I tried to keep my distance from him. Anyways, this female ended up calling my friend Kimmy a nigger when we went over there to get my mail from the house that had been being sent there. She asked us to leave the house, and as we were leaving, she came outside with a fire place poker running toward us before we could reach the drive way.

Kimmy wasn't going to tolerate any type of disrespect so she turned around to stand up for herself. There was the lady who was twice our age ready to attack. The lady then attacked my friend, putting her hands on a minor who wasn't even eighteen years old.

I didn't want any police contact because I had other misdemeanor warrants at the time for underage drinking that I caught a year or so prior and another one for driving on a suspended license.

Kimmy defended herself, fighting the woman all the way down the driveway. I stayed back against the fence as the psycho lady ran up to me when she got a chance pushing me down on my knees. I didn't want to defend myself because I didn't want any police contact. I was angry picking myself up off the ground. I pleaded for Kimmy to come on and get into her father's car that she was driving at the time.

Kimmy was so shaken up from having to fight for her life. She was so in shock and in frantic that she when we drove off we went around the block, she ended up losing control of the wheel and ended up hitting a neighbor's mail box, knocking it down. I grabbed the wheel and told her to focus. Once she focused, she dropped me off in front of the familiar apartments I had been living in with old school.

As the months then passed, I ended up catching another case for not waiting for the police to come when the incident with the crazy thirty-year-old woman had attacked Kimmy and I. Since she called the police and made a police report, I looked like the guilty one. The only reason I didn't wait there was because I knew I was going to go to jail for my other warrants and didn't want to deal with that at the time. Finally, the month April hit and it was four twenty, which was known as National Smoker's Day.

Kimmy invited me over to a girl named Slim's apartment. I had once hung out with Slim a couple years prior around the time she stayed in Mt. Clemens. Everyone who was there for the most part was messed up on Xanax, weed, and alcohol. I didn't do pills so I stuck to smoking since after my experiences drinking were a big issue for me. Pills just weren't my scene because, in my mind, it was still dope.

That was the day when I met Rob who was in the band Day 26. He was actually one of the other people who weren't doing any pills. Robs brother had a baby with Slim, but Slim knew him pretty well too. The singer that many girls fell all over was just a normal man with ambition and dreams. He wore some black polo boots that were most likely new. He sat on the ground with his back against the wall near the kitchen.

I introduced myself too him but wasn't interested in anything except who he really was as an artist. Around this time, I had been hanging out with this girl on Thirteen Mile and Gratiot that was from the hood. She wore green contacts in her eyes and was very confused about her sexuality. One minute when she was sober, she like girls and the next when she was drunk she acted like it was a shame to like girls, and unfortunately, I had been sleeping with her so I became her victim when she was drunk. She was going through a lot, and like most people I cared for from Michigan, I thought I could help them.

Kimmy met her a few days prior to the party and let me know she didn't like her, so I knew by bringing her to the party someone would end up fighting her, which caused me to not bring her with me. Since I was pretty much sober at the party, I was watching a lot of fakeness going around among the people at the party that claimed they were all good friends. All I really could do is laugh because these are the same people who acted as if they were so real but, in all reality, these people were haters who really didn't want me at the party either.

The boy Riley ended up pulling me into the bathroom, explaining, all intoxicated, that Slim and Kimmy really didn't want me at the party. I didn't understand why Kimmy would invite me if they didn't want me here.

Then again it didn't surprise me based on what I had went through in the past with Kimmy and the people she surrounded herself around. She was also a couple years younger than me, so I didn't expect much from her. I knew she had a lot of growing up to do.

I had known her since she was sixteen years old and seen her transition into so many different characters. I didn't know really who she was going to transition into next. I knew that was normal because many people were growing, including myself, so who was I to judge? I just didn't want to be around any fakeness. I had been hanging out with Riley that last few months pretty tough. He was a confident young man who liked other men. We got along great and he kept me laughing. At the party, after Riley pulled me in the bathroom, I kept my cool. Rob and I talked for a short time. I told him about my book and some of my music, and he told me about his music. I hadn't really heard anything much of his music so Slim put on a song of his on her X-box. I didn't know him or wasn't the type of goopy chick to be all in his face. I loved music but was never the type of chick to kiss up to him to get the answers that I had for him. My friend Terry had always been there for me. At the end of the night, I didn't have a ride out of there, so he picked me up. We ended up dropping off this girl and her child who had been there off at her house on Fifteen Mile Road.

I went back to the girl I had been messing around the house who lived on Thirteen Mile and Gratiot. The next month for me was a bit rocky. The girl who acted as if she didn't like girls but, was messing around with me came clean and told me that she was raised with Niki and her siblings in the hood on the east side. It seemed like this world was getting smaller and smaller.

I told the girl not to tell Niki she was hanging out with me because, I hadn't seen Niki since last thanksgiving. I knew Niki was going to be angry and made sure to tell the girl that Niki would be pissed off if she knew I was sleeping with her. The girl wasn't the type to admit she was bi- sexual but, just in case I warned her not to do so. It became an issue being around this girl, even though I had started staying at her house with her. She drank a fifth every day. I was trying to heal my body from the liquor and she was trying to forget her problems.

Jess had a sad story, and I started feeling sorry for her. I thought that she was real, but confused and wanted to be there for her. When I was staying at her house, I was pulling my own weight. I would put food in her house, and supply her and I with woman bathroom supplies that we both needed. I didn't mind doing any of that because, I knew it was the right thing to do and part of maturing. I helped her with what she needed because, her priorities were drinking her troubles away and I felt as if I could help save her. She told me her son had mentally challenged issues and lived with his grandmother. As the nights went by there was occasions where I would hold her tight while we laid in bed as she screamed and cried, "my baby, my baby!" I couldn't even imagine her pain but, knew everyone had their own story. All I wanted to do was help her. I couldn't understand her pain. Her pain was different from my pain and I felt maybe God wanted me to help her. I knew that her pain led her to drink, and that was familiar as my pain had lead me to drink as well. I knew when she was sober things were fine and she had good intensions.

The minute she got the alcohol in her is when things became a problem and her good heart turned into a cold one. When she was sober, she was very affectionate to me, saying how she wanted to be more than friends, and then the minute she drank, she flashed saying she wasn't into girls acting violent toward me. At one occasion, I had my friend Terry over for dinner and some drinks, that was the first time I had seen a change in her. She started acting as if she was better than me, the more she drank. By the end of the night, she ended up hitting on my friend and I didn't understand so I got mad at him, telling him to back off my girl, but in all reality, he had nothing to do with her drunken issues. My best friend who stayed on Eight Mile wanted to meet her.

The day came when my adopted dad picked me and the girl I had been staying with up, taking us over to Eight Mile Road to meet my current best friend. I don't quite remember what happened exactly, but they were sitting in the backseat together and ended up getting into a minor argument about something. All I could hear in from the front seat was Mimi, saying, "I'm your girl! You're not going to talk to me any type of way!" I guess Lea, the girl I had been messing around with, was trying to see how far she could push Mimi. Lea always kept a Taser in her purse at all time. I was a bit worried but knew my friend knew how to handle herself.

Most people who knew Mimi knew that she was the type of person who wasn't going to hold her tongue, and if someone had a serious problem, she would fight for what she felt was right. The two females almost started scrapping, in other words fighting in the backseat. I figured the girl was jealous of my best friend because she was a beautiful chocolate young woman who kept her nails and hair up, as well as always had nice materialistic clothes and jewelry.

I wanted my best friend to meet her based on how she was treating me, and I wanted my friend's advice. If the drama with her was worth staying in lea's life. It was clear that Lea was threatened by Mimi who was raised in the hood. Lea had my dad pull up in the parking lot next to her apartment complex because she didn't want Mimi to know where she lived. As she got out of the car, she started acting all loud, yelling for Mimi to get out of the car so she could taser her.

Mimi was already aware of the Taser so she didn't get out of the vehicle. Lea was so crazed, she then slammed the car door so hard that you would have thought the door would have fallen off. My dad was so mad he started yelling! He then said he wanted to leave to take my friend home. I knew I had to do the right thing by staying with my dad to drop off Mimi or she might not have gotten a ride all the way back to eight-mile road.

I told Lea that I had to go with them so my friend could get dropped off. She felt as if I was betraying her or picking my friends over her. It didn't matter much to me how she felt because, she had been mistreating me the whole time and all I had been trying to do is help her. A couple days passed and I decided to go back around Lea, checking up on her because. She was someone I was growing to care for. The day we had another terrible incident had finally come.

That day from early in the morning wasn't going so great. I did her a favor and cleaned up her kitchen. Then went grocery shopping for things to prepare for dinner. Riley said he wanted to come enjoy dinner with us, so I wanted everything to be nice. I had money to buy us food and even drinks.

Lea said she forgot her ID so when we went into the grocery store she decided to steal a gallon of vodka and a twenty-three–dollar package of shrimp. I was so angry that she was doing careless things when I offered to help her out. At the time she wanted me to walk out with her, which I had already told her I wasn't going to do based on my experience when I ended up in jail in Wayne County for stealing when I was eighteen years old.

My reaction to Lea was telling her "Oh hell no!" As we got outside I was so angry I started walking in the direction of her apartment just not with her. When we got to her house, I started lecturing her, telling her that what she did was unnecessary and childish after I told her I had money and not to do it. In the end, she hardly heard anything I said. She cooked the shrimp and didn't ask me if I was hungry or if I wanted any of it. I was very disappointed after all that I had did for her but learned a valuable lesson that if you do something for someone you are not to expect anything in return. Nine times out of ten people aren't what you think they are and won't care about you as much as you care about them.

I knew that our friendship was soon going to be over. Sad to say it but I really liked Lea and felt that in some ways we could have helped each other. A couple hours later, she was smashed off that gallon she stole from the store. I had one cup of liquor, which had me a little buzzed, but I was not drunk. Everyone including Riley was buzzed but mainly sober. No one was belligerent or drunk like Lea was. An hour or so passed and I don't know what came over Lea. She then had butt heads with me as hard as she could in my forehead.

Everyone including Lea and Riley were completely shocked of what she had done. After my experiences with Megz, I didn't want to put my hands on a woman I was involved with. My feelings were so hurt and I controlled myself very well. At that time, Lea started saying she wasn't gay. She started snapping pictures of me with her throw away camera as if she did something to be proud of herself about.

I started crying, saying, "You don't treat people you care about like that." In her kitchen she tried attacking me again. Something came over me and I snapped. I finally had enough of her abuse. As she shoved me against the wall, I shoved her back as hard as I could. When I shoved her back, she said, "That's what I want you to do." She then said, "I want you to stand up for yourself." I was so upset by this time. She started acting crazier and crazier. As I tried to talk some sense into her, we ended up in the living room. Lea started laughing hard and crazily as she snapped more and more pictures of me. I got mad and stood up! I was done with her. I jumped on top of her and started beating my fist into her face about twenty times without resting. I stopped when I heard one of her family members ask, "Who's bleeding Cali?" They were wrong. I wasn't the one bleeding—she was! Her face had been cut in a couple different places. Lea's blood was squirting in my eyes. I was even more scared of what she may have had in her blood. When she got up, she looked so hurt and shocked from her head and nose leaking blood everywhere.

All I could see was her blood was dripping down her face into her eyes. My forehead was as swollen as a softball. At that instant, Lea then ran and got her Taser that she carried around everywhere.

I didn't want to go to jail nor did I want to keep fighting the girl. I left her apartment immediately, as I was followed out by Lea with a Taser. Her family held her back while I ran across the street crossing a busy street called Gratiot, trying to get away from her as fast as possible. I was so weak I could hardly hold myself up. As I walked into a business where they rented tailors and dolly's to people to move their things, I asked the man out of breath if they had a bathroom. The man replied yes. As I was opening the bathroom door, I then fainted to the ground.

My body was sore and weak. I woke up on the ground about five minutes later and realized the guy at the front desk was going to end up calling the police because I had Lea's blood all over me. I suddenly washed my face and hands trying to wake myself up, still in shock. After I left the bathroom, I walked up to the clerk repeating myself, thanking the clerk twice without noticing it. I was still in shock mode. I asked the clerk if I could use their phone. He agreed and I then called Mimi explaining a little of what happened. I told Mimi that I needed to come to her house because I was too weak to walk anywhere.

Finally, I got to the nearest bus stop to wait for the 560 bus headed to Mt Clemens to Kimmy's house. When I got to Shady Side Park, I stayed for a while and walked to her house. Kimmy's family answered the door calling her to come to the front door to see why I was there.

Once she reached the front door, she saw the girl's blood all over my clothes and how swollen my forehead was. Her parents were very strict and started tripping out so I used her phone to tell Mimi I was on my way and to call riley to see what was going on.

I hopped back on the 560, which was the Gratiot bus heading for Detroit. When I got to Mimi's house, her mother gave me a stand back and allowed me to spend two days and two nights to rest. I ended up staying until I wasn't weak anymore. The last day I was at Mimi's mother's house, she gave me some clothes to change into.

Mimi and I knew that her mother wasn't going to let me stay any longer since they had a full house. I thanked Mimi and her mother for the help. I then took the 560 Gratiot bus headed to Twenty-Three Mile so that I could go to Cece and old school's apartment where I had been staying. It seemed as if every time I came back from visiting other friends, old school and Cece would tell me how much he had missed me. After I told them what happened, they had also told me some news. They told me that they had gotten evicted. They didn't tell me why they had gotten evicted, but I figured it was because, old school was always fighting with starting drama with Cece.

There was actually one occasion I could never forget when old school was fighting with Cece. I was laying on the couch when the police came in. I had four warrants and didn't want any police contact.

When I heard the police come into the apartment, I put a blanket over my face and pretended to be sleeping. I was so terrified. Old school knew my situation with the law. When the police asked old school, "Who is your friend?" Old school said nothing because the officers immediately turned to Cece and asked her, "Does this friend have anything to do with the problems between you and your father?" She then replied no. All I could do was continue to grind my teeth, and by this time, I was sweating patiently waiting for the police officers to leave. Once the officers, left I felt a sense of relief come over me.

Cece then told me that I was going to have to leave for the night because she was going to her mom's because she couldn't deal with her father any longer. Old school would always bring random things back with him from Detroit, such as clothes, shoes, and other random trinkets.

Old school would give me clothes and other things he found because he would have an overload of stuff. Even though at the time I had four misdemeanor warrants, I knew I didn't have an income so I was worried about being locked up. I started to hang out with a young athletic man who was about two years younger than me. I was tired of being abused by different woman. I explained to him how I wanted someone to care for me. He and I became very close around this time. I decided to bring him back to twenty-three mile to meet old school and Cece.

I started feeling that Will, the young man who I had been hanging out with, was someone special who could care about me. Next thing you know he was spending the night with me in my apartment.

I didn't want to be away from him but knew that I would end up hurting him because I didn't know how to commit to a guy because I was so used to being interested in a woman.

After some nights of us together, we ended up being intimate with each other. I could tell he had feelings for me as well and knew I had to push him away and fast! I was in the process of making a transition from living at old school's house. I knew that I needed to figure out a way to go off on my own to support myself. The last time I had hung out with Will was at old school's house, he helped me pack up my stuff so that I could move from there. I was introduced to a woman who called herself Paradise.

Paradise was about eight years older than I was. She had been living on the west side of Detroit her whole life. When she and I talked on the phone, we arranged and agreed that I could come stay with her in her mother's five-bedroom house on the Westside, but she told me about her current profession. She told me that she wouldn't pressure me to do anything I didn't want to do. Her profession was being a call girl on the west side of Detroit working out of different local rooms that were low key.

I had no real experience in the way she operated her business. I wasn't snooty or stuck up about her lifestyle. I knew that I had nowhere to live nor did I want to stay with just anyone. I knew that I needed a way to be able to feed myself and pay my phone bill so I could keep contact with my family in California. When I was done gathering all my things up at old school's house, I put them all in a thick black garbage bag. I then gave Will the very last hug and arranged for Old School and Cece to drop him off on the east side of Detroit where he lived.

Once everything was arranged, I called my adopted dad Jerry to pick me up so that he could take me to the west side of Detroit to live with a woman I hardly new. I enjoyed mine and Paradise's conversations. I loved both my daughter and my adopted dad very much. I was focused on enjoying the beautiful weather that was starting to bloom. I decided to have a BBQ at the local park that was off the water. I was excited to finally see Michigan's peaceful weather. The local park was just transformed into a mini water park with a jungle gym.

My daughter was almost two years old so I was excited to take her. I saw a little girl whose mother I knew, I then re-added her mother on Facebook to see how she was doing. Jerry and my daughter went to see her one day with me at her apartment on Ten Mile. When we got there it was very nice and welcoming inside. I haven't seen Diabla in a very long time. I thought she was something special. She was funny, very loving and had an idea of life in a positive outlook. She was in college and was trying to do the best she could for her child who was a few years older than mine.

Even though the children had a bit of an age difference, they gravitated towards each other right away. After a couple visits, I met one of Diabla's friends at my friend Jerry's house for a bond fire. There was only a friend of mine over from Port Huron, she was as beautiful as we all were. She had been over all day. We actually had a peaceful dinner. After dinner was when I talked to Diabla about bringing her friend by for a bond fire. I enjoyed where we lived because it was far from the Hood. At night you could see many stars. My favorite thing about living by life is that there was a marina down the street from our house.

New Baltimore was truly one of the nicest parts of Macomb, Michigan. It was the true country full of dreams and comfort. I answered the door for Diabla and Jess. I said, "Wow, Jess was cute!" She was Puerto Rican with big lips! I had a friend visiting though to get to know. Everything happened for a reason. As we all sat around the cute little bonfire, we laughed, and joked and laughed again.

Of course we were drinking a little southern comfort! That's what a lot of Michigan's people picked to drink around the summer time. Summer was just in the beginning and every night after that I could not stop getting Jess, loud, vibrant, beautiful ball of energy out of my head. Over the next few days, the girl from Port Huron went home. After talking to Diabla I decided to go to her apartment so our children could play. Jess was actually going through moving conditions with her child's father. Her past story was unbarring; she had been a heroin user in her past. Everyone was turning their back on her based on some of her past actions. Diabla was her only real friend when I met her that never turned her back on her when I met her, they actually called each other sisters. I know from spending time with them they truly loved each other dearly.

I loved being around both of them. When the three of us were around each other it completed me. I was grateful that we could get all of our kids together. Everyone was so caring towards one another. We stayed up that night. All the kids which were Jay, Jess' son, my daughter and Diabla's daughter were all asleep in bed. As for us mothers, we were sitting on the porch staring at the moon. The moon was full, yellowish-grey and the stars were really bright. Us three we enjoyed our own perception of music. We would drink and laugh and talk about our night. We all talked about our pasts, and past abuse that we went through.

We knew what other people did to us was wrong and we enjoyed our time together as one. It seemed that there was no realer love than a friendship that helped all of us heal. That night we almost stayed up all night when Diabla left and went to bed and left the couch for me and Jess to share. We had been both been mistreated throughout our lives by the family and people we loved at one point of time. It actually made us come together and get along so well. It seemed like we had plenty of things in common as women, mainly the good and the bad, as far as insecurities. That night we ended up making secret love that we had no idea that would bind us for life. That night I made a friend for life. As we made passionate love for each other I knew I didn't want anyone else after that point. I had been still waiting for something more to love since I had been back in Michigan.

The next morning when we woke up I told Jess that she and her son could come live at my house with my dad Jerry and my daughter and I. Diabla had her own life and really felt that she could only help Jess so much. Being the fact they had a lot of past situations that made their relationship like that I was very opened minded and really wanted to help the both of them. I wanted Jess and her son to have some stability.

As a woman I felt empowered to do the right thing when you love someone. I didn't know how long they would stay for but we were going to try a couple days out to see how it would go. The first stop was to my adopted Dad's house and the second stop was to see her mother which was really her ex-step mother who was a beautiful musician that played the guitar and sang with her loving twin sister.

Her twin sister was an awesome musician as well. I had never seen that type of love in my life between two sisters up until that point. It was nice as we approached the house and I met her family for the first time.

My Dad Jerry brought his guitar to play along with the band of twin sisters. I had a healthy laugh with Jess as we smiled at each other. Her mother and aunt helped her raise her son for most of his life. They were one of the strongest women I have met in my entire life. When Jess wasn't up north with her biological mother trying to make things right with her for the past abuse she had put her through she was home with her aunt and sisters and son. I loved seeing her happy. She started taking meaning in my life.

At that point in her life she was trying to find herself. She had so much to take hold of herself. It seemed over time as I nurtured her it made her stronger and want to do better for us all. I was a bit intense and over bearing. Any strong woman just isn't going to always keep quite when things aren't right. Then again silence in some situations is due when needed! When you love someone you just don't shut them completely out. I was willing to understand her for understanding me. It seemed like I wasn't the only one out there who felt they had a crazy life.

All of us woman and even men in the world had so much healing to do. I felt hurt and strong at the same time. I wanted to stay strong for the people I loved so I strived for them. Jess was one of the first person I had never gave up on. Wow did we have a past.

It still seemed we really didn't know each other's strengths and weaknesses. It took time for me to learn who I wanted to be. I had a plan but I didn't know how far my heart would need to go.

It seemed like at times I had no control over trying to heal people by loving them. I still found myself trying to reach my highest goals. All I could do is sit back and smile at jess. I was happy we had become so close, even as fast as it was. I knew Diabla was a great person too. I knew she would always have my best interest at heart. She was honest with me before I even left. She explained to both of us how she felt about what we had done.

Our secret wasn't a secret much longer. I was okay with that though and jess seemed so loving and ambitious. Everything was coming into place. We all sat around and listened to music as everyone accepted me and our situation for what it was. Our love was pure love! It was getting late as we drove by the local beach on the way home. The home was so beautiful.

Michigan had many different divisions of love it seemed. It just depended on where you seemed to adventure off too. Everyone had a great time. I was glad both of our families that we had built gravitated to each other with such great loving conditions. I felt truly happy at that time in my life. When we got home I started making bacon pepper jack cheese burgers. While I had the food on the stove I showed jess where to give the kids a bath at.

Once the kids were in the bubble bath and clean we all sat down at the table to eat. It was very nice to share my life with someone else who needed my love as much as I needed theirs. I loved her son as if he was my own. In a way it started feeling as if he was my son. He became my God-son! I built another room on the other side of the remodeled basement.

We put a bed together for Jay, with also a lamp and a fridge on that side of the basement. There was also a brand new remodeled bathroom the other side of that wall. I was so happy to be helping a woman find her strengths as a mother first and mostly important. I didn't want anything to happen to him.

My adopted dad got Jay a bike and we started teaching him how to ride it. I was so happy to be outside enjoying the summer rays with my beautiful new family. I gained a best friend that summer and love that would last forever that was mutual. It was like a seed that was planted. Our love was growing more as the summer grew stronger, and hotter. I was happy for once helping someone settle down and receive love from me. I could not ignore the pain in her eyes that I would see every time she glanced at me.

After getting close with Jess I learned that the pain she endured was from her child-hood memories of the abuse she had endured, and action that caused on herself when she was under the influence. I would never know everything though that had happened to that woman.

I knew I could tell she was still in pain and trying to mend her pain with a bottle of alcohol. At one point she would numb her pain with other drugs as well but, that all changed when she came into my path. I didn't do any other drugs besides drinking.

It seems like we were breaking down our lives to each other and helping each other stay stable. I knew I had to stay stable for my child's future. I knew jess and I both had a past that was messed up, but I never let that cause me to stop loving her though.

Our children were growing together and it was such a blessing from God to have the will in us to love hard. I did know my friend was worth so much that she couldn't see in herself. Throughout that time in our lives I stood by her. Jess was the happiest when she was outside with our kids in our beautiful back yard. We had such a beautiful life sharing with each other. I was very grateful for the chance to live in a nice area away from the city. I was ready to settle down after I had my daughter.

I enjoyed letting Jess get loud and act out as if she was the boss. I thought it was very cute but, I knew I was the back-bone. Then our other best friend Diabla was also our best friend who was just the cartilage in our body when it came to love and loyalty. I was grateful for the Lord's people. There was still some great people out there believe it or not. I figured the Lord was the one who would place these people in your life to bless you by loving you. The definition of love is very simple.

The definition of love is feeling, and then acting on your feelings. I learned that many people run from their love. You have to love yourself in order to love anyone else. I loved myself. I had a will in me that wouldn't give up. I wanted to live and stop surviving for once. I felt tired of being hurt. The experiences I shared with Jess were very spontaneous and beautiful. I was finally becoming strong woman.

Adding Diabla in our mix was the definition of crazy beautiful. I loved every second of the time we spent together. When we all spent time together, I felt a sense of peace come across all over my body.

I was in a more relaxed state of mind. I had felt some sort of security from loving Jess and my kids! In reality we were all God's kids. In that instant, something changed. In my mind I thought I could change other people's lives for the better.

I only wanted the best for them. The perception of love was simple to me. I felt in my mind that Jess was the one person who would never leave me. I had one friend who always called me for help. I always felt that I could help her! Even though we were both hurt in our life journey, we stuck it out learning that summer about ourselves and how to grow stronger, even if it caused us to eventually go part ways. We started to hold onto each other as long as we could. One of our favorite things to do was stare at the stars every night together. No matter what, Jess seemed to go out to have a smoke.

I would always run outside in the backyard so we could stare at the stars together. I appreciated all the time that we spent together. It seemed so nice and comforting to know I was loved. The most appreciation was really the effort of two people who were feeling so down through life coming together to live I try to heal.

It was something through a journey that we could not see. I was in the peak in a fresh chapter in our journey.

I was trying to find something new within myself. I wanted to try to change some of my ways to create a stronger play out for my future and everyone who was around me. I knew the only way to do that was to start with me! That was it. I was messed up and needed help myself. It was true I did loved another woman. Yes!

The world had worse problems, I felt than to worry about woman homosexuality. I always looked at my situation as beautiful. Besides the point I was mainly just trying to learn how to be a friend first before anything else.

Other than a friend, I was trying to be a great person. I wanted to be kind-hearted. I felt that I had been wrong within some times in my life for some things that I had done. I wanted God to forgive me so I felt that giving love was the only way to repent. I worked harder and harder as each day passed to show my friend Jess what love really was about. I wanted to show her what life could be like with hard work and dedication. We had bigger problems. Before she started really healing. She was very torn with herself. With me. She felt as if she really had a home besides her stepmom's for her first time. Over time I learned that life is what you made out of it.

If you had ambition to survive, you would as long as you would continue to progress in a positive outlook. I wanted the future to be positive for everyone who was around me at that time. I knew that all that would come over time with patience. It's funny as I think more and more about it I see that as long as we kept our communication open we had the greatest relationship.

The moment we started going our different ways was when I started pushing her too hard. She seemed to want to learn certain things on her own. Everyone has their own levels of wants and needs. I accepted them.

I was happy to find someone to use my positive energy with. There were some differences in our journeys, but we led the same ambition to love and receive love. I never met a woman who masked her pain more with her laughter. We worked on talking about our feelings a lot.

The sun was shining bright that next morning. I was always cautious, keeping a close eye on the kids because of Jess's and my experiences of being abused. I kept a high paranoid profile when it came to my babies.

I was very stuck in my ways protecting the people that I loved. My fear of anything happening to my children or anyone's children bothered me. I was always on alert mode whenever my daughter or Jay was around anyone. I wanted them to always be protected. The power in me was the will to want to show Jay to have strength. At night sometimes when Jess would leave, I would have to put him to sleep. I would hug him and tell him there was nothing to worry about. I showed him that there was nothing to be scared of. It was right around bedtime when she would leave this little boy. I was irritated with her most nights that she went off to learn hard lessons on her own.

After the days passed, I proved my loyalty and love to Jess and her son. That we were all a family and I loved them with my actions. Anyone can talk but a person who follows their word is real. Even though Jess would go out and party, I still loved her more and more. It seemed as if the more she would push me away the more I would be willing to stick by her side through thick and thin.

The worse argument we ever had was about her getting herself together.

I explained to her that putting her son as her number one priority had to happen. She would irritate me with some of her actions of going out partying. I knew she loved her child. It seemed that she would drink every day to cover her pain. I first didn't realize at the time that I was doing the same thing but, more focused on the kids. It was the prime time in my life.

I was very happy listening to beautiful music in the summer time. I could never forget. Jess and I would sit listening to music, wondering where our life would take us.

I was content in my heart with the love we shared together. We were so different in levels when it came to controlling ourselves. We had similar hearts though. She loved my daughter as if she was her child. There had never been a dull moment that summer. The fire would flicker as the bomb fire would flame nicely almost every night. Even the next-door neighbor boy who was around my age would hop the fence to come over and hang out with us. It seemed like people were drawn to our personalities and beautiful smiles.

It felt like I was in a real life lesbian relationship with this woman. It was nothing I had ever dealt with before. It seemed over time she took some of my advice and Diabla's. A better way to describe my relationship with Jess was a strong friendship that was followed with passionate love. I started working at the local phone store that was also half of a tanning salon. I would literally walk to my daughter's preschool with the stroller around one in the afternoon before work. Her school was so conveniently placed which was right next to my job! I could feel God's presence up lifting me with chance for a greater change.

The summer was almost over. Jess was talking about going up north to stay with her mother to rekindle their dull relationship. They would fight and argue a lot over the phone. It was sad to see them both drunk going toe to toe. I didn't want Jess to leave, but things were getting out of control with her at my house.

My adopted dad was starting to crush on Jess, which started making things a bit awkward at home. My adopted dad was goofy and funny so it was just kind of innocent but it started getting weird. Sometimes Jess would have my adopted dad take her to the store for alcohol and cigarettes. She would sweet talk him every time into paying for them. I was annoyed at times with Jess wanting to drink all day long. It seemed as if what we were both seeking was love. Jay's father had a great construction job that paid very well. After meeting him and seeing him make an effort with being in Jess and Jay's life, I could tell that he loved them regardless of what they all been through. He wanted to work out their relationship.

Jess seemed a bit out of control. I really didn't know him at all. He loved her so much and was more worried on her actions than spending time with her son. She said that he loved their son but his priorities were elsewhere while he seemed everywhere at times. Later on in life, I understood how Jess's child's father was feeling. Of course no one wants the woman of their child to be on drugs and alcohol all the time. At one point I found out later that they both had used together in the past. I was worried about Jess being around him but stayed focused on my daughter.

Before Jess came into my life, I heard that she had a really bad heroin addiction. The addiction Jess carried was so bad that Jay's father could not allow her to stay at his mother's home any longer. In that time in Jess's life, she was trying to stay focused but couldn't before she met me. I was glad to finally be making a change in someone's life for the better. It seemed crazy how life worked out sometimes.

I wanted to be strong for everyone around me. Jess opened up to me and told me she never wanted to use hard drugs again. She told me how bad she felt for hurting the people around her. She wanted to actually be a better mother. I knew she had a lot of dealings to handle before being healed. Life was hard! I understood that. I never witnessed her on hard drugs. I was grateful for that because it would have reminded me of my mother and hurt me. I was proud of Jess for never doing pills or any hard drugs when she was living with me.

This new situation showed me how to be stronger in many ways. Being strong for not just two people but now five completed me. I made sure to cook and clean all the time. I wanted to show Jess how to be stable.

My poor baby Jess was coming from a very unstable life before we started creating ours. I know I made a difference in people's lives besides Jess, but she was the first time in a long time that I wanted to be stronger to guide her with love. She was fighting her own demons within her inner self. I knew drug addiction was very hard to battle within ourselves. The only real reason I felt I understood about drug addiction was from not having my mother my whole life because, of her meth addiction for over thirty years.

Drugs had caused my mother to up and abandon me when I was a young child. I truthfully was trying to save Jess from herself. I worked every day with Jess's emotions and inner feelings she had bottled up. I wanted to show her it was going to be okay by loving her hard. Her healing process was starting! I started to see a clear view change in this woman. A rush came over my body like a lightning bolt of joy.

Our love was one of a kind. I was her protector and her provider. I would never forget how beautiful we were together!

I appreciated Jess's family's respect they had for me because I provided stability for them. I had to realize some of my friend's actions were her own. I could not control her. I learned at that point I couldn't control anyone but, myself. Jess ended up calling Diabla to come and get her. I loved her and didn't want them to leave. I was so confused to what my next feelings would bring out of my pores.

I was hurt that they were gone. I was considered an emotional wreck at that time. It seemed that we had some things we had to work out eventually later on. It seemed that I wanted love bad! I wanted to be happy with myself at the end of the day.

I knew I had done the best I could for Jess and Jay by providing them with a different life that they had never had. At the end of the day it was never my doings I would take credit for. The Lord works in really mysterious loving ways. It was the Lord who does his work through his people on this earth. The love provided by the Lord is very consistent love that I had to realize would only come from one source with in me.

Even though I was considered single I had no room to date when Jess and her son was living at my dad Jerry's house.

We seemed oblivious to what relationship we really had. The night before she left I could never forget. Jess wanted things her way all the time.

I started getting annoyed with her trying to control me when she was raging drunk. I told her I was going to invite some girls over for a bomb fire.

She told me that no one was aloud over! I was dominant and couldn't stand not having things my way so I actually told jess to move up stairs. She freaked out on me, and got even drunker as the night went on. At that point we were both upset. All I could remember is arguing with jess almost the whole night. I was trying to make things right with her. I was done arguing with my friend. I loved her so much that I forfeited the fight and started chasing her around the house trying to resolve the issues we had.

Literally the realest love I had ever felt was that night with a friend who needed me as much as I needed her. We loved each other no matter what the circumstances were. In the morning the next day we both woke up with our heads throbbing. She had already called Diabla to come and pick her up from my house. I was very hurt at this point and had to except thing for what they were. It wasn't until after she was gone It really hit me that she wasn't sleeping next to me at night any more.

Each day love grew more when we were away from each other. She and I kept contact while she took jay up north to stay with her mom. The love I shared with Jess boosted up my energy to continue live with no regrets of having her live with me at all.

Chapter Twenty-Eight

After Jess and Jay left, I wasn't the only one that was hurt. My dad Jerry wouldn't get out of his bed for almost two weeks. He seemed just as heart-broken as I was. He yelled at me, telling me that I made her leave. I felt so bad when I saw him so sick the way he was. I was still having a rewind of Jess leaving.

I knew we had unfinished business that we had to attend to. We loved each other and didn't know what we were doing except loving one another. The key was we both loved hard once we found it for people. We would always share love that seemed to always balance our heart's pain from our past.

After that day I knew I had to stay focused on my daughter. I started working at the phone service store/tanning salon more. There was a private pre-school my daughter went to. My main focus was to follow God's lead for what was going to happen next.

I felt nature of my body when I would walk my daughter to school. Even though Jess was up north with her mom, I still stayed in contact with her on Facebook. I really had mixed emotions about the whole situation based on her actions. I was still sad though when I was home passing our hangout areas in the house. I had to be strong to get passed all of that.

The whole goal for me was to lose weight and live healthier. I stopped drinking for a while when Jess left. It seemed that drinking was something we did together. I would still drink occasionally to take me back to the memories that I shared with my two wild free-spirited friends.

I loved Jess no matter the circumstances of how far away she was. I knew one day she would come back from her mom's house.

I wanted to work hard to improve Kyla's life by making sure I was stable. I wanted everything to work out in the best way. As time surely passed, things seemed to slowly progress for the better. Our lives seemed to be in God's hands. Things started changing when my heart started building walls up to learn how to protect my self's emotions by use "boundaries."

My new friend's name was Piph. Even though she was almost five years younger than me, we got along for the most part. I started talking to her not knowing that later on overtime my heart would be tampered with as the walls would come down.

We ended up becoming good friends. Spent over time, a lot of memorable cute moments. Jess moved on and was talking to other people. She was very high spirited and loved people in such a way that reminded me of myself. At this time, I was juggling two part-time walking-distance jobs and having a one-and-a-half-year-old. I was actually able to balance everything I had to go on successfully. In my free time I would still work on my book. I wanted the world to read my story in such a way that it would move themselves to inspire a change. My goal was to help the world heal from their pain that could have been similar to mine.

I had the understanding that people would have hard criticism and judgment toward my life. I would deal with anything that would come my way no matter how the world judged me. I only cared in my heart truly how God viewed me and of the people I loved.

Later on in life, it was more important for me to put my heart into God's true feelings of my future. The only thing is, I didn't know what the Lord had in stored for me next. The more that the years, passed I could see myself picking up strong character traits that helped me protect myself and my daughter. I realized that time would soon be the beholder of why I was evolving into something beautiful. I wanted to be a better person. Soon, I would see myself for who I really was.

I made sure that my daughter was my first priority. I always wanted to express how much I loved her more than anything else in this world.

Over the next couple months, I started meeting new people to try to get my mind clear from the feelings of being abandoned by my friend. I always had a feeling that one day Jess would come back to me. Again I could have been wrong about her returning. By the time Jess did want to come home from up north, I wasn't feeling the need to want to help her or deal with her at all. I was repellent to her love at that point.

Even though I was mentally settling down, I didn't want to ignore my feelings of knowing that I would be hurt if I allowed Jess to come live with me again. I knew dealing with her leaving all over again would crush me.

My heart couldn't stand the thought of being emotionally hurt again. I couldn't emotionally detach myself to Jess, but instead, I reattach myself all in one feel. All I kept telling myself that time would hopefully heal me.

I didn't doubt for a moment that Jess loved me. I just knew she was struggling with knowing where to start loving. There were things my dear friend had to deal with on her own as in with in her inner self.

Everyone was different and similar in way or another. The next step was clear. I needed to save my money. I was getting some help through the state, but honestly, it never seemed good enough. The help from the state barely helped me make ends meet. I had to survive for now, not just for myself but for my child. I would never deny my dad Jerry a meal if I was cooking at home. I felt I was always caring enough to know I had love in my heart. My heart was ready to help love people through my gift of cooking.

I was very gifted in more ways than I ever imagined. It was sad, but I never fully gave myself enough credit on how well I handled my relationships. I didn't realize what I had to offer the world. I just kept thinking in my mind about one thing and that was surviving. Survival always seemed to cross my mind.

I was insecure being overweight at this time in my life after having my daughter. I weighed roughly a hundred and sixty-five pounds.

I felt very out of shape. I knew God had a greater plan for me. Even though I was learning about who God was, I was opening my heart to wanting a closer relationship with my higher power. I didn't know where my journey was going to end up going next.

I was very willing to appreciate my higher power along through the rest of the road. I felt that karma was real in our world. I felt like whatever you gave out in this universe as an energy would come back around. I kept focus on my past mistakes and knew, even though I couldn't change them, I would never forget how hard it was while I lived through it all.

Even though I had a Bible, I would only use it to randomly turn to a page to receive a message from God. I knew I wouldn't be able to feel him any other way.

I wanted to stay positive all the time. I felt that I would get nowhere if I didn't stay positive. I wanted to know one day more from God. I felt that there was a higher power greater than myself. I felt that there was no way I would have made it through the storm the way I had without God. There were too many times I was close to death. There were too many times where I was lost and feeling alone. When I finally changed my train of thought and really focused on the important things in life, that's when everything came into place for me spiritually. I felt very blessed to be alive. I never wanted my child to go through the things that I had gone through.

My goal at that point was to try and do my best with everything God laid in front of me. From one point to the next, I would take the love I had still inside of me and make it grow each day that I strived for my daughter's positive future. I knew what I wanted to do with my life. I had love inside of me still that wasn't going anywhere. My joy came from watching my daughter grow and advance each day.

My clearest moments of joy were watching different aspects of my daughter's life that my mother was not around for in my life. It gave me joy to know I loved my daughter. It gave me joy to know I loved myself enough to love what was mine. Watching my child grow and grow would give me strength that came only from the power of love I shared for her. My daughter's most precious moments as a baby so far had been her first steps and the moment she had first started talking on her own. I was so proud to have an advanced child.

My daughter was sent to me from God. Even though what the circumstances were, they didn't matter. I loved my daughter and who is my pride and joy. The love I had for my daughter only came from the power of God. To me it had seemed that the Lord had been the only one who had loved me through all my struggles and pain.

The Lord had seen all my struggles from the lowest to my highest achievement of positive abundance. I would usually keep my head on the right path but, still kept that gleam in my eye. I would continue to always keep my head in the clouds and my eyes focused on the night sky. It was me that God was staring back at all those times.

Even though I acted high and mighty with so much to say, I knew that there was so much more in spirituality that I needed to learn. I wanted to learn and was willing to hear God's vows for me whenever they came due. I still would never quite bow down to some of my personal friends on most topics. That was something I had been struggling with over the years.

Every year I seemed to grow in such a beautiful way. All I could do was appreciate my life and take things in for what they were. I was able to change my life for the better if I tried to follow a positive lead.

I was still learning to deal with my own issues. I was human like everyone else around me. My heart beat just like the next person's. I started to pray more after that day. I knew there were more powerful things out in the worlds universe then myself. I wanted answers to how I was feeling. I wanted to keep my faith in something greater and more powerful than my selfish needs.

I knew I wasn't perfect. Although I didn't know exactly what God was, I was starting to learn that over experience and time.

The God that I created in my mind was a loving great, who loved me in return harder and stronger than any love out in the world that was afford.

Jess said she was coming to visit me from up north. I was feeling so many different emotions. I loved her so much and wanted to see her really bad. I just didn't want to deal with the chaotic ways she carried with her at times in her life. Although Jess was coming to see me, I was still remembering the feeling of pain when she left the first time. I did not want to feel that pain ever again.

I was willing to push her away from me, as a mechanism, so I wouldn't get hurt again. I was very cautious with my heart. That week Jess ended up coming into our area to visit all of her family and friends. I was very excited to see her and Jay, her son. I loved them so much and felt as if something was missing without them while they were gone.

Even though Jess was visiting, she wasn't staying at my house. There was only so much I could tolerate from Jess.

It seemed that Jess had her own agenda when she came down from up north to visit.

I didn't know what to do for her. I was in such a bind. The love we shared for one another was there, but I just felt as if we were both living two different lives.

We both two beautiful dreamers. I would always have kept myself searching in Jess's eyes for love. When the light in her would shine, it would shine bright. I loved that she still was a fighter and had love left in her heart too when she was feeling as if she was being loved correctly.

I loved watching Jess's eyes soar like mine would when I was in a daze dream. We talked about what Jess had been up to while she had been gone. We conversed about so much that day!

Up north, she was staying with her mom until they got into it, and then she started staying with a friend of hers and her brother. When she came back down from up north, she went right away to stay with this girl she was friends with in Wayne County. The chick and her got extremely close and she ended up getting out of line with the woman when she was staying there. Jess had a way of running her mouth when she was drunk. Unfortunately, it was something she couldn't help but to do. It was part of Jess's personality. Jess ended up getting punched in the eye by the chick and ended up leaving with the chick's brother. Funny thing was it was a small world. I knew the chick's brother from back in the day when I used to be at Old School's house.

The whole situation Jess put herself in was a mess that I wanted to stay out of.

Chapter Twenty-Nine

Now I was working at the corner liquor store right along with the tanning salon at Metro Pcs part time. Thank God all my jobs were in the same plaza. It was a real life blessing that God was providing before my eyes. I would work from one job to the next throughout the day. In between working full time, I was focused on taking care of my daughter as well as I could.

My heart was a child's heart still. I viewed things to be normal with a fairy tale ending. I was aware after a while that it was a dream that only the person living the dream could change themselves. Thanking God every day for loving me was all I could do to stay appreciative.

I really cared about my future. I wanted things that occurred in my past to make me stronger. That was the thing I didn't quite know what was going on with myself. The different experiences I had lived were actually making me stronger. I wanted my past to make, and the person reading my book stronger as well. I know that everyone is different, but some of the ways I handled my situations and learned about myself helped me become stronger than ever.

I learned that love is all around you if you just open your heart to it. Even though I loved Jess, I wanted to keep myself a great person by having boundaries. A lot had changed around this time. I had met a guy who was interested in getting to know me. We met randomly and I felt that he had been a blessing. I needed someone really bad to watch my daughter.

It was extremely hard for me to find people who I could trust. I took a leap of faith in this situation by praying to God that this new guy could help watch my daughter and keep her safe. I couldn't trust anyone and felt like I was always looking over my shoulder.

Around this time, my daughter's Godfather was in a relationship with a woman he was seeing on the Westside of Detroit. She was helping him watch my daughter sometimes and I wasn't notified or aware of it until later on. I wasn't in too much of a predicament to complain as long as my child was safe, which she was.

I didn't know what situation was to come out of this new guy being around. One thing I did know was that from my childhood abuse issues, I couldn't trust anyone fully. I was able to go meet Louis's mom. I was very pleased to see how fast my daughter took a liking to her. Louis was helping transport me to and from work. He also keep an eye on my princess at my adopted dads while I was at work.

One day that all ended when Louis flipped out on my adopted dad's child's mom for writing with a marker on some of our belongings in the bathroom. She was writing some weird name on it. He was so irritated! He flipped out when I was at work. I got a phone call from my dad saying I needed to rush over as soon as possible or he would call the police. I ended up getting out of work a little bit early and rushing right home! When I got home, I saw a huge hole in the kitchen wall.

Throughout all the cautious that had happened, my main concern was making sure my daughter was safe. I was happy to see she was okay. I grabbed her and put her in my arms. We gathered our stuff for the night to go stay at Louis's mother's house. I was happy to see the police weren't called. I talked with my dad and told him to calm down! I told him we were leaving for the night and we would be back. Everyone needed time to relax.

Louis had already called his mother and warned her that we were all coming.

I didn't really know what was going on here in this situation besides my adopted dad's kid's mother's mental state was a bit off. Everything else was seeming to work out in God's own way. It seemed to me like racism was involved here.

My adopted dad didn't seem racist, but he had been through a lot in the city of Detroit with different cultures of life. I think that my adopted dad's kid's mother was a bit racist or maybe not. Louis was a darker African American young man. I didn't really understand what was happening here. I knew my adopted dad was more anti-racist against people in general. I don't think color really took effect in his perception, then again, I didn't know what to think.

Louis's mother had cooked a roast. He told me every Sunday she would cook a pork roast, with some sides of baked macaroni and cheese, collard greens, and cornbread. I really enjoyed eating her food. It would really fill me up and give me a sense of comfort. It was nice having a mother figure to look up to. I had a good feeling that everything was going to work out for the best. My daughter got close fast to Louis mom.

My daughter was still very little. She was a little over two years old at this time. I loved watching my daughter learn more as each day passed. I could tell my daughter was going to be something great when she was older.

One night I got a babysitter so I could go out and hang out with Diabla and Jess. We finally all met up at Diabla's apartment. Jess had been back for a while now.

Diabla was still dating one of the top hustlers in Detroit. What's crazy is they called him D. He had family and friends that loved him everywhere. I wasn't accustomed really to what type of situation Diabla got herself into but I would soon learn. From what I heard from my home girls is that he had a lot of money. I wasn't worried about the money he had to offer. From all the little things I heard about him, I really didn't care for his company at all. I was still respectful of his presence and never disrespected him when we were all put into a situation where we all were hanging out that night.

I never wanted to jeopardize my friendship with Diabla based on him or anyone else ever. I could tell from all our encounters Diabla and I had a different special bond that I could only identify with her. I left my cell phone on Diabla's kitchen table. Jess, Diabla, and I jumped in D's all-black Cadillac truck. I sat in the back left hand side.

D was driving and Diabla was in the passenger seat. D's boy and Jess sat in the back behind me. The more we all drove around,

I really wanted to go back to the apartment to get my cell phone. Once I complained enough, they finally stopped back around to her apartment so I could grab my phone. I had been a bit emotional that day based on my own life events. The drunker we all got after eight bottles of Moet. Jess and I argued most of the night.

The guy that was hanging with Jess most of the night said that we seemed like we were having a lover's quarrel. We all started partying from one bar to the next in the day time and ended up back at the apartment at ten at night. I was a little nervous driving all around the city of Detroit going to all kind of different hood strip clubs.

The first strip club we went to was called Saph's. I was actually down to have a good time. I just ended up drinking way too much that night. It was interested in given a chance to see all different types of entertainers. The waitress was thick and cute with beautiful brown skin with hair that was so long! I was having a great time so far. After a while, I got so drunk that I ended going to the chicken place across the street to order fifty pieces.

I was so intoxicated that I wasn't aware that my friends were across the street in the club. I was calling people to pick me up feeling that they had left me. I honestly think that the liquor hit me while I was waiting for the chicken to be cooked at the fast-food place. I had a survival mechanism come all over my body. I felt that I was very scared to what was going to happen next.

The dancer who came to our table ended up coming across the street to buy some chicken when she saw me looking helpless. She ended up flirting with me and crossing me back across the street, telling me that my friends were over there still. I ran fast across one of the main roads to get to the club holding the woman's hand. I felt like that was a gift from God getting me safe back to my friends so I could get home. When we all got back to Diabla's house by ten, everyone was drunk.

After listening to Jess nagging me all night, I had enough. I started fighting Jess frustrated on how our whole night went wasted. We actually fought each other, but the moment I kicked her with my boots on, our other friend Diabla jumped in it by punching me. I looked at Diabla like 'wow', I couldn't believe she had punched me over her. I started feeling a sense of hurt take are over my body when I reacted in a strong way. I instantly hit Diabla in her forehead without a thought.

There we were all three fighting for no real reason but the fact we were drunk arguing over petty stuff. I was so irritated by then! D ended up putting Diabla in her room. We all said good night and went to sleep. Jess and D's friend slept on one couch and I slept alone on the other one.

Chapter Thirty

After we all fought it out, we ended up saying sorry before we all went to sleep. We really didn't talk, though everyone was tired and drunk. It seemed like a crazy night. We were all best friends that loved each other. I couldn't even think about the idea of us hurting one another. The alcohol was taking over the best of us. I felt like the alcohol was the devil. I would never forget that day because the most significant part of the night was when Jess woke me up at six in the morning when everyone was still in bed. She woke me up trying to tell me something. As much as I loved her, I was still very annoyed with her.

I decided to wake up and listen to her. I was really sorry when I saw the bruises all over her body from fighting me. She told me she was sorry for leaving my house. It was our chance to finally really talk. I was willing to hear her out for what she had to say. I was intrigued with knowing the truth of how she really felt in this situation. She told me that she loved me. She told me she finally figured me out. Said it took her some time and she couldn't understand me. Then she said it dawned on her in the morning.

I was happy to hear the words come out of her mouth. Jess said she finally understood that I just wanted to be loved. At first I thought she was still drunk, but listening to her speak the words that were true, I knew that something beautiful came over her.

I was surprised to waking up to Jess calling me baby, sweetly telling me to wake up. Even though I just looked at Jess with confusion of wanting to know what she wanted, I finally heard what I had asked for from her the entire time. It definitely was worth waking up at six in the morning to hear her out. I told her how sorry I was repeatedly.

I just let Jess talk to me while I didn't say a word until she got her point across to me. As the words slipped out of her mouth, "I finally get you," a spark inside me lit up. Even though I was still waking up drunk, I listened to my friend's words. She was teasing me telling me to kiss her calling me baby over and over again. I didn't want to kiss her because, I was still partly mad at her.

I felt bad seeing the bruises all up and down her legs from her fighting with me and falling down drunk throughout the night. After that we made up. I never wanted to fight her in the first place. She told me she was drunk and very sorry for pushing things to a fight. She admitted she egged it on and pushed me to react. I took responsibility for my own actions. I told her I loved her that I wasn't trying to use her in any way. We had basically talked about all our issues we had been going through. We had unfinished business to attend to. I told her I was still drunk. Everything I was telling her was true. I believed in the saying that went around which was a drunk man never told any lies. I wasn't telling any lies. Even if Jess didn't want to admit it, I knew she was still drunk as well. I believed Jess at that moment about wanting to be loved. I knew that we were both pouring our hearts to each other.

The truth was finally getting out. It seemed a bad situation had turned into a positive outcome. Listening to Jess making it clear to me that she wanted to be loved as much as I had made it clear that she loved me. I made sure to make it clear to her how much I had loved her too. Jess was never going to leave my life. I knew this was something for sure. She loved me and would always be around. The perception I had was that Jess would always be in my world.

At that moment, my perception was focused on being loved. It was true Jess was right. That was exactly what Jess was pointing out to me. In life there was so much I wanted to learn. It seemed that I wasn't alone in not wanting to end up alone in life. I knew Jess didn't want to be alone either.

The words from her saying over and over again that she loved me comforted me as she looked at me passionately into my eyes. I felt that everything was controlled by the Lord above. Everything happens for a reason. I still held my ground and never kissed her in her mouth though. I didn't trust Jess when it came to stuff like that. I wasn't clear on what she had done that night or before I had seen her.

I was sitting next to her when she called her child's father on the phone. She laughed and laughed while she told him how I kicked her butt. She told him that it was her fault. I was very happy to know that she wasn't mad at me. She told him that she was drunk, talking crazy and that's why we ended up fighting. I was feeling my anxiety go off.

I was ready to finally go home to Louis's house and get ready for the day. I called Louis to come and pick me up so I could rush home to see my daughter and shower. I told Jess and Diabla that I would see them later after I went home for a little while. I felt just as crazy as my two best friends were.

People said that I loved really hard. I could never see the friendship I shared with them ever ending. When I came back over to Diabla's house later that night, we all sat around talking about the night previous. We all laughed and laughed, because we didn't know how to feel about the whole situation even occurring.

Each one of us got brave that night we fought with each other. That next night as we all hugged and talked, it showed us how loyal we were toward keeping our friendship tight. We all felt stupid because we didn't know why we were fighting in the first place. After talking about the night before we all realized we were a trio of trouble who wanted love. We all had our own version of the night before. I was just happy to see no one was mad at each other.

I felt comfort knowing that I was loved. I was happy that the love we all shared was mutual between us. When I did go home earlier that day to shower, all I could do was stare at my daughter and kiss her. I was glad to be alive. I wasn't being dramatic it was just that people died every day in Detroit, and here we were enjoying it driving around, drinking. I know other people were scared to even go into the city of Detroit. A lot of people stayed out of the city. There was just too much going on that had many people alarmed and aware of their surroundings.

Chapter Thirty-One

The night we all partied, part of me felt like I was kidnapped because D was nervous about having me hangout with them. He was successful and kept his circle very small. I couldn't blame him for being paranoid. I could tell that they were testing my loyalty because D had doubt that I was going to stay loyal to Diabla. When D was worried about my loyalty, I was happy to prove to him wrong. I stayed honest no matter what came my way. For the first time in a long time, I had felt that my life was out of my control. I was feeling that God had my heart but the alcohol was taking over my mind. I felt that alcohol was truly sent from the devil himself to destroy lives. I knew that the devil was trying to knock me off my focus. My main focus was on God and raising my daughter at the best of my ability. I knew that God was the only one who could feel your heart and hear your deepest thoughts. Besides everything I had ever been through so far in my life, I knew the only way to work through the feeling that life brought into my life was to stay positive and be ready for a chance to change. I had some principles that I would live by. I was trying to work through all the negative encounters I had so far and was willing to do it with any means possible. I knew I had to put God first in order to heal from some thing's I had been through. I felt that once I put God first, everything else would fall into place. I was thinking hard about how God was still there watching over me. God was watching over my child too! I was so grateful to have a close relationship with God. Ever since my daughter was born, I was focused on having a better relationship with God. My priorities were in gear. I knew I had to make sacrifices to provide for my child's future. Partying was the last thing that was on my mind. I was working up at the store when Jess walked in with her son. A couple minutes later, two old familiar faces walked into the store. It was K.B and Stunner. I hadn't seen them in years. Jess was telling her son to say hi to me, referring to me as his stepmom. I could tell she had been drinking before she came into the store. I was frustrated with her because I couldn't leave work to tell her to come to my house. She was basically in survival mode. I was very stuck in between living and surviving myself. She asked me to go to Hamtramck with her to go to K.B. and Stunner's house. I knew that it would be a conflict of interest based on my daughter being Chip's daughter and that's all our old crew of friends. I was behind the counter and could not leave early. I didn't want to go over to their house. I made sure to express that to Jess.

Stunner tried to talk to me while I was behind the counter at the register. I wasn't interested at all in hearing what game she was trying to spit my way. I wasn't the same old Cali that they once knew. I was really irritated with Jess at this point. I knew the customers I was serving at the register could tell I was super irritated by this time. The neighbor boy that was hanging out that summer with Jess and I when we were having our backyard bomb fires who lived next door to my adopted dad's house witnessed the whole thing that happened to me while Jess was in the store. The boy's advice to me was to not let anything phase me. She was tripping and acting loud in my job. I was getting nervous with her making a commotion in front of my coworkers. I didn't want to lose my job over some petty drama. I grabbed my phone and texted Jess right away. I wanted to know what she was thinking by coming into my job. I was so angry with her. I told her that I wasn't going to be going out to Hamtramck. I told her that she was tripping by building a relationship with her girl's brother. I was under pressure trying to serve customers. Since K.B's sister kicked her out, she wanted to come back and live with me at my dad's. The only thing wrong with her idea was that I was moved out staying with Louis and his mom already. I couldn't handle living with Jess again. Part of me wanted to love Jess again, but my heart was scared to jump right into things again with her. I had already made arrangements in my life elsewhere. Jess was catching me in a cross road of my life. Part of me wanted to leave Jess in the situation she had got herself into. I was feeling that the situation I was in was going to teach her a lesson. I took responsibility for pushing K.B and Jess together by not allowing her to come and live back at my dad's with me.

I would get periodic phone calls after that from Jess. It seemed that K.B wasn't good for Jess. He was enabling her by drinking with her all the time. They enabled each other in many ways. Jess and I had a couple crazy encounters where she would call me to pick her up. I would remove her from any bad situations that I could whenever she called me for help. Her son stayed with her family while Jess stayed at Stunner's grandma's house with K.B. in Hamtramck. Everyone loved Jay. He was a smart little boy. The twin's raised him for jess for most of his life. I was happy to see how bright jay was. I was very impressed with how jay was fast at responding to doing whatever he was asked to do. He was a blessing from God. I was glad to see Jay's mind wonder. I had never seen such a smart boy in my life. God was great! I could tell that our little boy had a bright future ahead of him. I was determined to make sure he was successful with whatever his heart desired for him to become. I planned to stay in Jess and Jay's life. I knew Jess and I would have to stay on a friend level in order to keep boundaries between us. Regardless she would always hold a special place in my heart. I heard she hadn't seen her son for a little while since she had been staying with K.B in Hamtramck. Jess was always trying to get me to come check out her new home. I told her that I already knew them and I didn't have any interest in hanging out with them. I told her that was part of my past and I was only focused on the future. Jess needed money really bad, so she started dancing in the strip club. An agent for the club on the east side had helped her get a dance license that costed her two hundred dollars. The agent from the club fronted Jess the money for her dance license. The agent who helped her had been in the industry for over twenty years.

He was an agent also for a few other bars. Once he was able to get her a dance card, she started working right away. At the time I was still overweight. I wasn't mentally or physically prepared to start working in that type of environment with the size that I was. Jess actually went into work and did well at the strip club. I was proud to say she made almost nine hundred dollars that night. That was really good for her first night at the bar, I thought. I was happy for Jess for trying hard to have a positive outcome. Jess still talked to her child's father almost every day. Other people in jess's life were also proud of her. I would always love Jess regardless of her choices. Jess and her child's father were best friends. I loved Jess wholeheartedly. Jess called me a couple of times to pick her up and drop her off from a couple bad situations she had got herself into.

Chapter Thirty-Two

One time she was stranded at a hotel at Eight Mile and Gratiot. Any time Jess needed me I would jump to her rescue. Out of everyone in her life besides Diabla she knew I would always be there for her. One day, Jess called me randomly on the phone in frantic. Even though I was frustrated with her, I answered the phone for her anyways. All I could hear was Jess breathing, saying, "Baby, you have to come get me! This mother-f-err raped me!" I was in shock by this time, panicking, telling Jess to tell me where she was so I could pick her up. Jess immediately said she was at Taco Bell on Twenty-Three Mile. Even though I was caught up in my own world, I stopped what I was doing.

There I was running to her rescue again. This time I picked her up, I felt pained to know what she was dealing with. She said, some guy she met off the Internet who lived in Algonac named Steve had picked her up to take the ferry to Mackinac Island. She said once they were hanging out in a house, he slipped something in her alcohol.

Jess said it was some sort of date rape medicine because she ended up falling asleep. She said when she woke up her body felt torn apart, and she found blood in her underwear. The only reason Jess had gone to meet this guy was to try and get some money from him.

The guy with the red pickup truck lived on the island. Instead of Jess waiting for someone to go with her, she went alone. When I picked Jess up, she was wearing jeans, with brown boots and a black tank top. I still couldn't forget the look on Jess's face when I picked her up. When I pulled up to Taco Bell, I was so scared. I was nervous. What all had happened to Jess. Thank God her son had been at her mother and aunt's house. I was feeling overwhelmed. Glad that Jess had a lot of love for her son. I was grateful he was safe. Her aunt and mother always took great care of Jay. I was glad she had them to help her with him. I knew it was hard being a single mom. I drove Jess straight over to her mom and aunt's house.

I talked with Jess about what happened. Jess was trying to make money and ended up getting drugged then raped. She told me they only had a couple drinks and then she felt her body pass out. Listening to her tell me the story I got really scared for her. I felt a quiver all over my body as she told me the story. It seemed that I was always trying to save this woman when we got to her family's house, she started getting wound up in the kitchen, screaming as she told her aunt what had happened to her. Her family told her to try and stay quite because her son was there.

I watched her explain to her aunt how she was raped. Her aunt seemed to act as if she didn't believe her. Jess even took her bloody underwear off to show her. I believed her problem was her family didn't really believe her, because she had been away from her son.

I still believed her though regardless if anyone else believed her or not. I watched my friend try to make her point to her family but not getting anywhere.

Jess's family lived off the lake. I loved it where her family lived. I tried keeping Jess calm she argued with her family. She was starting to get upset with her aunt. I told Louis to take Jay and my daughter outside to play. There was too much craziness that I didn't want any of the kids to hear.

Jess told me that she had a warrant out for her arrest so she couldn't go to the doctors. My poor baby was so scared to file a police report because she didn't want to go to jail. I was honestly a wreck going through the movements with my girl I would always love.

Jess asked me to examine her vagina. I was really nervous about looking at her down there. She wanted me to examine her to make sure she wasn't cut. I knew I wasn't a doctor. I know there was only so much I could do for her. I told her to calm down. As I spread her legs, I went down and looked. I will never forget the sick smell that came out. The smell of smelling raw and bloody skin tissue made me sick. I was so sickened I told her to get up and get in the shower. She asked me to come into the bathroom with her to wash her and calm her down. I heard her repeat herself over and over again, saying this bastard raped her. She started crying and screaming! I just kept washing her, telling her everything was going to be all right. Jess was so beat up. I could see her body was bruised up. I just held her and washed her. I was so sickened by all this. I knew she was really going through it.

All I wanted to do was make her pain go away but I couldn't. Jess was in so much pain emotionally. She was an emotional wreck. I was so angry! She actually had the guy's debit card with his picture on it. I told her that once she cleared up her warrants, she would be able to go and make a report against him.

After that point I knew there was nothing we couldn't handle together. It was no shock that we went through hell together. It was even clearer to me that we had God to protect us. We had love in our hearts.

Love was the power of all positive energy. Out of all the bad things we both had been through, love was the potion of healing. I loved Jess and all I could do was love her past her pain. We were all steamed out. I even shed a couple tears with her. I just kept scrubbing her pain off her body.

I just kept telling her eventually the guy would get karma for what he had done to her. There were a lot of sick people out there in the world who would cause other people pain. That guy was sick in the head. Anyone who would have to drug a woman in order to have sex with them is disgusting. I told Jess over and over again that I loved her. I reassured her not to worry that she would get passed this dark time in her life. I went through a time in my life where I was sickened to my stomach by the thought of this happening. I didn't want to leave Jess's side. I told Jess to make sure that she stayed off the Internet. I wanted Jess to settle down. I knew we had a lot of fighting left in us to make it through any situation. We all decided to go over to Diabla's apartment for the most of the weekend. It seemed like when we were all together, we were all balanced out. I was attached to both of them in a way that captured my heart.

The friendship we all shared was unique. I told Louis that I needed to spend time with my family. They were a part of my family I had built in Michigan. The relationships that I had with my two friends was amazing.

It was great to feel love in my heart for another person. It was blessed to have them in my life especially since it was the same friendship in return. We all drank our problems away. Well, that's what we thought we were doing together. I was blessed to receive the same type of love in my heart from two friends who gave me the same type of love in return.

Louis and his mother kept safe watch over my daughter while I was gone. I was grateful not to worry about my child's safety. All day long we all would play music. Our dreams would be in our future loving one another. I ended up going home after I knew Jess was okay. She was planning on going back out to Hamtramck. I gave her a hug. Our hugs always seemed to be very long.

When Jess and I hugged, it always felt like we didn't want to let go of each other. I was very stressed out. Part of how I was feeling was traumatized, but I had so many life events that made me feel like I was bulletproof for different situations. It felt like I could take on any person's troubles. I could adapt quickly to other people's life styles. I went home after that to attend to my child.

After leaving, Jess and I stayed in contact. I stayed focused on my daughter more than anything else in this world. In my free time, I enjoyed cooking for Louis and my daughter. It was nice getting close to Louis but I could tell I really didn't know what I wanted to do.

My perception was that I was still young. I didn't know where the future would end up for me. I could feel the world staring at me. I started to plan my life out. I knew that from what I learned, life was based on choices and faith with a little chance. No one ever knew where they would end up. I had so much to learn. It seems like I was changing over and over again with time. I wanted more out of life so I kept my faith for a greater life. I held onto my heart's energy to help me strive for my dreams.

My heart stayed with helping people out any way that I could with using boundaries. I wanted to be a better me. Time had passed by so fast. I was out with Louis's car the night before when I got a call from Jess, saying to come out and see her in Hamtramck. I told her I didn't want to drive far out that way but I would try. I ended up at one of my ex-girlfriend's houses the night before. I felt so bad the next day when I got a weird text message from Diabla saying Jess was dead. I thought this was a joke when I first saw it. The text message didn't register clearly at first.

I ended up rereading the text. When I couldn't stand it any longer, I called Diabla's cell phone to find out what had happened to Jess. When I called Diabla, she answered after the fourth ring. I was in disbelief, hearing Diabla say Jess was dead out of her own mouth. I instantly hung up the phone. I could tell by the tone in her voice that she was not joking at all. It was true—Jess was really dead!

At that moment I knew something tragic had happened. When I called Diabla back on the phone, she told me that she got a phone call from K.B. early in the morning, saying that Jess wasn't breathing. They all had been drinking and partying the night before this happened. I wasn't aware of all the details from her death.

I started screaming. I felt so lost and empty. I threw my cell phone on the ground. I was so hurt into my best friend was gone. I felt weakness in my heart the moment it all soaked in my brain. It felt like someone was snatching my heart out.

Once I started screaming and crying, my daughter heard me. She started screaming and crying right along with me. It was a real mother-daughter connection. My daughter could feel my pain. I was so hurt that tears kept flowing. There was nothing I could do but let the tears flow. Jess was my best friend and I thought she would never leave my side but I was wrong about that.

Only God had control of my friend's fate. I asked God why would this happen to such a young soul. I was feeling confused to why God took Jess to heaven and not me. I had many close-to-death experiences and couldn't figure out why God took her. I was distraught from not being able to say good-bye to Jess. After finding out about Jess's death, I took things day by day. I missed her so much.

Every day that passed, I would miss her more. The next day, after finding out what happened, I went out to Jess's aunt and twin mother's house. Everyone at her family's house was very distraught. I picked Jess's son up to take him to get ice cream.

Jess's family was doing the best that they could with what they had based on what was going on. This was a time in Jess's family when she passed all who didn't get along ended up coming together for her funeral. It seemed like many families had their in's and out's.

I had my own experiences with my family so I could easily understand hers. That day Jay and I hung with my friend Piph. She helped comfort Jay. After I dropped Piph off, I went to hang out with Rissa. My friend Rissa grabbed Jay up in her arms and cuddled him. As I glanced in my rearview mirror at Jay, I was worried about him. I watched tears flow down the little man's face while he made little whimpers. My heart was crushed, watching her son so distraught. I didn't know what else to do in this situation but talk to Jay. I asked Jay if he knew what happened to his mother. He then said, "she died."

I was saddened to see this four-year-old child so hurt. It was hard for a child to be torn from his mother. I was a mother, just like Jess was, so I could understand how painful this was for Jay. I couldn't imagine my daughter feeling pain of me not coming home to her. All I could do was hug Jay to comfort him, telling him that it was going to be okay. I told him I loved him and I would always be here for him. Jess being gone was affecting everyone. I started opening my eyes to the world. My heart started molding like an old sponge.

I was feeling down and out but tried to pull it together. I ended up taking Jay back home. I didn't want to drop him off, but I told him I would see him again soon. After kissing Jay goodnight and telling him how much I loved him when I was leaving, my eyes gleamed right along with the brightest star. I was right where I wanted to be by the lake looking up at the stars. I was looking for answers from God. I just kept staring harder and harder wondering if my prayers would be answered.

The sky was pitch-dark black. I lived a distance away from where we were. I was still going through my own emotions from Jess being gone. Even if she wasn't living with me, she was always a phone call away. Now it seemed like she was lost and I couldn't find her. There was much love shared between me and Jess.

I never met someone with such a beautiful heart like Jess had concealed. Jess's child's father and I didn't come together as friends until after she was gone. Her child's father was really hurt by all of this too. The first time we all hung out was when he was staying at his cousin's house and I stopped by over there with my daughter to see Jay. He was excited to see us. That night while we were all hanging out was one of the first times I had ever felt Jess's spirit strongly around. The house I felt her in was her kid's father's cousin's house where I had actually been introduced to Jess by Diabla. I didn't want to ignore her presence.

After that high spiritual connection with Jess in that house, I felt that Jess was still on earth in spirit. After that moment, I started feeling my friend's presence all around me on a daily basis. It was very intense being able to feel my friend spirit around me. I wasn't ready to let her go. I was still distraught and always would be. I don't know what would heal me faster at this point then time.

The love I shared with Jess was one of the realest love I had ever had with another person other than my child. Our love would last a lifetime. Love was powerful and still lived in our hearts. I tried to fill my heart from being shattered by hanging out with other people.

God had stepped in to help me get through this hard time. The day of Jess's funeral, I went to Hamtramck to the house she died in. In my mind, I wanted to know the truth of what happened to her. I wanted answers and K.B. wanted a ride to the funeral so it seemed like everything was going to work out. When I got to the house, I could feel my friend's spirit. K.B. was still living in the house.

I had Rissa drive me because I was planning on drinking that day. I was in the house where Jess had last called it her home. I asked K.B. to start from the beginning and tell me what happened to my girl. K.B. told me that Jess went to work at the strip club that night. She told K.B. that after the club she went to see a friend who gave her a sack of pills. I found out from the time that Jess started dancing she ended up dabbling back with drugs and alcohol. I stayed distant from Jess mainly because of that reason, sat there and beat myself up about not allowing Jess to come back to my adopted dad's to live there. If I could have let her come back there, maybe she would still be alive.

My heart was very much torn. I was torn beyond all feelings. It was hard for me to have a spiritual connection with Jess's spirit. I started missing Jess so much that it was a point in my life where I started to drink more alcohol to try and mask the pain. Jess and I would drink together in our passed. Both Jess and I had comfort as we felt warm hit our throats as the whiskey was poured into our body's.

Usually women who were neglected drank to try and cope with the pain that came from their past abuses. It seemed that something that was extremely bad for us brought us closer together. I wanted to feel something that would calm my heart down. Around this time in my life I cried a lot.

I was destined to know what happened to Jess before she passed away. Saddened to say I was so intoxicated I never made it out of the car for the funeral.

My next turn in life wasn't a surprise at all.

One night, I was meeting some friends at a club in Pontiac when I drove myself there reassuring myself that I wasn't going to drink. I was wrong about that when I laid eyes on a beautiful Mia who was Dominican and Mexican. I was lost for words when Mia spoke to me, telling me everything that I wanted to hear at the bar.

Mia was extremely charming, and with one smile, she had me smiling right along with her. That night she ended up buying me drink after drink. She was really beautiful, telling me that she would help take care of my daughter. She told me everything that I wanted to hear. She was very aware of her latest achievements and made sure to point them out. I enjoyed listening to her, but as the drinks started kicking in, I was attracted to her curves. I enjoyed listening to Mia speak a little bit of Spanish. Although I loved hearing her speak, I met her off of lust at first sight. By the fifth shot of alcohol, I was drunk. Mia knew the bartender and he was making my drinks really strong. I was trying to show Mia how strong I was when I did a dumb thing. I ended up picking Mia up when I was in heels I twisting my ankle.

 I felt so stupid doing that, but I was drunk. Earlier that night this guy I was acquainted with met up with me at the bar. He ended up showing me a pistol he had just gotten. I had a really nervous feeling about the guy showing me his gun. The guy kept saying he wanted to drive me home and to leave the car there at the bar.

 The chick Mia said she was going to follow me home. I was so drunk I really shouldn't have been trying to drive myself home like that. I ended up on the wrong freeway toward the opposite way home. I looked behind me and I saw a car following me.

 I thought the car following me was the girl Mia, I was wrong! I started feeling my eyes slip into sleep. I then pulled off the side of the road. When I pulled over, I saw a car pull over with me. The car that followed me from the bar was the guy with the gun. Only thing is the guy wasn't alone this time. The guy had at least four other foreign guys with him. He came right up to my car and snatched the keys out of the ignition through my driver's side window that was down. I was drunk, getting sick, demanding him to give me my keys back. In this situation I felt like God sent me an angel to save me from a close to death experience.

 My vision was blurry after driving for a while. I didn't know what would happen next. I remember punching the guy in the face and wrestling him for my keys. After pushing the guy toward the freeway, he then called the police on me. The person riding with him took my ID. He wanted me to get into his car but I refused. Even though I was intoxicated I knew not to get into his car with all those guys. I didn't know how he kept up following me all the way onto the wrong freeway.

 The police came to see what was going on. Even though I passed the line walking test, the officer could still tell I was drunk. The guy handed my keys to the officer. I was getting angry. The police officer ended up taking me to jail. I was so upset sitting in jail. I didn't know what would happen next. I knew I had to wait to be boiled out. Thank God Louis's mother had come to bond me out of jail.

I instantly started crying and kissed my baby when I saw them when I was being released. When I got my phone back as I was walking up to my house, I got a weird text message, saying, "I hope you're okay." It was from the guy that called the police on me. I was super annoyed by this time and didn't reply to the guy.

Everything started making sense. I had started understanding everything. It had seemed that I had been blessed to be alive.

Chapter Thirty-Three

Things started to make sense. I looked at the situation as a blessing because who would have known what would have happened to me if I would have gotten into the car with all those guys or kept driving drunk on the freeway. It didn't seem good look my perspective.

I cut all ties with the that guy after that. I was really happy that Louis's mom bailed me out because I didn't have a solid relationship with my mom. I was grateful to have a strong woman by my child's side. I felt the Lord's presence all the way home that day shining on me with his light through my car window. I sat in the backseat with my daughter. I was glad to see Louis wasn't that mad at me anymore for getting his car impounded. Louis still seemed mad at me but didn't express that. He just seemed happy that I was home. I kept thanking God over and over again. I still felt a little lost.

I showered, scrubbing the days I spent in jail off me. I was in a holding cell in jail for most of the time I was locked up. I was struggling with myself. I was feeling so hurt and I had to get myself out of that state of mind.

Time would only tell what was going to happen next. I had a court date coming up. I was hurt inside from my past. When Jess was alive, she made me feel as if I helped her follow her dreams. She actually started writing her own book about her life before she died. I was happy to know that while she was alive, I inspired her to live better.

Jess was one of the many people that I was able to help through the love I had to offer to them. I was glad that my heart crossed over to her and many others over time. The next life event that would occur for me was getting sick from drinking. I didn't see this coming. I was at a great friend's house when I was feeling myself vulnerably sick. I was throwing up for six hours.

My drinking was going to change my life forever and I didn't even know it. After that day, I was driving in the city of Warren drunk. It was a rough time in my life. It had been almost three weeks after I had gone to jail and caught my first drinking while intoxicated. My feelings of being hurt seeped through me by my poor actions. This time when I went to jail I sat in there. In jail, people knew my friend Jess who had passed away.

Jess had such a story of her own that needed to be told. I was proud of her even in her transitioning weak points. I would always love Jess no matter what her journey led. When my original court date came up for driving while intoxicated, I was now facing two charges. I was feeling like a wrecked ship. Before going to jail, I was diagnosed with a gall bladder, running at four percent. When I went to jail in Macomb County, I was extremely sick and had been taking photonics. Being in jail was one of the worse experiences of my life.

In the holding cell, there were black maggots in the sinks. I was so disgusted I tried my hardest not to drink the water in jail. I was throwing up in the holding cell. When I told one of the nurses after passing out for hours to please get me to a hospital, she denied me that right to go to the hospital.

There were witnesses of other people who were incarcerated who heard me screaming for help. I ended up writing down all the women's names who had witnessed what I was going through.

Many different people told me that it was illegal for the jail to deny me medical treatment when I was diabetic. I could have died in jail because my sugar was acting up. I remember the nurse didn't give me my medicine either.

I kept throwing up repeatedly. Everyone that was in the holding cell with me was very terrified for me. Life was really changing for me. I felt that life was what you made out of it but also was out of our control. I felt that God was in control of our journey. Some things in life happen to people that is out of our control. Things I felt happened based on people's actions and perception on life. I felt that people's actions changed the course of how peaceful life could have been for them.

Many people do not understand or see what happens to them until God humbles them by removing the person out of the situation they are in. Everything happens for a reason. My experience at Oakland County ended up being the same type of treatment. The jail had no remorse for inmates.

The jail officials think that everyone was coming off drugs so they assume people are lying about being ill, so they can try and be sent to the hospital. Many officials take providing medical treatment very lightly. I learned that millions of people die over the years from being denied medical treatment. I felt my friend's spirit all around me. I felt like I was fighting a spiritual warfare. I felt as if the devil was trying to target me.

I had a scary experience when I was in the Oakland County Jail, which made me believe that I was fighting demons. I was sleeping on the a bottom bunk in a cell with another inmate who stayed on the top. In my sleep, I was fighting a spiritual warfare. It felt like a physical person was trying to cover my mouth when I was sleeping.

I felt my eyes rolling in the back of my head as I tried fighting to wake myself up. I remember saying I rebuke the devil over and over again. Finally, the trance let me go, and I woke up in a panic.

I started hyperventilating after I came to my normal consciousness. I started thanking God from the heavens above! Gasping for air until I calmed down, I prayed every day after that until I was bonded out.

Jess, before she passed away, knew a bondsman that had friended me online, inquiring to know what happened to Jess. When he found out that I was in jail, he did all he could to get me out.

The bondsman and I reminisced how beautiful Jess really was. The view I was getting was that Jess's spirit was sent to help by connecting me with people who loved her! I was grateful to get bonded out by Jess's friend. The bondsman bonded me out for five hundred dollars and never asked me to pay him back. Before I went back to jail, he visited me in the hospital when I was sick going through my changes. I was trying to focus on healing my heart. Nothing was going to change with me if I didn't put the effort into it myself.

Even though I sat there adjusting to my life, I was in a process of a game controlled by time and fate. My court date was coming up soon for my poor actions. After getting bonded out, I had the bondsman take me straight to the hospital because I had been denied medical treatment in jail. I needed to be seen by a doctor right away. They said that they would have me follow up with an outpatient doctor to schedule to get my gallbladder out. The next day, I went to put in a complaint with the sheriff in Macomb County.

I had witness and phone numbers to testify for me. My main concern was my health. I was focused on getting through the process. At court I was ordered to live in a rehab for thirty days. The rehabilitation center was known all over the state for helping people make a change in their lives. I was credited the time I did in jail. The county jail's van was to transport me from jail to rehab after court.

The rehab helped people make a turning point in their lives. I kept thinking of my daughter. On the way to rehab, I couldn't help but stare in the clouds for answers from God. Once the van got to the main office building, I went inside to register to sign documents.

The counselor who took my intake asked me almost fifty questions. After the process was documented and signed, I was told that I would be shuttled to another all-girls' location. I followed directions as I was told and got into the van. Outside, all I could see around me were trees and old buildings. The city was small. The roads had some windy areas.

By the time we reached the woman's headquarters, I was hungry and ready to rest. I had so much on my brain. Once we rode up to the old Victorian house, I was amazed by its appearance. Once I went inside the house, I was stopped to register with a counselor on the left-hand side office right when I walked in the door. After all the women were processed into the system, the counselor told everyone to eat until they were full. I ate so much pasta that day. Every day the system was to get the female clients out of their beds around six o'clock in the morning to do different chores.

For the first twenty-four hours, I had to go upstairs and pick clothes out of the clothes closet until Louis could bring some of my clothes to me. I was provided hygiene products and a clean towel to take a shower. Then everyone was assigned beds.

I made sure to call Louis's mom to tell her where I was. That week was a very interesting. There were so many different identities of people living in this old Victorian house. There were many women with different reasons of why they chose to stay in the program rather than leave any chance they got. The way the program was set up, anyone could leave whenever they wanted to from the house. The program wasn't designed to keep people in, but to want them to change their lives around to stay in to have a better outcome to all their issues.

The only person who could keep the people in the program was themselves. It was a mind-over-matter type of situation. Anyone who was in the program had to be strong enough to walk into sobriety.

God's presence was shining through every morning as the woman in the house woke up to meet downstairs for a group meeting. Sometimes in the morning, we all had group outside in the grass on the side of the house. The realest sessions I had been brought into was when the topics targeted addiction. Over time I was just living healthier.

My routine was just like clockwork as my days went on. The program that I was in was being ran by strong woman. The city where the rehab was kept had lots of crime.

I woke up every morning thanking God for being alive. I would pray to God for understanding and healing. I thanked God for my daughter. I wanted to get past my heartache and pain. I started learning stuff about myself that I never knew. I learned the worse type of heartache that I had ever felt. I was trying to understand what was happening to me but, I couldn't.

I knew something remarkable was happening. As I layed in bed praying to God, I knew that whatever was happening to me was remarkable. I would ask God to allow me to feel my friend's presence. The first time I felt Jess's spirit around me in rehab I could feel a presence on my covers.

When I looked, no one was there. Things were clearer to me now. As the days went by, I was learning about myself in so many different ways. The next thing that happened to me really hurt me inside. In my life, I was focused on the sexual abuse that I had been exposed to.

I didn't realize that there were other abuses I had to deal with. I wasn't focused on the physical abuse I had gone through with my predator who sexually abused me. When I would refuse to partake in the sick actions, my predator would hit me. I was tired of fighting my predator as a child and wanted to be loved. I wasn't getting the proper love and respect at home that other children got in their households. I learned to face the truth of my past abuse. As a child, I stopped fighting my predator and started running toward him looking for some type of love that I had been lacking. I started having therapy sessions with one of the counselors. She was actually a real therapist who was trained and educated. I opened up my brain at rehab to face the thoughts that I thought I erased.

I had a childhood flashback after seeing a hook nail hook lock on the laundry room and bathroom I shared with some other girls. My flash back was of me as a child being locked in a room by a hook nail lock. I remember the hook lock was on the outside of my bedroom door to prevent me from leaving my room. This ended up causing an issue with me later on in life. I felt as a child that I was caged as an animal. I was sickened by my childhood flashbacks.

I remember banging my fists on the wall, screaming to be let out of the room many times. I remember screaming that I had to use the bathroom and no one came to let me out of the room. I remember one time waking up to my grandfather changing my clothes from using the bathroom all over myself.

I was a very distraught child. The whole time I was blocking out the type of abuse that I didn't really focus on remembering. It wasn't until I was having flashbacks of my life that my memory came back.

I was willing to dig deeper and understand what I couldn't. I didn't understand why anyone would lock a child against their will in a room where they couldn't access the bathroom. That definitely was the definition of child abuse. In the rehab program I was in, the counselors had to watch you pee in a cup once a week for a random drug test.

I was always struggling to pee in front of the counselor. It seemed that my past was catching up to me. I could not relax my body enough to feel comfortable to pee in front of another person. I was very hurt mentally from being sexually and physically abused. I couldn't pee in front of the counselor and it wasn't the first time I had to strain pee out of me just to stay in this program. I was emotionally distraught, thinking that my body was damaged. As I sat on the toilet in front of Miss T, all that came out of me wasn't pee. It was tears!

The worse type of feeling for me was to have to deal with this type of pain all over again. I was very embarrassed but couldn't do anything about it. I didn't want to get kicked out of the program by not being able to pee in front of the counselor. I could have never felt more aware of my past abuse. When it was time to pee in front of the counselor, I tried my hardest until I couldn't and then I would wait till the whole line went to try again. I would even drink cups and cups of water until my stomach was so full, thinking that would help but it really didn't. I felt permanently damaged and scared mentally.

My counselor was very intelligent. Miss D wasn't just smart but had a degree in therapy. I was happy to be getting some therapy for my issues. My therapist had beautiful hair that was similar to my texture. Miss B was another counselor that everyone loved.

She was very sympathetic to other people's needs. These women were some of the strongest woman I had ever met in Michigan. I really enjoyed my time in my therapist's office talking with her. Even though, when I first met my therapist, she came off a bit intimidating so I asked her to transfer me to Miss B's file and she said no. After that I saw her face get extremely red. I ended up having to go back and apologize to her for being rude.

After that day, we got along great. I did some community service for her by cleaning her office. While I cleaned, we talked about life. She was very down to earth and real. She had her own story that led me to grow by listening to her experiences. I told my therapist that I might want to help people one day and become one too. It sparked my therapist to help me more with words of knowledge.

Thank God my therapist was a counselor and highly trained with a lot of experience. I was emotionally going through a lot. I needed a therapist and a counselor who specialized in alcoholism. Throughout the time I spent with my therapist, she was able to teach me strong values that would cross over with me for the rest of my life.

One major thing I learned through my therapist was how to have boundaries with people. I found myself very outspoken sometimes. I could see myself being honest with people even if the honesty hurt them. I learned from Miss D that it was better to speak when spoken to. She also told me it was wise to think before speaking. I listened to her with great concern to follow her advice. I felt that it was better to build proper structural thoughts that would turn into words of proper situation.

Miss D taught me that boundaries would keep me from being a bad person. She said that knowing how to protect your heart and others by making respectful choices would lie on everyone involved.

There was so much time on my hands in rehab to just think and evaluate my life to greater it. So much time had passed. Every Sunday, Louis would bring my daughter and his mother to come see me in rehab. I was very happy to see them all every Sunday on visiting day. I wrote Louis and his mother two long letters.

I expressed to Louis how I was sorry for impounding his car. I told him that I did love him and wished later that when I got home that we could work out our differences. Every time he came to see me, he was angry and didn't want to hear anything I had to say. It wasn't until the sixth visit when Louis stopped being so resentful toward me. I had another court date coming up. I was able to get a pass from my therapist to leave the premises.

Louis picked me up the day of court. I was feeling healthier inside from being clean and sober. I felt that God was helping me by keeping me clean. I heard people say that the Holy Spirit could show you things when your body was clean from smoke, alcohol, and drugs.

I never really knew who or what the Holy Spirit was until I had my own real life experience. It was the first time for me having the Holy Spirit pass through my body. I was in the shower when I felt cold water hit my body. I then instantly started feeling a bit dizzy when I started having a vision while the cold water was running over my face. I could see from my vision an old desert with a canal where there was an old ancient well.

For a moment, I could see what looked to me like Hebrew alphabet from the ancient days. After I saw that, I passed out in the shower for about thirty seconds then came back, breathing deep for air. It felt like the Lord was trying to tell me something. Later that night, I was searching for answers what had happened to me. I told one of the older spiritual women what had happened to me.

She was the late night watch for us women. I wanted a spiritual adviser to tell me what had happened to me that day when I showered and prayed. The woman looked me in my eyes and told me that what I was trying to figure out was clear. She asked me if I knew who the Holy Spirit was. I told her I didn't know at all.

The woman told me that the Holy Spirit was in everyone's body but couldn't connect with you while your body was clouded by smoke, alcohol, and drugs.

The woman also told me that the Holy Spirit could pop up through any time in your life. She had a powerful gift that was given to me from God. I didn't know what to think next.

I was anxious to what God was going to expose me to next. I was hoping that the information I was given was true. I didn't know this woman too well but I stayed positive. I finished my conversation throwing my guard up. I didn't know what to expect next. That night was actually the first time I tried using Miss D's boundaries technique and it worked! The program was almost over. I was happy to finally be able to go home to my daughter and get another chance to do things right. I mopped and cleaned the old Victorian house it seemed like daily. There were two bunk beds in each room. On my floor, there were six bunk beds. I was glad to know I inspired some woman in there with my story. Everyone knew I had a novel coming out soon and wanted to read it. I made sure I told everyone I came into contact with about my novel to help people in different ways. I wanted to help heal all women and men from their past abuse issues. In rehab, I listened to other women talk about their past abuse issues.

I stayed inspired by listening to other people's hardships. It was beautiful listening to people wear their hearts on their sleeves. I was able to feel a connection with the different women's stories about their life abuse even though I didn't even know them.

My enjoyment was listening to the different women speakers that would come in on the weekends to share their stories. I was able to connect spiritually with a woman speaker who came in. As I listened to the woman speak and tell her story about how she was struggling with being an alcoholic, the living room was very dim at that moment. The living room had hard wooden floors, which made the room a tad bit dimmer.

When I had seen the woman up close later after the AA meeting, her face was skinny again. I told the other speaker once they were done with their meeting what I had seen. I was staring at the woman listening to her testimony of God. All of a sudden, after hearing the woman cry, I saw her skinny face become whole. Her face looked rejoiced all of a sudden. The woman talked about her second chance God had given her by saving her life. I saw her suck-in face become whole again. I was confused at what I saw. I had been intrigued but quite scared of what I was seeking for. intrigued and told me that there was a verse to explain what I saw in the bible to verify what I saw. The verse in the Bible explained that when a person was willing to change and repent, they would be renewed of their youth. I was amazed by God's presence that was exposing love to me in different ways. I prayed hard every day when I was in rehab. Sometimes when I would have group sessions in the morning time, I would feel my friend Jess's spirit.

I was aware that the old Victorian house we were staying in had many different women come and go through the program who had ended up dying. I would feel my friend's spirit touch my face, making it itch. I knew that God had his hold on my life. I could feel positive spirits in the house that started feeling like not just my friend's presence being there. I was connected with positive energy. I rebuked the devil every day. I prayed very hard every day when I was alone.

Whenever a mean thought would come across my mind, I would immediately rebuke the thought to vanish. I was always trying to do better in life. I wanted a positive outcome. While I was in rehab, I watched a movie during one of the activity sessions that really inspired me! The movie was called *The Secret*.

The movie was about manifesting a person's thoughts to have a positive future. I was so determined at this point to change my life around. I had to stay living at the rehab for thirty days, court ordered. I also was ordered to have to pay almost fifteen thousand dollars in probation fees and court fines. I was ordered by the courts to also have random drug screenings for my probation period. I lost my driver's privileges for a little over a year. I was ordered to take a course called driver's intervention. It costs almost five hundred to stay in the hotel for the weekend in order to do the program.

At the program, everyone was ordered to listen to lectures. I was surprised when I watched a horrible film of real life car accident cleanups from drunk drivers. We were taught there were many deaths caused by alcohol overdoses.

I was shocked when I saw the dead bodies on the TV screen. It traumatized me and other people as we attended the class later on as I left rehab.

In rehab, I was working on building my mind and body up in the healthiest way.

Every day I would humble myself to get healthier. I was determined to get passed all my previous abuse issues.

I never wanted to do the dumb acts of alcoholic ever again.

The whole time I was in rehab, I struggled with my inner issues that caused me to drink.

I was taught in rehab, once you take the addiction away, the person was still standing there either a good or a bad person. People were always blaming other people for their problems for their addiction issues. I learned that being angry was a cover up for actually being hurt. I was so happy to have earned some money in rehab.

I was very open to change! I know I had to make some life changes if I wanted to live by God. I wanted to live healthier. One day, Louis picked me up to stop at his house so I could grab a couple of my belongings. The moment when I walked in front of the door, I felt another presence there with us that I could tell was friendly.

It was a strong force of wind that followed me inside the house that day. All I could do was smile because I felt loved.

I had a good feeling about whatever spirit was gravitating to me. I was very intrigued to know that God had a greater purpose for me. Once I was released from rehab, I had a lot of fixing to do. I had to mend certain relationships. I wanted to fix things about myself that I didn't like. I wanted to continue to fix my relationships with people that I loved. I gained so much extra body fat from drinking alcohol. When I got home after seeing my probation officer, I cleaned the house top to bottom until it was spotless. I cooked almost every night to try and regain a part of me that was still missing.

I didn't want to be hurt anymore. My life since birth had been painful throughout this journey.

Chapter Thirty-Four

My journey was unlike anyone's I had ever known. I couldn't feel sorry for myself. The will to better myself grew stronger and stronger as the days went by. I was grateful to be alive! As I looked back at all I went through, all I could do is fall to my knees to thank God for keeping me alive. I didn't know what my journey had in store for me.

I knew for a fact, whatever came my way, I would face it with honesty and love. I had many questions run through my mind on what happened to my friend Jess. For the next year, I fought and fought to search for answers to what really happened to her. It seemed that it wasn't just the devil trying to bring people down.

It was true that all the issues someone endured would cause pain in their lives to make choices that could potentially kill the person. If a person doesn't treat their pain, it starts to build up! Worrying about the past doesn't help anyone get healthy. I learned that after all that I had been through. Life is too short to live in regret. Life is so short. Holding onto pain will only kill you. Pain in your heart causes stress.

The repercussions of stress will kill you. The power of love will create a will in any a person's heart to want to change their lives around. I look back on my life and can say proudly that if it wasn't for the pain I had gone through, then I would have never been able to get so close to God, searching for healing. I didn't know where my faith would have been if it wasn't for my journey.

Remember it is true that it is you the reader who has the power to do right and change your life around. God in the end has the last say to what happens to you. Yes, I said it! There is a God! I wouldn't know how emotionally and mentally I would have ended up. Faith had helped me keep my light shining. The light in me shined where other people saw what at times I couldn't see. There was power inside everyone that gave people faith. There was a strong testimony that God was hearing.

Only God can hear my heart's and mind's true intentions. I felt that God worked in many ways to do wonders. God has control over a person's fate, but how you deal with your choices as a person builds great character through your spiritual journey.

My advice to my readers is please look deeper inside yourself for questions that can only be answered based upon your choices. If you are telling yourself as you read my words that you're feeling pain inside of you, it's because it is caused from being hurt from your experiences.

My readers, I can say that we both can relate to feelings of emotions, but everyone has a different story even when our experiences are similar. I will tell you the truth that your suffering has ended. Close your eyes so you can feel peace quiver all over your body. Take a moment to breathe in and out slowly. Relax so you can feel the power inside of you after you take God's air.

It's the power within all of you readers to push forward. It's up to you, the reader, to manifest your life to what you want it to be. Positive outlook gives a prosperous future. The only thing that can love you past your pain is God's love for you. Stop searching for love. God will provide it all for you when the time is right.

The Lord's love is there searching for you! I had seen unimaginable things provided from the Lord. If the Lord can do these wonderful things for my heart, I know he could do that for other people as well. Stay strong and willing for a positive change. In life everyone gets what they deserve. Remember that.

God is great with his all mighty rays of love. I know that his love's rays shine down on our world every day. As the world rotates fast than faster, I feel that the Lord's love rotates right along with our world's energy. Every one's energy is given to the people of God's world differently.

From my own experiences with using my energy in the most positive way, I was able to inhale my energy and exhale it with feelings connected with other people's hearts.

I wouldn't take my life journey back for anything in this world. I feel that all my experiences can help make our world greater by showing our population how to collect what they truly seek deep down inside their inner selves. If you choose a greater path in life for yourself, then you do have a chance to change your story into your own success that other's would learn the most from.

My readers, your stories matter, because you have a chance to change your world to form it the way you really want it to be. Life is based on how you treat the feeling's inside of yourself that send signals to your brain to cause you to act a certain way to react toward people, places, and things.

Please understand that your health is the main priority for your inner comfort of stability. Keep striving to live to love in ways of every emotion that is pouring out from your hearts to your hands.

You readers matter in our world and your energy is what makes our universe what it is today. Without all of you readers, our universe would stop spinning.

All we can do as human beings is keep our faith so that we can keep our world spinning to feel every emotion that helps us conquer our fears. Stay true to yourself to heal yourself. That's the only key to successfully loving yourself.

Don't give up on your peace. Eventually a day will come to you where you won't lose your own inner battle with yourself. The secrets of life are within this book through my journey. I feel that as long as you keep your own truth to your heart, soul, mind, and body, there will be no stopping you on your recovery of completing what you feel has been missing your whole life.

Good luck and God bless you all with the strength of love and faith with in the strongest power to help provide you with the right brightest future that you all deserve. Don't forget everyone has a second chance to live and finally stop surviving!

About the Author

Tianna Jones was born in Renton, Washington, and grew up in Texas until she was nine years old. Once her father was released from prison, she moved back to Campbell, California, where she learned to love again. As a child who went through different traumatizing changes. This young woman attended Gilroy High School in Gilroy, California, and then attended Westmont High School later on in Campbell, California. She has written her first autobiography, which took her nine years to complete. Seeking a vision of truth, the author, Tianna Jones, took up many different professions while she focused on her dream as a writer. These positions are included inside the story line as part of a hard-working woman's struggle to survive. Tianna Jones has always had an interest in writing but never imagined the wonders of how strongly impacted her story shall become. *Cali Girl, How Did You Make it in the Treacherous Streets of Detroit?* is her first Autobiographical novel. Tianna Jones currently lives with her daughter in the heart of Michigan.

CPSIA information can be obtained
at www.ICGtesting.com
Printed in the USA
FSHW010857220619
59327FS

9 781640 824744